Sale and Lease of Goods

BY DOUGLAS J. WHALEY
Ohio State University

Thirteenth Edition

THOMSON
＊
BAR/BRI

EDITORIAL OFFICES: 111 W. Jackson Blvd., 7th Floor, Chicago, IL 60604
REGIONAL OFFICES: Chicago, Dallas, Los Angeles, New York, Washington, D.C.

PROJECT EDITOR
Erin Johnson Remotigue, B.A., J.D.
Attorney At Law

SERIES EDITOR
Elizabeth L. Snyder, B.A., J.D.
Attorney At Law

QUALITY CONTROL EDITOR
Sanetta M. Hister

Summary of Contents

Text Correlation Chart

Gilbert Law Summary **SALE AND LEASE OF GOODS**	Benfield, Hawkland *Sales Cases and Materials* 2004 (4th ed.)	Farnsworth, Honnold, Harris, Mooney, Reitz *Commercial Law—Cases and Materials* 1993 (5th ed.)	Honnold, Harris, Mooney, Reitz *Law of Sales and Secured Financing* 2002 (7th ed.)	Jordan, Warren *Sales* 1992 (3d ed.)	Speidel, Rusch *Commercial Transactions* 2004 (2d ed.)	Whaley *Problems and Materials on Sale and Lease of Goods* 2004 (4th ed.)
I. INTRODUCTION						
A. Historical Background	Page(s) 2-9	Page(s) 1-19	Page(s) 2-5	Page(s)	Page(s) 6-8	Page(s)
B. Scope of Article 2	11, 13-34	2-9, 20-48	85		57-60	1-36
C. Basic Principles of the U.C.C.	7, 11-13, 49-52, 105-106, 110-126, 130-143	3-4, 12-14, 19-48, 357-360	5-6, 29-32		9-21	
II. THE SALES CONTRACT						
A. Subject Matter—What Goods Can Be Sold	11-25, 27-32	20, 358-359, 375, 540-544, 695-696	85-112	233-239, 240-243	57-60	4
B. "Sale" vs. Other Arrangements	26-27	396			464-466	
C. Formation—Offer and Acceptance	40-55		1-13		98-108, 110-119	58-96
D. Parol Evidence Rule	165-170	428, 452	116-117		179-181, 189-201	51-57
E. Statute of Frauds	57-74		103-108, 114	14-43	129-130	39-51
F. Missing Terms—The Gap-Filling Rules	130-180	523-526, 530-531	114		148-153	215-221
G. Revision of the Contract Terms	104-123		117	45-58	395-402	
H. Assignment and Delegation of Contract		500			490-494, 493-495	
III. TYPES OF SALES						
A. Cash Sale Transactions		31-38, 171, 173, 525, 531, 735-736	34-36, 49-51		463-464	
B. "Sale or Return" and "Sale on Approval" Transactions	234	909-924	811		464-466	
C. Auction Sales	30-32	410-413	158-159			
IV. WARRANTIES						
A. Background	493-502	361-364			203-207	
B. Warranty of Title	392-393	409-417	150-162	244-253	482-490	97-102

Gilbert Law Summary SALE AND LEASE OF GOODS	Benfield, Hawkland *Sales Cases and Materials* 2004 (4th ed.)	Farnsworth, Honnold, Harris, Mooney, Reitz *Commercial Law—Cases and Materials* 1993 (5th ed.)	Honnold, Harris, Mooney, Reitz *Law of Sales and Secured Financing* 2002 (7th ed.)	Jordan, Warren *Sales* 1992 (3d ed.)	Speidel, Rusch *Commercial Transactions* 2004 (2d ed.)	Whaley *Problems and Materials on Sale and Lease of Goods* 2004 (4th ed.)
D. Damage or Destruction of Goods—Risk of Loss	211-229	687-719	516-518	294-314	421-446	224-238, 281-285
VIII. REMEDIES						
A. Seller's Prelitigation Remedies	503-540	38-39, 571-587, 619-621, 732-743, 1080-1095	32-50	94-99, 385-411	458-460, 463-470, 497-511, 526-529, 555-562	307-319
B. Buyer's Prelitigation Remedies	394-502	101-102, 539, 563-570, 589-598	168-169, 429-430	315-318, 318-320, 320-338	451-457, 471-477, 511-515, 516-524	307, 319-342
C. Preserving Evidence Where Condition of Goods in Dispute					497-511	
D. Seller's Litigation Remedies	475-485, 490-519	571-587		355-374, 385	527-577	307-319
E. Buyer's Litigation Remedies	466-475, 519-530	365, 396-400, 509-519, 538-539, 546-559, 589-598, 1019-1020	168-169, 194-202, 214	338-354, 375-385	566-595	306-307, 319-342
F. Limitation of Remedies	475-485, 490-519	417-423, 436-447	51-54, 1113-1119	165-179, 375-385	639-652	154-168
G. Statute of Limitations		22-30, 462-476	353-377	207-218	670-679	343-355
IX. DOCUMENTS OF TITLE						
A. Bills of Lading	641-663	71-83, 108-116, 119-120, 529-530, 603-618	71-73	266-275	315-316	369-392
B. Warehouse Receipts		69-72, 76-83, 108-120	71-73	263-266, 275-293	313	358-369
C. Rights of Third Parties	582-621	78-82, 889-890	71-73	257-262, 422-458	425-428, 455-456, 461-462, 467-471, 471-478	
X. LEASE OF GOODS						
A. Scope of Article 2A	30	754-755, 761, 874, 890-908	776-777		9-10, 60-64, 317	33-36
B. Article 2 Rules Copied						
C. Warranties		387-396, 416-417	203	140-142	209	205-214
D. Remedies					495-497	280-281, 318-319
E. Priority Disputes		895, 946-947, 1007	793-794		447-450, 456	
XI. THE INTERNATIONAL SALE OF GOODS						
A. United Nations Convention for the International Sale of Goods	29-30	16-17	137-149		198-199	280
B. Scope of the Treaty	29	15-16, 359-360	11-13, 21-22		22-24, 73-74	37

Gilbert Law Summary **SALE AND LEASE OF GOODS**	Benfield, Hawkland *Sales Cases and Materials* 2004 (4th ed.)	Farnsworth, Honnold, Harris, Mooney, Reitz *Commercial Law—Cases and Materials* 1993 (5th ed.)	Honnold, Harris, Mooney, Reitz *Law of Sales and Secured Financing* 2002 (7th ed.)	Jordan, Warren *Sales* 1992 (3d ed.)	Speidel, Rusch *Commercial Transactions* 2004 (2d ed.)	Whaley *Problems and Materials on Sale and Lease of Goods* 2004 (4th ed.)
C. Some Substantive Issues	73, 91, 122, 192, 299-300	401-408, 417, 477, 520-521, 533-537, 598-601, 621-650, 690, 709-710, 722-725	139-140, 378-383, 427		121-122, 591, 454-455, 531	51-52, 59-96, 280, 340-341

Capsule Summary

I.   INTRODUCTION

A.   HISTORICAL BACKGROUND   §1
In the late nineteenth century, the Uniform Sales Act codified the common law of sales. However, commercial development made the Act outmoded almost from its promulgation. Accordingly, a new uniform act was drafted in 1951 and now appears as *Article 2 of the Uniform Commercial Code* ("U.C.C."). All states except Louisiana have adopted Article 2. A number of states have also adopted U.C.C. Article 2A, which is similar to Article 2 but governs leases.

1.   Revision of Articles 1 and 2   §4
Article 2 was revised in 2003 but probably will not be adopted by many states. Revised Article 1, containing general U.C.C. principles and a large definition section, has a similar problem. It is *essential* that students use the *correct version* chosen by the instructor. Revised versions are identified by the letter "R" (*e.g.*, 2R-302; 1R-201). This Summary generally focuses on the pre-revision versions.

2.   United Nations Treaty   §6
The United States is also a signatory to the United Nations Convention on Contracts for the International Sale of Goods ("CISG"), which applies law similar to that of Article 2 to international contracts for the sale of goods.

B.   SCOPE OF ARTICLE 2   §7
Article 2 applies only to *transactions involving "goods"* (basically tangible chattels). Although not covered in Article 2, *documents of title* are also discussed in this summary because of their close relation to the law of Sales. Article 2 does *not* cover the additional problems involved when a seller or lender claims a security interest in the goods.

C.   BASIC PRINCIPLES OF THE U.C.C.

1.   Good Faith   §13
The U.C.C. imposes an unwaivable obligation of good faith in the performance of enforcement of contracts or duties within its scope; good faith is generally considered a condition precedent to U.C.C. protection.

a.   Honesty in fact   §14
Good faith is defined *subjectively* as "honesty in fact"; *i.e.*, not the reasonable person test. Revised Article 1 includes an objective component

to good faith: "honesty in fact *and* the observance of reasonable commercial standards of fair dealing."

    b.   Merchant's standard   **§15**

Merchants are held to an *objective* standard that includes the observance of reasonable commercial standards of *fair dealing in the trade*.

2.   Construction Terms   **§16**

Courts look to the following circumstances in constructing the meaning of contract terms.

    a.   "Usage of trade"   **§17**

This means the *custom within the industry* and binds all who should know about it—sometimes even consumers.

    b.   "Course of dealing"   **§18**

This refers to the *parties' past contacts* with each other.

    c.   "Course of performance"   **§19**

This refers to what the parties do when performing *this particular contract*.

    d.   Hierarchy of terms   **§20**

Express contract terms (unless waived) *control* over course of performance; course of performance controls over course of dealing which, in turn, controls over usage of trade.

3.   Unconscionability   **§21**

The U.C.C. purposely does not define an "unconscionable" contract. Generally, it is one so *grossly unfair* that it *shocks the conscience* of the court. Often courts find unconscionability where there is both *procedural* (bargaining process) and *substantive* (terms in resulting contract) *unfairness* in the transaction.

    a.   Effect of unconscionability   **§23**

If a court finds a contract or any part thereof unconscionable, it may (i) *avoid* the whole contract; (ii) *enforce* the contract *without* the unconscionable clause; or (iii) *limit* the application of the clause so as to avoid the unconscionable result.

    b.   Application of doctrine   **§24**

The U.C.C. requires a hearing before a finding of unconscionability is made. In determining unconscionability, a general guideline is that the terms bargained for (*i.e.*, those to which both parties *voluntarily and knowingly consent*) will not ordinarily be deemed unconscionable even if they are unfair. Note that printed-form contracts that are unfair by virtue of economic power are more likely to be held unconscionable.

    c.   Commercial contracts   **§25**

When buyer and seller are both *business entities*, the resulting contract is *almost never* held unconscionable.

4.   Merchants   **§26**

Article 2 distinguishes between merchants and nonmerchants and holds merchants to higher standards.

(b) Knock-out rule §86

Other courts find that both parties have objected to the differing terms so that a contract is concluded without an agreement on the matter. The court will then apply the Code's *gap-filling rules*.

(c) No contract §87

If the disagreement concerns a major term of the contract, some courts will find that no contract ever arose. However, if the parties begin to perform, section 2-207(3) would be used to create the terms of the deal (*see infra,* §89).

(3) Writings that do not create a contract §88

In response to U.C.C. section 2-207, forms now typically contain "objection" clauses. The offeror's form objects to any new terms, (a proviso clause) and the offeree's form proposes new terms and states that it is *not* an acceptance unless the offeror consents to the new terms. Accordingly, there is no contract *unless performance begins*.

(a) Effect of performance §89

If the parties behave as if they have a contract by beginning to perform, there *is* a contract. The contract consists of all the terms on which the *writings agree* plus terms supplied by the U.C.C. where the parties are silent.

b. 2003 Revision of Article 2 §90

Section 2R-206(3) drops the proviso and the mirror image rule of the original Article 2. Instead, section 2R-207 provides that beginning of performance before agreement on all terms results in a contract containing terms that have been agreed upon by the parties and supplementary terms provided by the Code's gap-filling rules. Contradictory terms are stricken.

D. PAROL EVIDENCE RULE

1. Common Law §91

The parol evidence rule *excludes* evidence of *oral representations* or understandings made *prior to the signing* of a contract that would *alter or vary the written terms*.

2. Sales Contracts §92

However, under the U.C.C., before the writing can operate to exclude parol evidence, a court must find that the *parties intended* the writing to be the *complete and exclusive* statement of the contract's terms. If the court does not so find, parol evidence is allowed concerning *consistent, additional* terms. Moreover, even if the writing was intended to be the complete and exclusive statement of the terms, parol evidence may be used to *explain or interpret* terms.

a. Common law exceptions §95

The common law exceptions to the parol evidence rule (*e.g.*, fraud, mistake) are also good in sales transactions.

E. STATUTE OF FRAUDS

1. In General §96

Certain sales contracts are *unenforceable* unless there is a sufficient *writing* or some other act that evidences the existence of a contract.

2. Basic Code Provision §97

The U.C.C. Statute of Frauds applies only to contracts for a sale of goods having a *price of $500* or more ($5,000 under the revised version).

3. Effect of Code Provision §98

A sales contract that does not comply with the Statute is *unenforceable*. However, if the parties choose to perform, enforceable rights may be created.

4. What Constitutes Sufficient Written Memorandum §100

There must be a writing signed by the party to be charged (*i.e.*, the party refusing to perform).

a. Terms that must be contained in written memorandum §101

The writing is sufficient if it indicates that a contract for sale has been made and specifies the *quantity* term. Note that a quantity in terms of *output* (*e.g.*, "all the steel you produce") or *requirements* is sufficient.

b. Form of memorandum §104

No particular form is necessary as long as it contains the required terms. A *buyer's check* with a notation as to subject matter and quantity suffices to bind the buyer; a *seller's indorsement* when cashing the check will also bind seller.

c. Signature §106

Any mark with the *intent* to authenticate the writing is a signature. Many cases hold that a *printed letterhead* satisfies the Statute, as does an *agent's signature*. However, some states have "equal dignity" statutes requiring the agent's authority to make contracts to be in writing if the Statute of Frauds requires a memorandum of the contract.

d. Written confirmation from other party §109

Under the U.C.C., where *both* parties are *merchants*, a written confirmation not signed by the party to be charged sufficiently satisfies the Statute unless the receiver *objects in writing* within *10 days* after receipt. Although such a confirmation satisfies the Statute of Frauds, it does not necessarily show that a contract exists.

5. Exceptions to Statute of Frauds §114

Exceptions include *partial acceptance*, but only to the extent of the goods received and accepted; *partial payment*, enforceable as to goods for which payment has been made; and where a *substantial beginning* on the manufacture of, or *commitments* for, the procurement of *specially manufactured goods* has been made.

a. Pleading and testimonial admissions §120

A party against whom enforcement of a contract is sought that admits in pleadings or testimony that a sales contract was made loses the Statute of Frauds defense to the *extent of the quantity admitted*. Note also that a court may apply the doctrine of *estoppel* to a Statute of Frauds defense where *detrimental reliance* has been shown.

F. MISSING TERMS—THE GAP-FILLING RULES

Payment is due at the **time and place** at which the buyer **receives** the goods. "Receipt" occurs upon taking physical possession of the goods.

a. Document transactions   §153
Payment is due at the time and place the buyer receives the documents (*e.g.*, warehouse receipt).

b. Open credit   §154
The general rule in credit transactions is that the credit period begins to run from the **date of shipment**, unless the sending of the invoice is delayed.

7. Other Open Terms   §157
The purchase of mixed or bulk lots entitles the **buyer to specify** the assortment. If **no shipping arrangements** have been agreed upon, it is the **seller's** duty to make such arrangements.

8. One Party to Specify Missing Terms   §159
Where details of performance are to be supplied by a specified party, that party must perform in **good faith**. Usage of trade, course of dealing, and course of performance are also used to fill in missing contract terms.

G. REVISION OF THE CONTRACT TERMS

1. Modifications   §161
The U.C.C. does **not** require new **consideration** for a sales contract modification, and no writing is required unless the contract **as modified** is for the sale of goods priced at $500 or more. Note that **good faith** does not permit a party to demand a change without a **legitimate commercial reason**.

2. Waivers   §165
An attempted modification, although ineffective, may operate as a waiver of contract rights where the other party has **changed position in reliance** on the attempted modification.

a. Retraction   §166
A waiver is retractable by **notice** from the waiving party **unless** the other party has materially changed position.

H. ASSIGNMENT AND DELEGATION OF CONTRACT

1. Delegation of Duties of Performance   §167
The U.C.C. provides that all duties are delegable, **unless** the parties agree otherwise **or** the obligee has a **substantial interest** in the **personal performance** by the original obligor. However, delegation of performance does **not** relieve the delegator of either the duty to perform or liability for breach.

2. Assignment of Rights   §168
Either party can assign contract rights unless it would (i) materially change the other party's duty; (ii) materially increase that party's burden of risk; (iii) materially impair the chances of obtaining return performance; or (iv) violate a nonassignment clause. Note that **after** performance, the performer may **always** assign **payment** rights.

IV. WARRANTIES

A. BACKGROUND §210

Originally, breach of warranty was a tort (fraud). Later cases recognized the liability as **contractual** so that fraud or bad faith is immaterial. More recent cases also recognized implied warranties, a concept adopted by the U.C.C. The U.C.C. categorizes warranties of title and warranties of quality.

B. WARRANTY OF TITLE

1. What Is Warranted by the Warranty of Title §212

The U.C.C. provides an automatic warranty that the seller will convey **good title**, that the transfer is **rightful**, and that the goods are **free of any claim** of the seller's creditors of which the buyer has no knowledge. This warranty is not classified as either express or implied.

2. No Warranty of Quiet Possession §214

The warranty of title does **not** contain a warranty as to freedom from all lawsuits or threats thereof.

3. Warranty Against Infringement §215

The seller, if a merchant, warrants that goods shall be delivered free of the rightful patent or trademark claims of third persons.

4. Disclaiming the Title Warranty §217

The title warranty does **not arise** where a buyer should reasonably know that the seller makes no claim of title (*e.g.*, judicial sale), and it may be disclaimed by **specific, conspicuous** language in a contract disclaiming title warranty.

C. EXPRESS WARRANTIES

1. Creation of Express Warranty §220

A statement of fact or promise that **relates to the goods** and is **part of the basis of the bargain** creates an express warranty that the goods shall conform thereto. Descriptions, samples, and models of the goods may also create an express warranty. No technical words are needed and the warranty may be **written or oral**.

    a. Seller's intent or culpability immaterial §223

No intent to warrant is required, and where the warranty is breached, the seller is **absolutely liable**.

    b. Fact vs. opinion §224

A seller will be held liable only for statements of fact or promises, **not** for mere "puffing." There is an **apparent trend** for courts to narrow the scope of permissible "puff," thus expanding the scope of warranty. The **relative knowledge of the parties** is a principal factor considered by courts.

2. Basis of the Bargain §225

This means that the statement must have been part of the deal and must have played some part in the buyer's decision to buy. Under the U.C.C., the buyer's reliance is no longer a significant factor.

cumulative and consistent whenever possible and reasonable. If the results would be unreasonable, the parties' *intent* determines which warranties dominate. "Intent" is determined according to three rules: (i) exact or technical *specifications* control over general language; (ii) *samples* prevail over an inconsistent general description; and (iii) *express* warranties displace inconsistent implied warranties (except for fitness for a particular purpose).

G. PRIVITY

1. Early View §306

Traditionally, privity was required for a person to sue for breach of warranty (*i.e.*, one must be a party to the sale).

2. Modern Law §307

Today, the privity doctrine is being abandoned by nearly every state; it was first discarded in foodstuff cases and is now disregarded by courts under several theories; *e.g.*, advertisements are considered **express warranties** to the **entire public**, or the courts find **strict liability** or general **tort liability**. Note that the revision codifies express warranties created by advertisements (*supra*).

a. Significant distinctions between tort and warranty actions (product liability) §318

A strict liability tort action is generally available only for **physical harm** to person or property; a warranty action allows recovery for such harms **and economic** losses. A strict liability action is permissible only where the product is inherently or **unreasonably dangerous**, whereas the warranty action is available for **all** products. A tort action is subject to a **short statute of limitations** (usually, one year); the U.C.C. has a **four-year** limitation for warranty actions. Note that a **wrongful death** action is applicable where the death was **tortiously** caused, but cannot be based on a breach of warranty.

b. Trend §323

There is an apparent trend to recognize the similarities and ignore the distinctions between tort and warranty actions, so as to have a single cause of action in product liability cases.

3. Effect of U.C.C. §324

The Code is of little or no use in this area. It offers three "alternatives," which have been given broad judicial interpretation.

H. ACTION FOR BREACH OF WARRANTY—REQUIREMENTS

1. Breach Must Be Proximate Cause §329

In an action for breach of warranty, the buyer must always **prove** that the breach is the **proximate cause** of the loss sustained.

2. Requirement §330

To recover, the buyer must **plead and prove** that notice to the seller was given within a **reasonable time** after the breach should have been discovered. If no notice is given, recovery is barred. Notice may be written or oral. Courts are split as to whether filing of a suit constitutes sufficient notice.

(tender) conforming goods to the buyer. Tender may be accomplished in several ways.

a. **Manual transfer of possession** §404
Tender must be made at a *reasonable* hour and at a place agreed upon. If there is no such agreement, the place is the *seller's* place of business or residence. Tender must be held open for a reasonable time to enable the buyer to take possession.

b. **Constructive tender** §410
Goods may be tendered to the buyer without an actual offer to transfer physical possession (*e.g.*, seller tells buyer to get a pile of lumber at a railroad siding).

c. **Goods in possession of bailee** §411
This is another occasion where tender of delivery can occur without a manual transfer by the seller (*e.g.,* by delivery of a document of title).

d. **What constitutes sufficient tender** §414
The U.C.C partially retains the common law rule of *perfect tender*. The U.C.C. rule states that if goods fail to conform *in any respect*, the buyer *may* reject the whole, accept the whole, or accept part and reject part.

   (1) **Rule mitigated** §417
However, other U.C.C. provisions mitigate the harshness of this rule by allowing the seller to *cure* the defective tender in some circumstances. Also, *substantial performance* of a sales contract is sufficient in *installment contracts*. Substantial performance is also adequate in *shipping arrangements* unless *material delay or loss* occurs.

e. **Curing improper tender** §423
If the original tender is rejected because it is nonconforming, the seller may promptly *notify* the buyer of an intention to cure, and then *within the contract time for performance*, remove the defect or breach.

   (1) **Surprise rejections** §426
If the seller provides nonconforming goods and has *reasonable grounds* to believe that they will nevertheless be accepted (*e.g.,* because the buyer accepted such goods in the past), but the buyer rejects the tender, upon notice the seller has a reasonable time in which to substitute conforming goods, *even if the time for performance has expired*.

   (2) **Variation—2003 revision** §427
The revision permits cure in all cases where the seller, having made an improper tender, acted in *good faith* and in circumstances where cure is *appropriate*. This provision gives courts great latitude in cases where substition of goods is the best solution.

B. PERFORMANCE BY BUYER

1. **Facilitating Receipt of Goods** §428
The buyer's first duty is to furnish facilities reasonably suited to receive the goods.

the seller's account. In all cases, the buyer must make reasonable efforts to sell *perishable* goods. The buyer is entitled to reasonable *expenses* from the seller for caring and disposing of goods, including a selling commission.

6. Revocation of Acceptance §483

A buyer cannot reject goods after acceptance. However, where serious flaws in the goods are discovered after acceptance, the buyer can revoke the acceptance (at common law, this remedy is called rescission). The flaw must be one that *substantially impairs* the value of the goods.

a. Buyer must justify acceptance §486

The U.C.C. allows two ways that a buyer can justify acceptance of the defective goods: (i) the buyer knew of the nonconformity but assumed the seller would cure it; or (ii) the defects were difficult to discover.

b. Notice §489

The buyer must give notice of the revocation of acceptance to the seller within a reasonable time after the buyer *should have discovered* the defect.

c. Effect of change in goods §490

If, prior to revocation, the goods have substantially changed for some reason *other than the defect*, the buyer *cannot* revoke the acceptance; damages is the appropriate remedy.

d. After revocation §491

The buyer has the same duty to care for the goods as if they had originally been rejected (*i.e.*, not use them, reasonably care for them). A buyer who rightfully revokes is entitled to *damages* (purchase price paid plus consequential damages not preventable by cover).

VII. BREAKDOWN OF THE BARGAIN

A. ANTICIPATORY BREACH

1. Repudiation—In General §494

An unconditional repudiation by either party of some future performance (other than the payment of money) is a breach of contract and creates an *immediate* right of action.

2. Rights of Aggrieved Party §495

Contrary to common law, the aggrieved party may remain inactive only for a *commercially reasonable* time and then must take action in *mitigation*. The aggrieved party may seek *any remedy* for breach, even after notifying the repudiating party that the aggrieved party would await the contracted-for performance.

3. Retracting Repudiations §500

The repudiating party may retract the repudiation unless the other party has *materially altered* her position in reliance on the repudiation.

B. DEMAND FOR ASSURANCE OF PERFORMANCE

D. DAMAGE OR DESTRUCTION OF GOODS—RISK OF LOSS

1. **Background** §521
   Traditionally, when goods were *accidentally* destroyed or damaged, the risk of loss was borne by the party with *title* to the goods. Generally, the U.C.C. provides that risk of loss follows *possession* of the goods. Note that if a party has caused the damage or destruction, that party remains liable for obligations under the contract.

2. **U.C.C. Rules**

   a. **Risk of loss shifts when parties agree** §523
      The parties can agree as to when the risk of loss shifts, or sometimes the parties' intent will be *implied* from the nature of the transaction (*e.g.*, risk of loss is on buyer in *sale or return* transactions; seller has the risk in a *sale on approval*).

   b. **When parties have not agreed** §526
      Control is the determinative factor where there is no agreement.

      (1) **Where goods are shipped via carrier** §527
          In *shipment contracts*, the risk of loss passes to the buyer *upon the seller's delivery* of conforming goods *to the carrier*. In *destination contracts*, risk of loss passes to the buyer only when the goods *arrive* at the destination *and* are duly *tendered* to the buyer. Unless *expressly* designated a destination contract (*i.e.*, F.O.B. destination), a contract is construed as a *shipment contract*.

      (2) **Where goods are held by bailee** §531
          Where the goods are covered by a *negotiable* warehouse receipt, the risk of loss passes to the buyer upon *receipt of the negotiable document*. Where the goods in possession of a bailee are covered by a *nonnegotiable* document of title, risk of loss passes upon receipt of the document *or other written directions* from the seller to the bailee. If there is *no* document of title, risk of loss passes when the bailee *tenders* the goods *or* otherwise acknowledges the buyer's right to immediate possession.

      (3) **In all other nonbreach situations ("catch-all" rule)** §535
          In all other nonbreach situations, the result generally depends on whether the seller is a merchant. If so, the U.C.C. shifts the risk to the buyer only upon actual *receipt* of the goods. If the seller is *not* a merchant, the risk of loss passes upon mere *tender of delivery* by the seller. The revision's default rule drops the merchant distinction and provides that risk of loss passes to the buyer upon *receipt* of the goods.

      (4) **Different rules apply where party in breach** §537
          Where a seller ships *nonconforming* goods, the risk of loss remains with the *seller* until cure or acceptance. Where a buyer has *wrongfully repudiated* (or otherwise breached while risk of loss is still on seller) and the goods are damaged and not covered by the

seller's insurance, the seller may treat the risk of loss as resting on the buyer "for a ***commercially reasonable period of time***."

3. Right to Sue Third Parties for Damage to Goods §543
Where third parties (*e.g.*, warehousers, carriers) are responsible for loss or damage to goods, the U.C.C. provides that until the goods are ***identified***, only the ***seller*** has the right to sue the third party. However, upon identification, the buyer has an "insurable interest" in the goods and obtains a right of action. Note that either party may ***consent*** to the other to file suit for the benefit of the proper person. The ***party who bears the risk of loss*** has the primary right to sue and retain whatever is recovered.

VIII. REMEDIES

A. SELLER'S PRELITIGATION REMEDIES

1. Right to Withhold Delivery or Demand Cash Payment §549
A seller can demand cash payment in lieu of agreed-upon credit where the seller learns of a ***buyer's insolvency***. Also, an unpaid seller in ***possession*** of the goods can withhold delivery when the buyer ***wrongfully rejects***, ***rescinds***, fails to make a ***payment when due***, or ***anticipatorily breaches***.

2. Reclamation of Goods §552
The U.C.C. permits an unpaid seller to reclaim goods (i) where the buyer's check is returned for insufficient funds (***cash sales***), and (ii) where, after delivery, the seller discovers the buyer is insolvent (***credit sales***). In the credit sale situation, the seller may demand ***in writing*** the return of the goods within ***10 days*** after receipt by the buyer.

   a. Exceptions to 10-day rule §555
If, within three months prior to delivery, a buyer misrepresents solvency in ***writing*** to the ***particular*** seller, the 10-day limit on demand is inapplicable. The ***revision*** contains ***no 10-day rule*** and substitutes a ***reasonable time*** provision. Neither does the revision require a misrepresentation of insolvency.

   b. Enforcement of right §559
If, after ***written*** demand, the buyer does not return the goods, the seller must reclaim them through legal action; self-help is ***not*** permitted. Note that successful reclamation ***excludes all other remedies***.

   c. Rights of third parties §563
A transfer to a ***bona fide purchaser*** cuts off the seller's right of reclamation. Generally, a perfected security interest in the debtor's ***after-acquired*** goods is treated as a "good faith purchase." A buyer's trustee in bankruptcy is ***not*** a BFP. The Bankruptcy Code permits reclamation of goods sold to an insolvent buyer ***if*** the seller makes written demand within 45 days after delivery, and this right ***prevails*** over the trustee in bankruptcy.

3. Stoppage in Transit §567
A seller can stop goods while they are in transit where the ***buyer's insolvency*** is discovered ***after*** shipment ***or*** where the buyer ***repudiates*** a ***large order*** (*e.g.*,

a truckload or planeload). The *revision* has no big shipment requirement and permits stoppage in *all* cases where the buyer is insolvent, fails to make payment, or the seller has any right to withhold or reclaim the goods.

good a position as performance would have (*e.g.,* because seller can obtain as many goods as seller can sell and so loses sales volume as a result of the breach), recover for ***lost profits***.

a. Incidental damages §641
In all of the above measures of damages, the seller is entitled to recover incidental damages. However, the seller must ***deduct*** any expenses ***saved*** as a result of the buyer's breach. The ***revision*** expands a seller's potential recovery, for the first time, to ***all foreseeable consequential damages***.

b. Deduct expenses saved §642
Any expenses saved as a result of the buyer's breach must be deducted from any recovery by the seller.

E. BUYER'S LITIGATION REMEDIES

1. Possessory Actions

a. Replevin §644
The U.C.C. permits replevin (*i.e.,* an action to recover the goods) when the buyer is ***unable to cover*** or in ***satisfaction of a security interest*** in the goods.

b. Specific performance §647
Under the U.C.C., this remedy is appropriate where the goods are ***unique*** or in other proper ***circumstances*** (*e.g.,* goods are in short supply or damages are inadequate).

2. Action for Damages for Nondelivery §653
There are several measures of damages when the seller fails to deliver the goods. The buyer may recover (i) the ***contract-cover differential*** at the time and place the buyer learned of the breach; (ii) the ***contract-market differential***; (iii) ***consequential damages*** where, at the time of contracting, the seller ***had reason to know*** additional losses would result from a breach, and which could ***not reasonably be prevented*** by cover or otherwise; and (iv) any reasonable ***incidental damages***. (***No*** punitive damages are allowed.) Here too, the buyer must deduct any expenses saved by the breach.

3. Restitution of Payments Where Buyer in Default §664
The U.C.C.'s "***rule of thumb offset***" permits a buyer to recover advance payments when the buyer's default has not caused much damage to the seller; *i.e.,* buyer can recover the amount by which the advance payments ***exceed 20%*** of the purchase price ***or $500***, whichever is smaller.

a. Effect of valid liquidated damages provision §666
This rule may be inapplicable if the contract has a valid ***liquidated damages clause***.

b. Rule of thumb offset eliminated by revision §667
Instead of the original U.C.C. offset, the revision allows the breaching buyer to recover ***any*** amount paid that exceeds the liquidated damages provision or, if no such clause, that amount which exceeds damages proved by the seller.

c. Other damages §668

The seller can recover greater damages, if proved, rather than the rule of thumb offset. Even if the seller is *unable to prove any damages*, in addition to the offset, the seller can recover *incidental damages* and the value of any *benefits received* by the buyer.

F. LIMITATION OF REMEDIES

1. Liquidated Damages Provisions §671

The U.C.C. allows the parties to provide liquidated damages clauses *if* the amount is *reasonable* and there is *no unconscionability* (e.g., disparity in bargaining power).

a. Revision variation §678

The revision also provides for recovery of liquidated damages for reasonable amounts. However, in *consumer contracts only*, the validity of the clause is measured by the difficulty of proving loss and the inconvenience of obtaining another adequate remedy.

2. Limitations on Damages §679

The parties may limit damages (including consequential damages) between themselves if the limitation or exclusion is *not* unconscionable. Note that unconscionability is *presumed* in *consumer goods* cases. Limitations are often found in warranty disclaimers.

3. "Exclusive Remedy" Provisions §684

The parties may choose their own remedies as long as *adequate minimum remedies* are available. Exclusive remedies must be clearly stated, or courts will interpret around them.

4. Failure of Essential Purpose of Remedy Limitation §686

When an exclusive or limited remedy fails to function as contemplated by the parties, the injured party can *ignore that remedy* and have recourse to remedies under the U.C.C.

5. Consequential Damages and Limitation of Remedies Relationship §688

Courts have reached differing results in deciding whether the failure of a limitation's essential purpose permits recovery of consequential damages or whether the aggrieved party must still prove that the disclaimer is unconscionable. Courts are more likely to find the provisions *dependent in consumer cases*, thus making it easier to obtain consequential damages, and *independent in commercial cases* so that the commercial party must also prove unconscionability.

G. STATUTE OF LIMITATIONS §690

The U.C.C. provides a *four-year* statute of limitations on sales contract actions (*oral or written*). (Note that several states have not adopted this provision.) The statute starts to run when the cause of action *accrues*. There is a presumption that the period starts to run *at delivery* in breach of warranty actions; however, *express warranties of future performance* start to run when buyer *should have discovered* the breach (implied warranties are *always* breached on delivery).

showing that it received goods not actually received. In these cases, the carrier can limit its liability by noting on the document, "shipper's weight, load, and count," or similar language.

4. Bills Drawn to Seller or Seller's Order—Divided Property Interests §737
A seller may *consign the goods to seller*, thus reserving title and protecting seller until payment is received from buyer. This practice is called *shipment under reservation*.

X. LEASE OF GOODS

A. SCOPE OF ARTICLE 2A

1. Lease Defined §742
Article 2A is limited in application to transactions for the lease of goods (including subleases).

2. Lease vs. Disguised Sale on Credit §743
If a so-called lease is actually a disguised sale on credit, the seller must take steps under Article 9 for perfection of a security interest to ensure priority to the subject goods in case of default.

    a. Tests for distinguishing sale from lease §744
If a contract contains a *clause* permitting the lessee to *terminate* the lease at any time *and return the goods*, the transaction is a *true lease*. If the lease is for the *entire economic life* of the leased goods, the transaction is a *disguised sale*. All other cases must be determined on an individual basis.

    b. Protective Article 9 filing §749
Where it is uncertain whether a transaction is a lease or sale, it is prudent for the lessor to perfect a security interest under Article 9; section 9-505 permits a lessor to do so under the designations "lessor" and "lessee" rather than "secured party" and "debtor."

B. ARTICLE 2 RULES COPIED §750
Article 2A generally follows Article 2 rules with the following exceptions:

1. Statute of Frauds §751
The lease must be evidenced by a signed writing describing the goods and the lease term if the total payments under the lease will be *$1,000 or more*.

2. Battle of the Forms §752
Article 2A has *no* battle of the forms provision.

3. Consumer Protection

    a. Option to accelerate §754
Clauses permitting acceleration of the entire lease obligation at the lessor's will are enforceable only if exercised in *good faith*.

    b. Unconscionability §755
Article 2A's unconscionability rule goes further than Article 2's rule, mainly

to benefit consumer lessees. Consumer leases can be declared unconscionable if *induced* by fraud (there is no additional requirement of substantive unfairness). Consumers can recover *attorneys' fees*, but if the court finds the consumer's action to be groundless, fees can be assessed against the consumer. In a consumer lease, a *disclaimer of liability for consequential damages* for personal injury is *prima facie unconscionable*.

C. WARRANTIES

1. Few Distinctions from Article 2 §759
The lessor generally makes all of the usual warranties that are made by a seller under Article 2, except regarding a finance lease.

2. Finance Lease Defined §760
In a finance lease, the lessee has the lessor purchase the goods from the seller (*"supplier"*) and then leases the goods from the lessor. The lessee is the one who selects the goods—not the lessor.

3. Warranties in a Finance Lease §763
The finance lease lessor makes *no implied warranties*, but any *warranties made by the supplier* to the lessor are *passed on* to the lessee, who may bring a direct action against the supplier for any breach.

4. "Hell or High Water" Clause §764
Except in consumer leases, a finance lease imposes an *absolute duty* on the lessee to make payments to the lessor no matter how badly the leased goods perform or break down.

D. REMEDIES

1. Default by Lessor §766
Default by the lessor gives the lessee the same rights and remedies that the lessee would have if the transaction had been a sale and Article 2 applied; however, revocation of acceptance is *not* permitted in a finance lease for *quality problems* first arising after acceptance, but only for substantial breaches of the lease agreement between the lessor and lessee.

2. Default by Lessee §767
Default by the lessee gives the lessor remedies similar to those given to a seller under Article 2. The lease can be cancelled only if the lessee's breach is *material*; an action for damages is the remedy for nonmaterial breaches.

3. Repossession by Lessor §768
Under Article 2A, after repossession, a lessor can recover *only actual damages*. Thus a lessor *cannot* repossess, sue the lessee for the entire amount remaining under the lease, and relet the goods.

a. Action for rent §769
The lessor can sue for the entire amount of rent due under the lease when the goods have *not been repossessed or tendered* by the lessee (*e.g.*, where the goods are worthless or have been destroyed) or where return of the goods was in no way a mitigating factor (*e.g.*, where the lessor has lost volume by the lessee's refusal).

C. SOME SUBSTANTIVE ISSUES §786

The following provisions under CISG vary from the corresponding Article 2 rule.

1. Statute of Frauds §787

CISG recognizes oral contracts; there is **no** Statute of Frauds provision.

2. Mailbox Rule §788

Under CISG, an acceptance is not effective until **received**, but the offeror is not permitted to revoke an offer once an acceptance has been dispatched.

3. Battle of the Forms §789

Under CISG, a reply to an offer purporting to be an acceptance but containing additions, limitations, or other modifications is a rejection and a counteroffer. However, a reply to an offer purporting to be an acceptance but containing additional or different terms that do not materially alter the terms of the offer is an acceptance unless the offeror timely **objects orally**. If there is no objection, the modifications in the acceptance are included in the contract.

4. Fundamental Breach and Notice §790

CISG gives a broader range of remedies for fundamental breach than for other breaches. Fundamental breach is similar to material breach. The buyer must give seller a **notice** of breach within a reasonable time, but no longer than **two years** after receiving the goods.

5. Remedies

a. Specific performance §792

CISG has a **presumption** in favor of specific performance but does not permit it where the court asked to grant it would not do so under local law.

b. Rejection by buyer §793

The buyer may not reject goods and require delivery of conforming goods unless the seller's original tender was so deficient as to constitute a fundamental breach.

c. Grace periods to resolve disputes §794

CISG gives parties (buyers and sellers) an opportunity to propose a grace period (called "Nachfrist notices"), during which time no action can be taken, thus giving the breaching party a chance to remedy the problem.

Approach to Exams

The issues on your Sales exam can be broad questions such as "Buyer sues Seller; who wins?" or very specific questions like "who bears the risk of loss where the contract requires F.O.B. seller's factory?" A helpful approach to the broad question follows; for more specific questions, use the appropriate parts of the following approach and the detailed chapter approach sections at the beginning of the relevant chapters.

1. Is There an Enforceable Contract?

By definition, a "sale" is a contract by which title to goods is transferred from a seller to a buyer. Therefore, begin your analysis by determining whether there is an enforceable contract. To do this, consider the basic principles of Contract law: Is there an *offer*, an *acceptance*, *consideration*, and *certainty of terms*? (*See* Contracts Summary.) In addition, remember that Article 2 of the Uniform Commercial Code ("U.C.C.") has engrafted onto the law of Contracts certain exceptions and modifications which may result in upholding and enforcing a contract for the sale of goods which otherwise would be unenforceable at common law, *e.g.,* "firm offers" (*see infra,* §§59-62), "open" terms (*infra,* §§119-157), etc. Therefore, you must consider *both* Contract law and the U.C.C. modifications.

2. What Are the Elements of Contract?

Under the law of Sales, the elements of a contract may derive from three sources, ranked in order of priority:

(i) **Agreement of the parties:** The parties' agreement is of *paramount importance*, and if problems arise in the performance of a sales contract, reference must always be made first to the agreement. If the agreement covers the problems, it will govern (subject to limitations of "unconscionability" and "good faith").

(ii) **Custom and usage:** If the agreement is *silent or incomplete* (as is often the case), reference is then made to the prevailing custom in the industry.

(iii) **U.C.C. rules:** Finally, the U.C.C. has *"gap-filling" rules* that attempt to supply terms overlooked by the parties.

But remember: The more gaps there are in the contract, the more likely the court will find that there was no real contract intended by the parties.

3. What Performance Is Required Under the Contract?

If you have gotten this far (in other words, if you have determined that an enforceable sales contract exists and determined the nature of the sale intended), the next issue is whether each of the parties has performed the obligations imposed by the contract:

a. Has the seller performed?

If the contract required the seller to ship the goods to the buyer *via carrier,* has the seller done so in the method contemplated by the contract or otherwise as allowed by law? If the contract required the seller to deliver the goods *directly to the buyer* (or allows the buyer to pick up the goods from the seller), has the seller made a valid tender of delivery of *conforming* goods (be sure to think about whether the goods must conform perfectly or whether something less is allowed)? Finally, if tender is defective in some way, can it be *cured*?

b. Has the buyer performed?

Basically, the buyer must accept the goods and pay for them when due.

(1) Regarding *acceptance,* remember that if the buyer interfered in any way with the seller's tender of delivery, the buyer has not properly performed under the contract. Other acceptance issues concern whether the buyer properly exercised the right to inspect or reject the goods. Keep in mind that the buyer can *waive* either of these rights and often does so by failing to act.

(2) As to *payment* issues, you need to consider when payment was due and what method of payment is proper.

4. If a Party Has Not Performed, Has Performance Been Excused?

Watch for situations where one party is excused from performance by the other *party's breach* or *anticipatory breach*, by *"unforeseen" circumstances* (*e.g.,* outbreak of war), or by the *damage or destruction* of the goods without the fault of either party. Obviously, if performance has been excused, the party cannot be in breach for not performing. If either party's performance appears doubtful, consider whether the other party has the right to *demand assurances* of counterperformance before performing.

5. If Nonperformance Constitutes a Breach, What Remedies Are Available to the Injured Parties?

a. Prelitigation remedies

(1) *Seller's remedies* include the right to demand cash, to reclaim goods already delivered, to stop goods in transit, to cancel the sale, to resell the goods, etc.

(2) *Buyer's remedies* include the right to reject goods, to "revoke" acceptance, to cover, to retain delivered goods in order to recover prepayments on the purchase price, to set off damages against the price, etc.

b. Litigation remedies

(1) *Seller's remedies* include an action for full purchase price or for damages for nonacceptance;

(2) ***Buyer's remedies*** include suits for possession, for specific performance, for damages for nondelivery or breach of warranty, or for restitution of prepayments on the purchase price.

c. Remedy limitations

The usual U.C.C. remedies may be altered by a valid ***liquidated damages clause*** in the contract or other clause limiting the remedy or disclaiming certain kinds of remedies. Also, remember that if the statute of limitations has run, the remedy may be eliminated by law.

6. What Are the Rights, If Any, of Third Parties?

If someone other than the buyer or seller claims an interest in the goods, consider:

a. Did the seller have valid title to the goods?

If not (*i.e.*, the transfer to the seller was fraudulent or unauthorized), is the seller's title totally ***void*** or merely ***voidable*** (so that the seller can still pass effective title to a bona fide purchaser)?

b. Does any third party claim priority as to the goods?

Even assuming that you find that the seller had valid title, think about whether a third party purchaser or creditor can assert rights to the goods because the goods were subject to a negotiable document of title (*see infra, §§700 et seq.*).

7. Is It Possible that Other Laws Apply?

a. Lease of goods

Article 2A of the U.C.C. covers the lease of goods and has rules remarkably similar to those found in Article 2. If the transaction creates a true lease, Article 2A must be consulted and its rules applied.

b. International sales

International sales are covered by the United Nations Convention on Contracts for the International Sale of Goods. Most of its rules are similar to those found in Article 2, but there are major differences on some matters. If the parties are in different countries, each of which is a signatory to the treaty (as the United States is), the treaty will govern the sale unless the parties agree to the application of some other body of law.

Chapter One:
Introduction

CONTENTS

Chapter Approach

The first issue to consider in any Sales problem is whether the Uniform Commercial Code ("U.C.C.") applies to the transaction. If so, of course you must follow the U.C.C. rules. If not, the common law rules of Contracts will be in effect. However, even if your question is a common law Contracts question, you should not ignore the U.C.C., because courts are often swayed by the U.C.C. rules and might apply the U.C.C. by analogy. Therefore, you should consider the U.C.C. in any Sales question.

This chapter introduces you to some of the basic principles used throughout the U.C.C. (*e.g.,* good faith, usage of trade, etc.). You must master these concepts before the details of the Code can be considered, because you will find that they turn up time and time again in Sales questions.

Note that Article 2 of the Uniform Commercial Code was substantially rewritten in 2003, and the changes made by this revision are discussed in this Summary, as well as the original rules. Your instructor will tell you which version to study.

A. Historical Background

1. **Origins of Sales Law [§1]**

   The law of Sales developed as part of the common law of both England and the United States, largely after the year 1800. At the end of the nineteenth century, these common law principles were codified in England as the Sale of Goods Act, and in the United States as the *Uniform Sales Act*, which was largely patterned after the English statute.

2. **Uniform Sales Act [§2]**

   Although the Uniform Sales Act was a well-drafted statute in its time, it was essentially outmoded almost from promulgation. It purported to codify the common law of Sales developed in the nineteenth century, but these principles proved inapplicable to many of the problems posed by the mass distribution of goods to consumers and businesses in the twentieth century.

3. **Uniform Commercial Code [§3]**

   As a result, a new uniform Act was drafted in 1951 by the Commissioners on Uniform State Laws, and this new Act now appears as Article 2 of the Uniform Commercial Code. Article 2 of the U.C.C. has now been enacted in every American jurisdiction except Louisiana, and it completely replaces the Uniform Sales Act. Article 2A of the U.C.C., also in effect in most jurisdictions, covers leases of goods. It is modeled on Article 2 but has certain rules peculiar to lease transactions alone.

a. **Revision of Article 2 [§4]**

In 2003 the drafters produced a new version of Article 2 of the Uniform Commercial Code, and sent it out to the states for adoption. Unfortunately, the revised version has powerful political enemies, and at this writing does not have much chance for widespread adoption. For that reason, this Summary concentrates on the rules of the original version and explains the 2003 revision only as relevant. In cases where the numbering is different between the two versions (which happily is not often), a citation that uses the letter "R" as part of its numbering refers to the 2003 revision only. Thus, a citation to section 2-302 refers to that section in both the original Code and the revision, but a citation to section 2R-302 refers only to the revised section.

b. **Revision of Article 1 [§5]**

Article 1 of the Uniform Commercial Code has a similar problem. Article 1 is a general Article whose rules are applicable to all the Articles that follow (unless they state otherwise). It contains general principles such as a section explaining how the Code is to be construed [§1-102], a section preserving the common law unless obviously changed by the Code [§1-103], a command that *good faith* be imposed in all U.C.C. transactions [§1-203], and, most importantly, a huge definition section [§1-201] explaining the meaning of terms used throughout the rest of the statute. Article 1 itself was rewritten in 2001, and it also has so far failed to be widely adopted. Consequently, unless otherwise noted, citations in this Summary are to the original numbering of Article 1 (and those containing the letter "R" are to the revised version).

c. **Correct version essential**

When looking up citations in the U.C.C. itself, make sure that you are looking at the correct version of the relevant Article. The original versions of Articles 1 and 2 are probably referred to in your statute book as the "pre-revision" versions.

EXAM TIP

gilbert

Be sure to note whether *your instructor* expects you to use the original or revised versions of Articles 1 and 2 for your exams, or if you will be required to discuss both variations.

---

4. **United Nations Treaty [§6]**

Effective January 1, 1988, the United States became a signatory to the United Nations Convention on Contracts for the International Sale of Goods (often called "CISG"). As discussed *infra* (§§780-793), the treaty applies whenever two parties to an international sale are located in different countries, each a signatory to the treaty, and they do not agree that some other body of law applies to the transaction. The rules of CISG are similar to existing American law, although there are some important differences.

B. Scope of Article 2

1. Concentration on U.C.C. Provisions [§7]

This Summary will focus almost exclusively on the U.C.C. provisions dealing with Sales. Common law and Uniform Sales Act provisions will be noted only where essential to understanding the operation and effect of the U.C.C. All references to and discussions of the U.C.C. are to the Official Text of the Uniform Commercial Code. However, it should be noted that many states have made changes from the Official Text in adopting the Code, and, therefore, attention must be given to local variations from the rules set forth herein.

2. Transactions Involving "Goods" [§8]

The law of Sales is applicable only to transactions involving "goods." This term is discussed in detail *infra* (§§37 *et seq.*), but basically covers *all tangible chattels*.

a. Other property outside the scope of Article 2 [§9]

The Sales provisions of the U.C.C. do *not* apply to *real estate* or any interest therein [U.C.C. §2-304(2)]; nor to *choses in action* (*i.e.*, the ability to sue for breach of contract other than those involving goods) or *investment* securities (stocks, bonds, promissory notes, etc.) [U.C.C. §2-105(1)].

TYPES OF TRANSACTIONS COVERED BY U.C.C. ARTICLE 2	gilbert
COVERED	**NOT COVERED**
The sale of: • **Goods**, *i.e.*, tangible chattels	The sale of: • **Real estate** • **Choses in action** • **Investment securities** • **Secured transactions**

3. Related Transactions [§10]

Because of their close connection to the law of Sales (Article 2), this Summary also covers *documents of title* (U.C.C. Article 7, *see infra*, §§700-741).

4. Secured Transactions Excluded [§11]

On the other hand, Article 2 deals only with *unsecured* sales transactions, and therefore this Summary does not cover the additional problems involved where a seller or lender claims a *secured interest* in the goods (*e.g.*, a chattel mortgage or conditional sales contract). Such problems are dealt with in Article 9 of the U.C.C. (*See* Secured Transactions Summary.)

C. Basic Principles of the U.C.C.

1. **In General [§12]**

   Before delving into the various rules comprising the law of Sales under the U.C.C., certain basic principles that permeate, and in some instances override, the U.C.C. rules should be kept in mind.

2. **Good Faith [§13]**

   First, and most important, every contract or duty within the scope of the U.C.C. imposes an obligation of good faith in its performance or enforcement. [U.C.C. §§1-203, 1R-304] This obligation *cannot be waived* by the parties. [U.C.C. §1-102(3)] There are a number of court decisions holding that good faith is an absolute condition precedent to any protection by the other U.C.C. provisions. Hence, if a person's action is clearly in bad faith, that person cannot claim the benefits of the U.C.C. rules.

   a. **Honesty in fact [§14]**

      "Good faith" is defined *subjectively* as "honesty in fact." [U.C.C. §1-201(19)] This is *not* a *reasonable person test*, but a test of subjective honesty, whether or not reasonable. *Note:* Under the revised version of Article 1, the definition of "good faith" has been expanded to include an *objective* component, so that it now covers both "honesty in fact *and* the observance of reasonable commercial standards of fair dealing." [U.C.C. §1R-201(b)(20)]

   b. **Merchant's standard [§15]**

      A merchant (*see infra,* §26) is always held to a higher objective standard that includes "the observance of reasonable commercial standards of *fair dealing in the trade.*" [U.C.C. §2-103(1)(b)]

3. **Construction Terms [§16]**

   In construing the meaning of contract terms, the courts will look to usage of trade, course of dealing, and course of performance.

   a. **"Usage of trade" [§17]**

      "Usage of trade" means the *custom within the industry*. It binds all of those who *should* know about it, sometimes even including consumers. [U.C.C. §§1-205(2), 1R-303(c)]

   b. **"Course of dealing" [§18]**

      "Course of dealing" refers to the *parties' past contacts* with each other. If the parties have dealt together in the past, what they did then is thought to give insight to their current agreement. [U.C.C. §§1-205(1), 1R-303(b)]

   c. **"Course of performance" [§19]**

      "Course of performance" (called "practical construction" by the common law) refers to what the parties do when *performing this particular contract*. It is particularly apropos when there are repeated occasions for performance without objection, as in an installment contract. [U.C.C. §§2-208(1), 1R-303(a)]

THE U.C.C. INSTRUCTS COURTS TO CONSIDER FIRST THE MOST SPECIFIC, PROGRESSING TO THE MORE GENERAL TERMS:

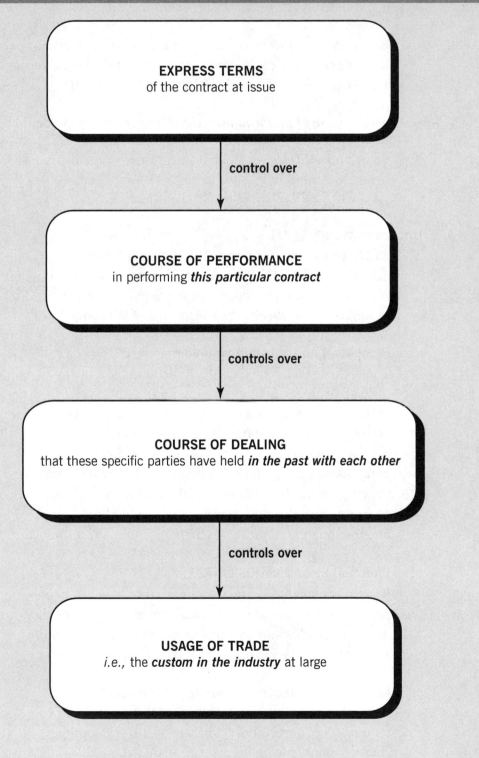

EXPRESS TERMS
of the contract at issue

control over

COURSE OF PERFORMANCE
in performing *this particular contract*

controls over

COURSE OF DEALING
that these specific parties have held *in the past with each other*

controls over

USAGE OF TRADE
i.e., the *custom in the industry* at large

d. Hierarchy of construction terms [§20]

If the usage of trade conflicts with the course of performance, which is most important in deciding the meaning of the contract? The U.C.C. answers this and related questions by *preferring the specific over the general*, so that the more closely related the term is to the transaction at issue, the more weight is given to it. Thus, the hierarchy is:

(i) *Express terms* in the contract control over course of performance (unless the course of performance shows that the express term was *waived* by the later conduct [U.C.C. §§2-208(3), 1R-303(f)]);

(ii) *Course of performance* controls over course of dealing; and

(iii) *Course of dealing* controls over mere usage of trade.

[U.C.C. §§1-205(4), 2-208(2), 1R-303(e)]

4. Unconscionability [§21]

The U.C.C. brings into the law of Sales the equitable concept of the unconscionable contract. [U.C.C. §2-302] The Code deliberately refrains from defining what constitutes an "unconscionable" contract. In general, it may be said to be one that is *so grossly unfair* that it *shocks the conscience of the court*.

a. Procedural and substantive unfairness [§22]

The courts have become fond of a definition of unconscionability first proposed by Professor Arthur Leff in a famous article. [115 U. Pa. L. Rev. 485 (1967)] Leff said that a court should never make a finding of unconscionability unless it finds both *procedural* and *substantive* unfairness in the transaction. "Procedural unconscionability" means unfairness in the bargaining process, typically because one party, having a superior bargaining position, will not bargain at all and presents the contract to the other on a "take it or leave it" basis (the so-called adhesion contract, whereby one party must adhere to the will of the other). "Substantive unconscionability" means a harsh term in the resulting contract.

b. Effect of unconscionability [§23]

If it finds that the contract or any part thereof is unconscionable, the court is permitted to (i) *avoid* the whole contract; (ii) *enforce* the contract *without* the unconscionable clause; or (iii) so *limit* the application of the clause that it will avoid the unconscionable result. [U.C.C. §2-302(1)]

c. Application of unconscionability doctrine [§24]

Before finding that the contract is unconscionable in whole or part, the U.C.C. requires the court to hold a hearing as to the commercial setting in which the charge of unconscionability arose. [U.C.C. §2-302(2)] Most courts have held such a hearing to be a condition precedent to a finding of unconscionability. [**State v. AVCO Financial Service**, 50 N.Y.2d 383 (1980)] It is impossible to state with any degree of assuredness just what is or is not an unconscionable clause. About the only guideline that can be offered is that the "dickered" terms of the bargain—those to which both parties *voluntarily and knowingly consent*—will ordinarily not be deemed unconscionable, even though they may be unfair. On the other hand, printed-form contracts that overreach the bounds of fairness by virtue of economic power will more likely be held unconscionable. There are cases saying that an extraordinarily high price alone can be unconscionable. [**Murphy v. McNamara,** 416 A.2d 170 (Conn. 1979)]

EXAM TIP   **gilbert**

Remember that so long as the terms of the contract are *bargained for*, they will not be deemed unconscionable, even if unfair.

---

d. Note—commercial contracts rarely held unconscionable [§25]

There has been almost no application of the doctrine of unconscionability to commercial cases. When buyer and seller are both *business entities*, they are usually treated as being on an equal footing, and thus even when the terms seem unfair, the courts will honor them. [**Keystone Aeronautics v. R.J. Enstrom,** 499 F.2d 146 (3d Cir. 1974)]

5. Merchants [§26]

U.C.C. Article 2 draws distinctions between merchants and nonmerchants and holds merchants to higher standards than those for nonmerchants.

a. "Merchant" defined [§27]

Under the U.C.C., a "merchant" is a party who:

(i) *Regularly deals* in goods of the kind sold;

(ii) Otherwise *holds himself out* as having *special knowledge or skill* as to the practices or goods involved; or

(iii) Employs an *agent* who fits within these categories.

[U.C.C. §2-104(1)]

(1) Special knowledge as to goods [§28]

Under this definition, a person clearly need not be a dealer or merchant in the traditional sense. Any person with special know-how or experience as to the goods involved may be so treated (*e.g.*, an auctioneer or broker who regularly sells goods of the type in question). [**Regan Purchase & Sales Corp. v. Primavera,** 68 Misc. 2d 858 (1972)]

(2) Special knowledge as to practices [§29]

Likewise, a person with special knowledge or experience regarding the practices involved in the transaction (or who employs an agent with such knowledge or experience) may be treated as a "merchant" for U.C.C. purposes. Under appropriate circumstances, a lawyer, bank president, or other professional person might be so classified; indeed, almost every person in business could be classified as a "merchant" with respect to certain practices (*e.g.,* responding to mail).

(3) Application—farmers [§30]

Is a farmer a merchant? It would seem so. Except perhaps for amateurs or "casual" growers, most *professional* farmers have special know-how regarding the crops they raise and sell. Following this reasoning, a number of courts hold them to be "merchants." [**Campbell v. Yokell,** 313 N.E.2d 628 (Ill. 1974)]

(a) But note

An equal number of courts disagree, usually reasoning that farmers' know-how is limited to growing, not selling, and that it would be too disruptive of farm sales transactions to impose on farmers the higher standards required of "merchants." [**Cook Grains, Inc. v. Fallis,** 395 S.W.2d 555 (Ark. 1965); **Sand Seed Service, Inc. v. Poeckes,** 249 N.W.2d 663 (Iowa 1977)]

b. Significance of distinction [§31]

As mentioned, the U.C.C. imposes higher standards on "merchants" than nonmerchants. Among the most important are the following:

(1) Fair dealing vs. honesty standard [§32]

Merchants are held to a standard of "fair dealing in the trade" [U.C.C. §2-103(1)(b)], whereas nonmerchants owe only a duty of "honesty in fact" in the transaction involved. [U.C.C. §1-201(19); *and see supra,* §14]

(2) Implied warranties [§33]

A merchant-seller is held to certain implied warranties as to the goods sold; nonmerchants have no such liability. [U.C.C. §2-314; *and see infra,* §§233-244]

(3) Oral contracts [§34]

A special exception to the Statute of Frauds makes oral agreements enforceable against a merchant, regardless of the price of the goods involved, if the merchant has failed to reply to a letter from the other party in confirmation of the deal (the "merchant's confirmatory memo rule"). No such exception applies to nonmerchants; *i.e.,* nonmerchants cannot be held to oral agreements for the sale of goods priced at $500 or more. [U.C.C. §2-201; *and see infra,* §§96-121]

(4) Battle of the forms [§35]

Where form contracts are exchanged, the Code permits merchants to add nonmaterial terms to the acceptance without the consent of the other party in certain circumstances. [U.C.C. §2-207(2); *see infra*, §§76-83]

SUMMARY OF DISTINCTIONS FOR MERCHANTS

LISTED BELOW ARE THE PRINCIPAL U.C.C. ARTICLE 2 SECTIONS DISTINGUISHING *MERCHANTS* FROM OTHER BUYERS AND SELLERS.

SECTION	TOPIC
2-201(2)	Statute of Frauds—merchant's confirmatory memo rule
2-205	Merchant's firm offer
2-207(2)	Additional terms in acceptance or confirmation—"battle of the forms" rule for merchants
2-209(2)	Agreement excluding modification except by signed writing—form supplied by merchant
2-312	Warranty against infringement
2-314	Implied warranty of merchantability
2-316(2)	Disclaimer of implied warranty of merchantability
2-403(2)	Entrusting goods to merchant gives her power to transfer rights to buyer in ordinary course
2-509(3)	Risk of loss in the absence of breach (noncarrier cases)—passes on buyer's receipt if seller is not a merchant, otherwise on tender of delivery

6. Reasonableness [§36]

Finally, it should be noted that the U.C.C. in effect establishes a rule of reason. Throughout the Code and particularly Article 2, the words "reasonable," "reasonably," and "commercial reasonableness" are repeatedly found in provisions setting forth standards of conduct. Again, no definition is given, on the theory that if the terms are defined, corner-cutters might find a way to comply with the letter but not the spirit of the law. Instead, by omitting definitions, the Code puts the parties to commercial contracts on notice that they are expected to behave properly, on penalty of having their actions judicially declared "unreasonable" at a later date with the consequent imposition of whatever sanctions are appropriate.

Chapter Two:
The Sales Contract

CONTENTS

Chapter Approach

Chapter Approach

As mentioned, the first issue in any Sales problem is whether Article 2 applies. To resolve this issue, you must determine whether the *transaction* involves *goods*. This chapter introduces you to the very broad U.C.C. definition of "goods" (basically, anything movable).

Once you have determined that Article 2 applies to the transaction at hand, the *scope* of the agreement must be determined. The U.C.C. codifies the common law rules of offer and acceptance but adds some special variations. Furthermore, the Code has its own Statute of Frauds and parol evidence rule, and makes some changes to the assignability of sales contracts. Therefore, for all these areas, you need to know the basic Contract law *plus* the U.C.C. variations, both of which this chapter highlights for you.

A. Subject Matter—What Goods Can Be Sold

1. **"Goods" Defined [§37]**

   "Goods" include all tangible chattels—basically anything *movable* at the time it is identified to the contract of sale. Excluded by this definition are transactions involving real property (but crops are included, *see* below); transactions in paper rights (*e.g.*, promissory notes, stocks, or bonds); the sale of services (*e.g.*, a membership in a health spa); and the sale of intangibles (*e.g.*, insurance). [U.C.C. §2-105(1)]

   a. **"Goods" attached to realty [§38]**

      As discussed above, Article 2 does not apply to the sale of land itself or any interest therein. However, it does apply to the sale of certain kinds of property attached to land, if severed and sold apart from the land:

      (1) **Crops [§39]**

          Growing crops, whether natural to the land itself ("fructus naturales") or cultivated ("fructus industriales") are within the scope of Article 2.

      (2) **Minerals, structures severed by seller [§40]**

          Minerals, ice, water, or any structure on the land, *if to be severed by the seller*, are covered by Article 2. If not, the contract is not subject to Article 2.

   EXAM TIP   **gilbert**

   Remember that who (buyer or seller) severs the property from the land is a *threshold inquiry*—consider this first to determine whether Article 2 or the common law should be applied.

(a) **Timber [§41]**

Under the original Code provision, standing timber also fell under this "seller's severance" rule. However, the provision has now been revised, so that timber is treated the same as "growing crops" above (*i.e.,* it does not matter whether the seller or the buyer is to sever the timber; either way Article 2 applies). However, not all states have adopted this change.

(3) **Fixtures [§42]**

Anything else attached to the land which can be removed without material harm thereto ("fixtures") is covered by Article 2, whether it is to be severed by the buyer, the seller, or some third person. [U.C.C. §2-107(1), (2)]

b. **Must be in existence [§43]**

The one major limitation on what can be "goods" is that goods must be presently in existence. Thus, for example, goods to be specially manufactured, or a work of art to be created, become subject to Article 2 only when actually created or manufactured.

(1) **Unborn young—in existence [§44]**

"Goods" also include the unborn young of animals. [U.C.C. §2-105(1)]

EXAMPLES OF GOODS SUBJECT TO ARTICLE 2   **gilbert**

CERTAIN GOODS ASSOCIATED WITH REAL ESTATE MAY FALL UNDER ARTICLE 2:

☑ *Crops*, either natural or cultivated

☑ *Minerals*, if to be severed by the seller

☑ *Water* or ice, if to be severed by the seller

☑ *Timber* to be cut, regardless of who severs

☑ *Animals*, including the unborn young of animals

☑ *Fixtures* so long as they may be removed without material harm to the land

---

2. **Nonexistent or Destroyed Goods [§45]**

If the parties purport to make a present sale of identified, *specific* goods (*i.e.,* this horse, that chair—not "a horse" or "a chair"), but unknown to them the goods have been *totally* destroyed or otherwise are nonexistent, the contract is *void* from the outset. [U.C.C. §2-613(a); *and see* Contracts Summary] Similarly, if the parties make an *executory* (unperformed) contract to sell identified, specific goods, and before the risk of loss passes to the buyer the goods are totally destroyed, the contract is avoided. [U.C.C. §2-613(a)]

> **Example:** Seller contracts to sell "Man of Battle," a famous racehorse, to Buyer. Unknown to either party, the horse died the previous day. The contract is automatically void.

3. Damaged and Deteriorated Goods [§46]

If the goods are damaged or have deteriorated but are not totally destroyed *at the time of sale*, then slightly different rules apply: The contract is not void; rather, the *buyer* has the *option* to void the sale. [U.C.C. §2-613(b)]

a. Option to accept goods and deduct for damage [§47]

Alternatively, the buyer may choose to accept the goods, even though they do not conform to the contract. The buyer doing so is entitled to a "due allowance from the contract price" (*see infra*, §617), but *waives all other rights* against the seller.

> **Example:** Seller contracts to sell a specific carload of foam rubber pillows to the buyer for $2,500. At the time the sale is made, but unknown to either party, water seepage had destroyed 20% of the pillows and damaged 40% of the remainder. Buyer can treat the contract as avoided or Buyer can elect to proceed. If so, Buyer is entitled to an appropriate price adjustment of at least $500 for the 20% destroyed, and a reasonable amount for the deterioration to the 40% of the remainder.

> **Compare:** If goods are damaged or destroyed *after* the sale is entered into, the rights of the parties depend on whether the *risk of loss* has passed to the buyer. If it has, the buyer is liable for the *full price* notwithstanding. If the risk of loss has not passed to the buyer, the seller must replace the goods. (*See* detailed discussion *infra*, §§521 *et seq.*)

4. Fungible Goods

a. Definition [§48]

"Fungible" goods are those in which each unit by its very nature, or by mercantile usage, is the *commercial equivalent* of every other unit. [U.C.C. §1-201(17)] Common examples of fungible goods are bushels of wheat, barrels of oil, and bags of jelly beans.

(1) Equivalent fungible goods [§49]

Goods that may not otherwise be fungible may be treated as fungible to the extent that a particular agreement treats unlike units as equivalents. [U.C.C. §1-201(17)] For example, a sale of "50 automobiles of any make or variety" from one junk dealer to another could, under the proper circumstances, be treated as a sale of fungible goods.

b. Sale of unidentified fungible goods treated as present sale [§50]

Fungible goods may be either identified (*e.g.,* "all the wheat in my silo") or unidentified (*e.g.*, "600 bushels from the wheat in my silo"). Ordinarily, there can be no present sale of ***unidentified*** goods. However, an exception is recognized where those goods are fungible. An agreement to convey an undivided ***interest in an identified mass*** of fungible goods is effective as a present sale—even though the goods are unidentified and the total number of units in the mass is undetermined. [U.C.C. §2-105(4)]

c. **Buyer of interest in mass of fungible goods becomes owner in common [§51]**
    Although title does not pass to any specific units, the buyer of a portion of a mass of fungible goods is treated as an owner in common with the owners of the remainder of the mass. If the contract is for sale of a *specific quantity* from the mass, the buyer becomes an owner in common of a portion of the mass, based on the proportion that the number of units of the sale bears to the number of units in the mass owned by the seller. [U.C.C. §2-105(4)]

 Example: If the seller sells to buyer "600 bushels of the wheat in my silo," and there are 1,200 bushels of wheat in the silo, the sale is effective to transfer title immediately to buyer of an undivided 50% interest in all the wheat.

---

5. **Services [§52]**
    Although contracts to perform services are not transactions in goods, many courts apply Article 2 to such contracts, either on a Restatement of Contract basis or "by analogy" to Article 2.

6. **Service Contracts Including Goods [§53]**
    If a contract involves the sale of *both* goods and services, does Article 2 apply? For example, if a contractor agrees to install roofing as part of the construction contract, or a hospital supplies blood to a patient as part of an operation, does Article 2 apply? In deciding such cases, the courts tend to ask whether the sale of goods aspect *predominates* over the sale of services aspect. The courts apply the U.C.C. only if the sale of goods is the predominant factor. [**Perlmutter v. Beth David Hospital**, 308 N.Y. 100 (1954)]

7. **Sale of Software [§54]**
    There is a major battle going on over whether the original version of Article 2 applies to the sale of software, with courts taking all possible positions. [*See, e.g.,* **Honeywell, Inc. v. Minolta Camera Co.**, 41 U.C.C. Rep. Serv. 2d 403 (D. N.J. 1991)—not sale of goods, common law applies; **I. Lan Systems, Inc. v. Netscout Service Level Corp.**, 183 F. Supp. 2d 328 (D. Mass. 2002)—not sale of goods, but Article 2 applies by analogy; **Softman Products Co., LLC v. Adobe Systems, Inc.**, 171 F. Supp. 2d 1075 (C.D. Cal. 2001)—is sale of goods] The 2003 revision of Article 2 has a controversial provision defining "goods" to exclude the sale of "information" [U.C.C. §2R-103(1)(k)], but no one is quite sure what this means, particularly in situations where software is sold along with some physical product (a geo-positioning device,

for example). The confusion over this issue has made the adoption of the new Article 2 controversial and much opposed by major commercial powers.

B. "Sale" vs. Other Arrangements

1. "Sale" Defined [§55]

A "sale" is a contract under which title to goods passes from a seller to a buyer for consideration called a price. [U.C.C. §2-106(1)]

a. Distinguish—other arrangements

A "sale" is different from a lease, bailment, pledge, consignment, etc., because in those arrangements there may be a delivery of possession of goods, and perhaps even the right to use the goods, but *no transfer of ownership*.

2. Nonsale Transactions Subject to U.C.C. [§56]

Remember, however, that Article 2 is expressly made applicable to any "transaction in goods." [U.C.C. §2-102] Thus, unless a Code provision expressly restricts its application to a *sale* of goods (as the warranty provisions all do), Article 2 also applies to leases, bailments, franchises, consignments, etc., involving goods. However, if the relevant state has adopted Article 2A of the U.C.C., that Article will govern disputes involving the *lease* of goods (*see infra*, §§742-779).

a. And note

Even if the Code requires a *sale* of goods, some courts have been willing to apply Article 2, by analogy, to nonsale contracts. Thus, for example, the U.C.C. *warranty* provisions have been held to apply in leases, construction contracts, sale of realty, etc. [**Cintrone v. Hertz Truck Leasing & Rental Service**, 212 A.2d 769 (N.J. 1965)]

C. Formation—Offer and Acceptance

1. In General [§57]

The requirements of offer and acceptance applicable to ordinary contracts are, of course, applicable to sales contracts. A sales contract need take no specific form. Under the U.C.C., the manner in which a contract is formed is not limited to an oral or a written agreement. Instead, the Code focuses on the element of agreement between the parties and provides that a sales contract can be formed in *any manner sufficient to show an agreement*, including conduct by both parties that recognizes the existence of such a contract. [U.C.C. §2-204(1)]

2. Contract Creation—Two-Pronged Test [§58]

Those in business sometimes do business in a very elliptical fashion, leaving out important matters. Nonetheless, the Code creates a contract if (i) the parties so *intend* and (ii) the court can fashion an appropriate *remedy*. [U.C.C. §2-204(3)]

3. Irrevocable ("Firm") Offer

a. Common law [§59]

At common law, to create an offer irrevocable for a specified period of time (*i.e.,* an option), the promise to keep the offer open has to be supported by *consideration*. If the requisite consideration is absent, the offer can be withdrawn at will, even if the offeror expressly promises not to revoke. [**Stamper v. Combs,** 176 S.W. 178 (Ky. 1915)]

b. U.C.C. rule [§60]

The U.C.C. changes this rule and provides that "firm" offers are irrevocable, even *without consideration*, if they meet the following requirements:

(i)   The firm offer must be made in connection with a contract to sell *goods*, as the Code does not purport to revise the general body of contract law outside its scope;

(ii) The firm offer must be made by a *"merchant"* (*see supra*, §27); and

(iii) The offer must be in a *signed writing* and must state that it will be held open.

[U.C.C. §2-205]

(1) How long irrevocable [§61]

If the above conditions are met, the offer is irrevocable ("firm") despite the absence of consideration for (i) the *period of time specified* in the offer, *or* (ii) if no period is specified, a *reasonable* time—but *in no event longer than three months*. Thus, even if the offer specifies a period longer than three months, the offeror will be bound only for three months. [U.C.C. §2-205]

(2) Form supplied by offeree [§62]

If the statement that the offer will be held open is on a form supplied by the offeree, the *offeror* is *not* bound by it unless this statement is separately signed by the offeror. [U.C.C. §2-205]

4. Medium of Acceptance

a. Common law [§63]

At common law, if the parties communicated with each other at a distance, the offeror could specify the medium of acceptance (*e.g.,* "reply by return mail"), and if the offer was limited to this medium, use of it was the only possible way of making an acceptance. The courts sometimes read the offeror's statement as permitting similar means of acceptance (*e.g.,* "reply by return mail" meant "reply by return mail or any medium as fast," so that a telegram or fax would do).

b. U.C.C. rule [§64]

The U.C.C. continues the liberal reading of the offeror's specification of the medium of acceptance, providing that "unless unambiguously indicated by the language or circumstances, an offer to make a contract shall be construed as inviting acceptance in any manner and by *any medium reasonable under the circumstances.*" [U.C.C. §2-206(1)(a)]

5. Acceptance by Shipment [§65]

When a buyer offers to purchase goods for *prompt or immediate* shipment, must the seller first notify the buyer that the offer is accepted (*i.e.,* making a *promise* to ship), or is the actual prompt shipment by the seller a sufficient acceptance to create a binding contract?

---

e.g. **Example:** Buyer sends the following order to seller: "Ship 750 Regal Computers by July 1." This offer is received by Seller on June 20, and Seller ships the requested merchandise to Buyer the same day. If the following day (before Buyer receives the shipment), Buyer faxes a cancellation of the order, is there a contract?

---

a. Common law [§66]

It was generally held at common law that an offer requesting prompt or immediate shipment *impliedly invited acceptance by shipment* or by notice. Seller's shipment of the goods, therefore, was an effective acceptance, and Buyer was bound by the offer, even though Seller had not given a return promise in so many words. [**Port Huron Machinery Co. v. Wohlers,** 221 N.W. 843 (Iowa 1928)]

b. U.C.C. rule [§67]

The U.C.C. takes the same position. An offer for prompt or current shipment is accepted either by a *prompt promise* to ship *or* by the *act* of shipment. [U.C.C. §2-206(1)(b)]

c. Effect of shipping nonconforming goods [§68]

The U.C.C. also deals with a problem not considered with any clarity by the common law cases—the effect of shipping nonconforming goods. For example, if in response to Buyer's order for prompt shipment of "750 Regal Computers," Seller had immediately shipped 650 Regals and 100 Overwoods, has Seller made an effective acceptance?

(1) Issue

Has Seller accepted Buyer's offer by doing something different than requested? Or has Seller merely made a *counteroffer* to Buyer by shipment of nonconforming goods, which Buyer is free to accept or reject on arrival?

(2) U.C.C. solution [§69]

Under the U.C.C., the shipment of nonconforming goods may be treated *either* as an acceptance or as a counteroffer, depending on Seller's actions in conjunction therewith.

(a) Mere shipment [§70]

If the seller merely ships nonconforming goods, then shipment constitutes both an *acceptance* of the offer *and a breach* of the contract formed thereby.

(b) Shipment plus notice [§71]

If the seller ships nonconforming goods and also *promptly notifies* the buyer that the seller is not accepting the offer but is merely shipping the substituted goods as an *accommodation* to the buyer, then the seller has made a *counteroffer* and no contract is formed. The buyer remains free to accept or reject the counteroffer shipment. If accepted, a contract is created. [U.C.C. §2-206(1)(b)]

6. Acceptance by Beginning Performance [§72]

Can an offer to form a sales contract be accepted through the commencement, but not completion, of performance?

---

e.g. **Example:** Buyer offers to purchase from Seller 200 high-speed drill bits. Immediately upon receipt of Buyer's purchase order—but without notifying Buyer of acceptance—Seller starts to assemble material and machines 30 of the drill bits. Then, Buyer sends a notice of revocation. Is there a contract binding Buyer?

---

a. Common law [§73]

At common law, whether the seller's commencement of performance constituted an effective acceptance depended on the *foreseeability* of the buyer's revocation once the seller had started to perform. [**Quick v. Wheeler**, 78 N.Y. 300 (1879); *and see* Contracts Summary]

b. U.C.C. rule [§74]

The U.C.C. clarifies this area by providing that commencement of the performance specified in the offer constitutes acceptance of the offer, *provided* that the offeree-acceptor *notifies* the offeror *within a reasonable time* that performance has commenced. [U.C.C. §2-206(2)]

(1) Note

The *notice* is not the acceptance; rather, acceptance (and thus formation of the contract) stems from commencing performance. Thus, any attempted revocation by the offeror *after performance has begun* but before the notice is received (if received within a reasonable time) is a nullity.

7. **Time of Acceptance Uncertain [§75]**

Situations arise in which the parties dickering for a deal exchange writings, but the interchanged correspondence does not disclose the exact point at which the deal was closed. In other words, it cannot be said with any certainty that one specific communication was the offer and a specific response the acceptance. Yet the parties thereafter act as if a contract had been closed. Under such circumstances, the U.C.C. takes the position that a binding contract exists even though the moment of its making is uncertain. [U.C.C. §2-204(2)]

8. **Counteroffers—Battle of the Forms [§76]**

Modern business transactions are often conducted largely by forms. A buyer, for instance, will dispatch to a seller a purchase order on which there are typed certain basic terms (*e.g.,* a description of the goods, price, quantity, delivery terms) and on which there are *printed* terms drafted by the buyer's attorney. Naturally, these printed terms favor the buyer. Upon receiving this order, the seller responds with a written acceptance or confirmation that usually contains the same basic terms as were typewritten on the buyer's order, but that also contains a number of printed terms. These printed terms, however, have been drafted by seller's counsel, and they favor the seller. Has a contract been formed between these two parties?

a. **Common law—"mirror image" rule [§77]**

Standard contract doctrine holds that the offeree's acceptance must conform to the *exact terms* of the offer (*i.e.,* there must be a "mirror image") and that *any* variance therefrom—material or not—constitutes a counteroffer, *i.e.,* a rejection of the original offer.

b. **U.C.C. rule under the original version of Article 2 [§78]**

Adopting the premise that both parties are relying on the existence of a contract despite their clashing forms, the U.C.C. establishes a general rule that a contract can be formed under such circumstances, *unless* the responding offeree (here, the seller) *specifically states* that there shall be *no contract unless the original offeror expressly accepts the second set of terms.* Such a clause is authorized by section 2-207(1), which provides that a written confirmation with different terms operates as an acceptance "unless acceptance is expressly made conditional on assent to the additional or different terms" commonly called the "*proviso*" part of this subsection. If the offeree specifically limits the contract to these new terms, the response is treated merely as a counteroffer, and no contract has been created (until the offeror expressly accepts). [U.C.C. §2-207(1)]

---

e.g. **Example:** Buyer sends a purchase order, and Seller replies with an acknowledgment form that agrees with Buyer's order except it disclaims all warranties. This is an acceptance in spite of this difference. As to what happens to Seller's new term, *see* below. However, if Seller's form had stated that it was *no*

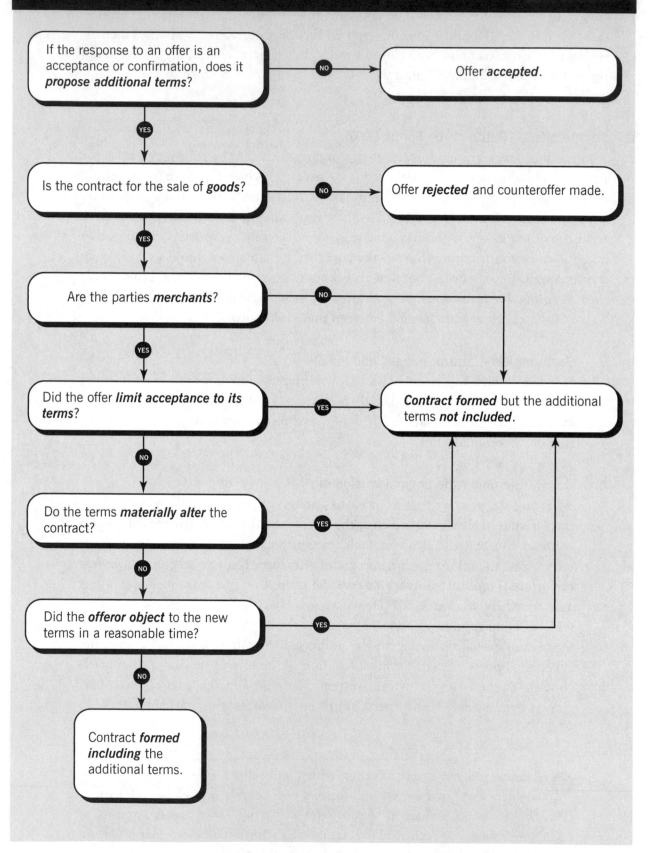

If the response to an offer is an acceptance or confirmation, does it **propose additional terms**?

— NO → Offer **accepted**.

YES ↓

Is the contract for the sale of **goods**?

— NO → Offer **rejected** and counteroffer made.

YES ↓

Are the parties **merchants**?

— NO →

YES ↓

Did the offer **limit acceptance to its terms**?

— YES → **Contract formed** but the additional terms **not included**.

NO ↓

Do the terms **materially alter** the contract?

— YES → **Contract formed** but the additional terms **not included**.

NO ↓

Did the **offeror object** to the new terms in a reasonable time?

— YES → **Contract formed** but the additional terms **not included**.

NO ↓

Contract **formed including** the additional terms.

acceptance unless Buyer expressly agreed to this change, then Seller has used the language of the *proviso* to avoid making an acceptance. All Seller has made is a *counteroffer*, and there is *no contract* unless Buyer expressly accepts the new terms. If Buyer says nothing and the contract proceeds, the contract is created under the default rules of section 2-207(3) (*see infra*).

EXAM TIP	gilbert

Recall that the U.C.C. changes the common law rule. Thus, for an offer for the purchase or sale of *goods*, an acceptance with additional terms is still an acceptance and a *contract is formed* (with or without the new terms). If the offer is for something *other* than the sale of goods (*e.g.*, land), an acceptance proposing additional terms is a rejection and a counteroffer; *no contract* is formed.

(1) New terms—where proviso is not used

(a) General rule [§79]

The new terms are construed as mere *proposed additions* to the contract; *i.e.*, they do *not* become part of the contract. These new terms must be separately accepted to modify the original offer. However, course of performance (*see supra*, §19) might show that these terms were impliedly accepted by the original offeror. [U.C.C. §2-207(2)]

(b) Merchants—special rule [§80]

If *both* parties to the contract qualify as merchants, the new terms *do* become part of the contract, unless one of the following happens or has happened:

1) Prior objection [§81]

If the original offer objected in advance to the addition of terms, the new terms are not part of the contract. [U.C.C. §2-207(2)(a)]

2) Subsequent objection [§82]

If the original offeror objects to the new terms within a reasonable time after notice of them is received, the terms are not part of the contract. [U.C.C. §2-207(2)(c)]

3) Material alteration [§83]

If the new terms would *materially* alter the original terms, the new terms are automatically stricken and do not become part of the resulting contract. Official Comment 4 to section 2-207 gives examples of terms that are material alterations and hence stricken. A *disclaimer of warranties* is the most obvious (and common) example. Most courts have held that a clause requiring arbitration is a material alteration. [**Universal Plumbing &**

Piping Supply, Inc. v. John C. Grimberg Co., 596 F. Supp. 1383 (W.D. Pa. 1984)]

a) **But note—contract formed without new terms**
If new terms are proposed that materially alter the original terms, *only* the material alterations fail to become part of the contract; the other parts of the offeree's form *do* act as an acceptance and *do* create a contract. [U.C.C. §2-207(2)(b)]

Example: Buyer sent Seller a purchase order. In reply Seller sent his acknowledgment form, which clearly disclaimed any warranty on the product. There is a contract, and Seller's disclaimer is of no effect.

---

b) **Policy**
The U.C.C. drafters are telling someone in the seller's position: Don't try to add material variations by boilerplate language in forms. If a point is important to you, negotiate it with the other party; otherwise, the U.C.C. will strike the material variation from the original offer.

(2) Different terms [§84]

The Code is less than clear about whether its battle of the forms rules apply to *different* terms. Official Comment 3 suggests that these rules do apply, while Official Comment 6 suggests the contrary. Suppose, for example, that a buyer's purchase order specifies one delivery date, but the seller's acknowledgment form changes the date. The courts have responded to this difficulty in three ways:

(a) Use of section 2-207(2) [§85]
Some courts, following the invitation in Official Comment 3, apply the rules of section 2-207(2), so that the different term in the seller's form is *stricken* if it *materially alters* the buyer's purchase order or if the *buyer objects* to it.

(b) Knock-out rule [§86]
Other courts have accepted the invitation of Official Comment 6 and find that both parties have objected to the differing terms, so that the contract is concluded *without agreement on the matter.* The so-called knock-out rule provides that the conflicting terms in the offer and acceptance are knocked out of the contract, and the knocked out terms are replaced by the U.C.C. gap-filler provisions instead. If, as in the above scenario, the parties cannot agree as to the delivery date,

resort is made to section 2-309, which says that delivery must be within a "reasonable time." [**Daitom, Inc. v. Pennwalt Corp.**, 741 F.2d 1569 (10th Cir. 1984)]

(c) No contract [§87]

If the disagreement concerns a major term of the contract, some courts will find that *no contract ever arose*, so that section 2-207 is irrelevant. However, if, in spite of this misunderstanding, the parties begin to perform the contract, section 2-207(3) is used to create the terms of the deal (*see infra*, §89). [**Continental Grain Co. v. Followell**, 475 N.E.2d 318 (Ind. 1985)]

EXAM TIP   **gilbert**

On an exam, when you see a question where the proposed acceptance does not mirror the offer, recall that there is a difference between *additional or new* terms and *different* terms. For *additional* terms, there is a clear rule for merchants: The terms become part of the contract unless the offer was limited to its terms, the terms are objected to within a reasonable time, or they materially alter the original terms. However, if the terms are *different*—*i.e.*, contradicting the original terms, not in addition to them—the rule is not clear: Some courts strike the terms if they materially alter the original terms or if the offeror objects, some courts knock out the conflicting terms and use gap-filler provisions instead, and some courts find that there is no contract at all.

---

(3) Writings that do not create a contract [§88]

Once the machinery of U.C.C. section 2-207 was in place, lawyers adapted to it. The original offeror's form now typically contains a clause objecting in advance to the addition of any new terms (a "proviso" clause; *see supra*, §82), and the offeree's response proposes new terms and states that the response is *not* an acceptance unless the original offeror expressly consents to the new terms. Now what? There is clearly no "meeting of the minds" here, and no contract arises *unless performance begins*. Prior to performance, either party may back out of the deal with impunity.

(a) Effect of performance [§89]

However, if the parties who have exchanged these nonmatching forms begin to perform, under the U.C.C., a contract has been created. Section 2-207(3) states that where the writings of the parties do not create a contract, but the parties behave as if they have one (*i.e.*, begin to perform), there *is* a contract consisting of all terms on which their *writings agree*, plus the supplementary terms supplied by the U.C.C. whenever the parties are silent (*e.g.*, if the parties omit the price, the Code presumes a reasonable price; *see infra*, §§122 *et seq.*). These supplementary terms also include the construction terms (*see supra*, §§16-19).

SOME IMPORTANT DIFFERENCES IN CONTRACT FORMATION BETWEEN COMMON LAW AND U.C.C.	gilbert
COMMON LAW	**U.C.C.**
Option contract requires consideration or promissory estoppel.	*Merchant's firm offer* is irrevocable *without consideration*.
Acceptance must conform to the *exact terms* of the offer; *any variance* will be treated as a rejection and counteroffer ("mirror image" rule).	Proposal of additional terms *does not constitute rejection*; terms may become part of contract per battle of the forms rule.
Offeror may specify *medium of acceptance and limit* to that medium, so that its use was the only possible manner to accept.	Offers construed as inviting acceptance by *any medium reasonable* under the circumstances, unless unambiguous language to the contrary.

c. 2003 Revision of Article 2 [§90]

The original version of section 2-207 proved so confusing to the courts that the 2003 revision tries to simplify matters. It drops any reference to the original version's proviso (*see supra*, §82). Instead section 2R-206(3) now provides that an acceptance need not be the mirror image of the offer. If the parties begin performance of the contract without express agreement on all the terms, section 2R-207 creates a contract out of the terms on which the parties have agreed (orally or in writing), plus the supplementary provisions supplied by the Code's gap-filling rules. Terms that contradict each other would be stricken.

 Example: The order form from the buyer says nothing about arbitration, but the seller's acknowledgment form requires it. The goods are shipped and prove defective. When the buyer complains, the seller demands arbitration. Since the seller's acceptance can add new terms, it is an acceptance. Whether the arbitration clause is part of the contract depends on whether it would be added by the Code's supplementary provisions. Most courts have said no to this, unless arbitration is so common in the industry that it is part of the usage of trade. [**Aceros Prefabricados, S.A. v. TradeArbed, Inc.**, 282 F.3d 92 (2d Cir. 2002)]

D. Parol Evidence Rule

1. Common Law [§91]

The parol evidence rule is a substantive rule of law. In spite of its name it is not a rule of evidence, but is instead a method of construing the contract. It operates to exclude evidence of *oral representations* or understandings made *prior to the signing*

of a contract that would *alter or vary the terms of a written instrument*. The underlying assumption is that if the parties have executed a written agreement, they intended it to be the complete and final integration of all their dealings. (*See* Contracts
Summary.)

2. **Sales Contracts [§92]**

In a sales contract, the U.C.C. rejects the assumption that because a writing has been
worked out that is final on some matters, it is to be taken as including all matters
agreed upon. Instead, before the writing can operate to exclude parol evidence, the
court must specifically find that the *parties intended* the writing to be the *complete
and exclusive* statement of the terms of the agreement. [U.C.C. §2-202(b)]

a. **Consistent, additional terms admissible [§93]**

If the court does not find that the writing was intended to be a complete and
exclusive statement of the terms, it may receive parol evidence of *consistent,
additional terms* (*i.e.,* terms not expressly or impliedly contained in the writing). [**Norwest Bank Billings v. Murnion,** 684 P.2d 1067 (Mont. 1984)]

(1) **Application**

A term is *not* a consistent, additional term (and is therefore barred by the
parol evidence rule) if it is the sort of thing that if true would *certainly*
already be in the writing. However, if it is the sort of thing that might
naturally be left out of the writing, it is a consistent, additional term and
may be admitted. [U.C.C. §2-202, Official Comment 3]

b. **Parol evidence may explain or interpret terms [§94]**

Even if the court finds that the writing was intended to be the complete and
exclusive statement of the parties' agreement, the terms of the writing may still
be *explained or interpreted* by parol evidence as to *course of dealing, usage of
trade*, or *course of performance*. [U.C.C. §2-202(a); *see supra*, §§17-19]

EXAM TIP   **gilbert**

It is important to note that there is *no requirement of ambiguity* in the writing before allowing an explanation by course of dealing or performance or usage of
trade.

---

c. **Common law exceptions to parol evidence rule [§95]**

Although the U.C.C. is silent on the subject, the common law exceptions to the
parol evidence rule (fraud, mistake, etc.; *see* Contracts Summary) also apply in
Sales transactions. U.C.C. section 1-103 preserves the common law except to
the extent clearly supplanted by the Code. [**Franklin v. Lovitt Equipment Co.,**
420 So. 2d 1370 (Miss. 1982)]

E. Statute of Frauds

---

1. **In General [§96]**

   Certain sales contracts are *unenforceable* unless there is (i) a *writing* sufficient to indicate that a contract has been formed or (ii) some other *act* deemed sufficient to evidence the existence of a contract and thus obviate the need for a writing.

   a. **Rationale**

      The policy of requiring some tangible evidence indicating the existence of a bargain in connection with certain kinds of contracts is designed to avoid the unfair results that frequently accompany decisions based on allegations of oral contracts. However, the Statute often resulted in fraud itself, by permitting the avoidance of contracts that could have been clearly established. The U.C.C. responded, both by retaining the Statute and by making changes that minimize the technical formalities, in order to prevent the protection of "avoiders."

2. **Basic Code Provision [§97]**

   The U.C.C. Statute of Frauds applies only to contracts for the sale of goods having a *price of $500* or more. [U.C.C. §2-201] The 2003 revision increases the threshold amount to $5,000. [U.C.C. §2R-201(1)]

3. **Effect of Code Provision [§98]**

   A sales contract that does not comply with the Statute of Frauds is *unenforceable—i.e.,* neither party can force the other to proceed therewith. However, the contract is not void; if the parties choose to perform, enforceable rights may be created.

   > **(e.g.) Example:** Where there is an oral contract for the sale of goods priced in excess of $500, neither party can be compelled to proceed with the sale. However, if the seller does deliver the goods and they are *accepted by the buyer*, the Statute is satisfied and the oral agreement may be enforced (*see* below).

   a. **Statute can be asserted only by party to contract [§99]**

      The lack of writing can be asserted only by the parties to the contract. A third party (*e.g.,* a creditor) *cannot* raise the objection. [**Blowers v. First National Bank,** 232 So. 2d 666 (Ala. 1970)]

4. **What Constitutes Sufficient Written Memorandum [§100]**

   One method of satisfying the Statute of Frauds, and thus rendering the contract enforceable, is the production of a written note or memorandum signed by the party to be charged (*i.e.,* the party sought to be held to the contract). [U.C.C. §2-201(1)]

EXAM TIP   **gilbert**

For the Statute of Frauds to be satisfied (and the contract to be enforceable), you need to look carefully for a writing signed *by the party to be charged* (*i.e.,* sued). Often the facts of a question will show that only one party signed the memo. Check first to see if the signature is of the party you need to hold liable. If not, consider the *merchants' confirmatory memo rule* (*see infra,* §109)—it may provide the answer. Be sure, however, that the contract is between *merchants*; if not, the rule does not apply and the signature of one party cannot bind the other.

---

a. **Terms that must be contained in written memorandum**

(1) Common law [§101]

At common law, it was required that the memorandum state with reasonable certainty *all the essential terms* of the transaction to which it related—*i.e.,* parties, subject matter, time for performance, and price.

(2) U.C.C. rule [§102]

The U.C.C., however, takes a different position: The writing is sufficient if it indicates that a contract for sale has been made and *specifies the quantity term*. The Code drafters felt that quantity is the one term that is impossible to imply by law. [U.C.C. §2-201(1)]

---

e.g. **Example:** "I agree to sell Buyer 200 wrenches, (signed) Seller" is a sufficient memorandum under the Code, even though there is no mention of price, time for delivery, etc.

(a) Output and requirements contracts [§103]

A quantity stated in terms of the seller's "output" or the buyer's "requirements" (*e.g.,* "all the steel you produce," or "all the steel you need") is sufficient to satisfy section 2-201. [**Gravlich Caterer, Inc. v. Hans Holterbosch, Inc.,** 243 A.2d 253 (N.J. 1968); *and see* further discussion, *infra,* §§137-143]

b. **Form of memorandum [§104]**

No particular form of writing is required, as long as it evidences the requisite terms (above).

(1) Buyer's check [§105]

A number of cases have held that the buyer's check, if it bears a notation describing the subject matter and quantity (*e.g.,* "deposit on purchase of 200 Regal computers"), is a sufficient memorandum to satisfy the Statute in an action against the buyer. If the check is cashed by the seller—thus bearing the *seller's indorsement*—it will render the contract enforceable against the seller too.

c. **Signature [§106]**

It is essential that the memorandum be signed by the party to be charged. No particular form of signature is required (it may be typed, stamped, etc.), and it need not appear at the bottom of the writing. Any mark made *with the intent* to authenticate the writing is a "signature" under the U.C.C. [U.C.C. §1-201, Official Comment 39]

(1) Printed letterhead [§107]

A number of cases hold that a printed letterhead may satisfy the Statute if it was *intended* as the equivalent of a signature. Thus, if the buyer sends the seller a purchase order on a printed form bearing the buyer's name and address, this may be treated as a "signed" writing, although not actually signed by the buyer, *if* it is shown that the buyer *intended to be bound* by the order. [**Southwest Engineering Co. v. Martin Tractor Co.,** 473 P.2d 18 (Kan. 1970); **Evans v. Moore,** 205 S.E.2d 507 (Ga. 1974); **Associated Hardware Supply Co. v. Big Wheel Distributing Co.,** 355 F.2d 114 (3d Cir. 1966)]

EXAM TIP	gilbert

To be sufficient for the Statute of Frauds, note that the writing may be informal and need not be contained in a single document. The "signature" can be any symbol meant to adopt or accept a writing. Thus, a note on a letterhead can be enough (the letterhead acts as a signature). *But remember:* A **quantity must be stated** in the writing.

---

(2) Agent's signature [§108]

The signature may be supplied by an authorized agent or broker. *But note:* Some states also require that the agent's authority to enter into the contract itself be in writing—under the so-called equal dignity statutes. (*See* Contracts Summary.)

d. Written confirmation from other party as binding on merchant to whom sent [§109]

The U.C.C. contains a novel provision whereby a written memorandum can become binding on the party to be charged even though that party never signed anything. Before this provision can apply, *both* parties must qualify as *"merchants"* in the goods or practices involved (*see supra,* §27). If the merchant sends a written confirmation of the contract to another merchant, and the writing would be sufficient to satisfy the U.C.C. Statute of Frauds were the sender being sued, the merchant who receives this writing *must object* to its terms within *10 days* or the recipient loses any defense based on the Statute of Frauds. [U.C.C. §2-201(2)]

Example: Seller sends Buyer a letter reading, "This will confirm our oral agreement yesterday for the sale to you of 200 pounds of refined aluminum at $3 per pound, (signed) Seller." This writing satisfies the Statute of Frauds and is therefore sufficient to bind Seller to the contract. It follows that *if Buyer is a merchant*, within 10 days after receiving this letter, Buyer must object to its contents or may not raise the Statute of Frauds.

---

(1) Caution—does not prove contract [§110]

Of course, such written confirmation satisfies only the Statute of Frauds requirement. It does not by itself prove the existence of a contract. The burden is still on whichever party is suing to show that an oral agreement was made and that the writing correctly reflects its terms. [**American Parts Co. v. American Arbitration Association,** 154 N.W.2d 5 (Mich. 1967)]

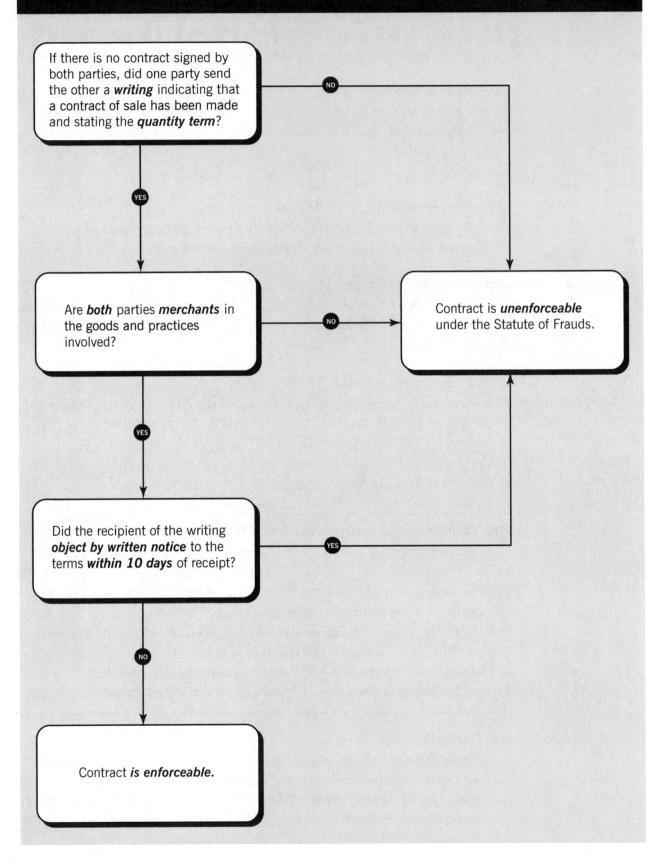

If there is no contract signed by both parties, did one party send the other a *writing* indicating that a contract of sale has been made and stating the *quantity term*?

NO → Contract is *unenforceable* under the Statute of Frauds.

YES ↓

Are *both* parties *merchants* in the goods and practices involved?

NO → Contract is *unenforceable* under the Statute of Frauds.

YES ↓

Did the recipient of the writing *object by written notice* to the terms *within 10 days* of receipt?

YES → Contract is *unenforceable* under the Statute of Frauds.

NO ↓

Contract *is enforceable.*

(2) What is a "confirmation"? [§111]

Although the U.C.C. does not define "confirmation," the term assumes the preexistence of an agreement. Thus, any writings that precede the oral agreement are not confirmations. If a "confirmation" states an additional or different term from the alleged oral contract, then section 2-207 (about new or different terms in an acceptance) should apply (*see supra*, §78).

(3) What is "receipt"? [§112]

It is not enough to establish that a confirmation was sent. The plaintiff must establish that defendant *received* it. However, the defendant need not actually have read it, as long as the defendant had *reason to know* its contents.

(4) What is an "objection"? [§113]

The recipient (defendant) may nullify the confirmation by sending *written notice* of objection within 10 days after receiving the confirmation.

5. Exceptions to Statute of Frauds [§114]

Both at common law and under the U.C.C., it is recognized that oral contracts that are otherwise violative of the Statute of Frauds may still be given enforcement under certain circumstances.

a. Partial acceptance [§115]

At common law, acceptance of any portion of the goods took the contract out of the Statute entirely. The U.C.C. modifies this rule; it provides that a contract not otherwise enforceable because of the Statute of Frauds is made enforceable by the receipt and acceptance of goods but *only to the extent of the quantity of goods actually received and accepted.* [U.C.C. §2-201(3)(c)]

---

e.g. **Example:** Seller orally agreed to sell 10,000 bushels of soybeans to Buyer at a set price per bushel. Seller delivered 4,000 bushels, but the market value of soybeans then increased so much that Seller refused to deliver the balance. Seller then sued for the price of the 4,000 bushels delivered. Buyer counterclaimed for damages on the 6,000 bushels not received. *Held:* Seller is entitled to the contract price on the 4,000 bushels accepted and received by Buyer. Otherwise, however, the contract is unenforceable under the Statute of Frauds, and, therefore, Buyer cannot recover damages for Seller's nondelivery. [**Del Hayes & Sons, Inc. v. Mitchell,** 230 N.W.2d 588 (Minn. 1975)]

---

(1) Rationale

Receipt of a specific number of goods serves the same evidentiary function as a written memorandum, but only with respect to the goods received. It would be illogical to exempt the balance of the contract from the Statute merely because of partial receipt, since there is no evidence as to the size of the balance.

b. Partial payment [§116]

The U.C.C. treats the effect of partial payment in the same manner as partial acceptance; *i.e.,* a contract not otherwise enforceable because of the Statute of Frauds is enforceable with respect to goods *for which payment has been made.* [U.C.C. §2-201(3)(c)] Again, the rationale is that the payment serves as evidence of the existence of a contract, but only as to the goods paid for.

(1) Down payment on indivisible item [§117]

The courts have found that where a down payment is made on an indivisible item, the partial payment shows that there is at least a quantity of one; thus, the Statute of Frauds is satisfied for that one item.

---

e.g. **Example:** When the parties enter into an oral contract whereby Seller agrees to sell Buyer Seller's car for $1,500, and Buyer pays $100, the Statute of Frauds is satisfied by the down payment and Buyer gets the entire car (not just a *part* of the car). [**Songbird Jet Ltd. v. Amax Inc.,** 581 F. Supp. 912 (S.D.N.Y. 1984)]

---

c. Specially manufactured goods

(1) Common law [§118]

An exception to the writing requirement of the Statute of Frauds was recognized at common law where goods were to be manufactured specially for the buyer and were not suitable for resale to others in the seller's ordinary course of business. In such a case, an oral purchase agreement was enforceable against the buyer; the Statute of Frauds was no defense.

(2) U.C.C. rule [§119]

The U.C.C. is in general accord, although it is somewhat more stringent. It is not sufficient merely that the special goods are "to be" manufactured for the buyer. Rather, the seller must have made either a *substantial beginning* on their manufacture or *commitments* for their procurement before receipt of the buyer's notice of repudiation. Only in such cases will the contract become enforceable. Furthermore, it must be obvious that these goods are meant for this particular buyer. [U.C.C. §2-201(3)(a)]

d. Pleading and testimonial admissions [§120]

A trap for the unwary lurks in U.C.C. section 2-201(3)(b). That section provides that if the party against whom enforcement of a contract is sought admits in the pleadings, testimony, or otherwise in court that a sales contract was in fact made, then that party loses the benefit of the Statute of Frauds defense *to the extent of the quantity admitted.* [**Garrison v. Piatt,** 147 S.E.2d 374 (Ga. 1966)]

(1) Trial tactic

A party seeking to enforce an oral agreement can sue on the oral agreement and put the other party on the witness stand at trial. If the other party admits the oral agreement, it is enforceable. (Even an involuntary admission waives the Statute.) If the party denies it, the witness runs the risk of perjury (assuming there is other evidence to support the plaintiff's claim of the agreement).

e.   **Estoppel [§121]**

Even if none of the above exceptions is applicable, courts may estop either party from asserting the Statute as a defense where, by word or conduct, that party has caused the other to *rely detrimentally on the oral promise* so that to deny enforcement would cause "unconscionable injury or loss." [**Atlantic Wholesale Co. v. Solondz,** 320 S.E.2d 720 (S.C. 1984)]

CHECKLIST OF EXCEPTIONS TO THE STATUTE OF FRAUDS — **gilbert**

ORAL CONTRACTS MAY BE ENFORCED DESPITE THE STATUTE OF FRAUDS IN THE FOLLOWING CIRCUMSTANCES:

☑   *Specially manufactured goods*—if the seller has made a substantial beginning on their manufacture or commitments for their procurement;

☑   *Confirmation in writing* by a merchant to a merchant;

☑   *Admission* by a party of the existence of the contract in pleadings or court testimony—to the extent of the quantity admitted;

☑   *Partial acceptance* of goods—to the extent goods were received and accepted;

☑   *Partial payment* with respect to the goods actually paid for;

☑   *Estoppel*—if one party has *relied detrimentally* on the oral agreement so that failing to enforce it would cause unconscionable injury or loss.

EXAM TIP — **gilbert**

An acronym for remembering when a writing signed by the party to be charged is *not required* for a sale of goods, even if for $500 or more, is *SCAPE*:

Specially manufactured goods,
Confirmation by a merchant in writing,
Admission in court,
Performance—partial acceptance or payment,
Estoppel (detrimental reliance).

F.   Missing Terms—The Gap-Filling Rules

1. **Introduction [§122]**

   It is the rare sales contract that covers every term that might subsequently be a source of dispute. Sometimes the deletion is deliberate, as when the parties cannot fix the term at the time but nonetheless wish to proceed with the contract. More often, however, the omission is accidental, as where the parties never considered the problem that has arisen and made no terms regarding it. Under such circumstances, the law steps in and provides rules to fill the blanks left in the contract by the parties.

   a. **Caution**

      Courts will "read in" missing terms only when it appears that the parties were intending an enforceable contract. The more "gaps" that exist, and the more vague the language, the more difficult it becomes to establish real bargaining intent. [**Arcuri v. Weiss**, 184 A.2d 24 (Pa. 1962); **Evans Implement Co. v. Thomas Industries Inc.**, 160 S.E.2d 462 (Ga. 1968)]

   b. **Methodology [§123]**

      In determining the terms of a contract, consider:

      (i) *Express terms* written or oral (these prevail over implied terms unless there is a contrary U.C.C. mandate); then

      (ii) *Course of performance*; then

      (iii) *Course of dealing*; then

      (iv) *Usage of trade*; then

      (v) *The Code* itself.

      If the above cannot "fill the gap," the missing term will not likely be supplied by the court.

2. **Open Price Arrangements [§124]**

   A fixed price is not essential to a valid sales contract. The purchase price may be specified in the contract, or it may be left open. Of course, the fact that the parties omitted the price term may be considered evidence that they did not intend to enter into a contractually binding agreement. However, in all cases, the parties' *intent* is paramount; if it is determined that the parties *did* intend to form a binding contract, the omission of the price term is not necessarily fatal. [U.C.C. §2-305(1)] In that case, the following U.C.C. rules apply.

   a. **Contract silent as to price [§125]**

      When a contract is silent as to price, it is assumed that the parties intended the sale to be at a *reasonable* price at the time and place of delivery. [U.C.C. §2-305(1)(a); **Interstate Plywood Sales Co. v. Interstate Container Corp.**, 331 F.2d 449 (9th Cir. 1964)]

b. Agreements to agree [§126]

Sometimes the parties agree to agree (*e.g.*, "price to be determined next January 1"). The issue then is whether a contract has been formed.

(1) Common law [§127]

The common law rule was that a price to be determined by future agreement of the parties was so indefinite as to render the contract unenforceable. [**Shayeb v. Holland**, 73 N.E.2d 731 (Mass. 1947)]

(2) U.C.C. rule [§128]

The U.C.C. reverses this rule and provides that if the parties are later unable to agree on the price, then it is to be a *reasonable* price at the time and place of delivery. [U.C.C. §2-305(1)(b)]

(a) Rationale

Entering into a contract in and of itself creates reliance and expectancies on the part of both parties which deserve judicial protection; the fact that the parties are later unable to agree on the price should not mean that these reliance interests cannot be judicially protected.

c. Inoperative reference to third party [§129]

Where the price is to be set by a third person or in accordance with some contractually defined standard (*e.g.*, prices in a trade journal), and for some reason—without the fault of either the seller or the buyer—the price is not set, the price is a *reasonable* price at the time and place of delivery. [U.C.C. §2-305(1)(c)]

d. Party reserving right to fix prices [§130]

If the agreement is that one party has the right to fix the price at a later time (*e.g.*, "price to be fixed by seller at time of delivery"), is there a contract?

(1) Common law [§131]

At common law, an agreement that provided that either of the parties had the power to fix the price was void. The rationale was that if either party retained unilateral control over the price, that party would, because of selfish financial interests, act in bad faith when setting it. [**Reiter Foster Oil Corp. v. Bodovitz**, 138 P.2d 95 (Okla. 1943)]

(2) U.C.C. rule [§132]

The U.C.C. rejects both the rationale and the rule, providing instead that such a contract *is* valid, but that the party who retains the right to fix the price must do so *in good faith*. [U.C.C. §2-305(2)]

(a) If bad faith [§133]

If the person setting the price does not act in good faith, then the other party may *either* treat the contract as canceled or exercise the same option and set a reasonable price. [U.C.C. §2-305(3)]

(b) If no price fixed [§134]

Similarly, if the price is not fixed for some other reason attributable to the fault of either party (*e.g.*, sending the third party who was supposed to fix the price on an extended trip to Antarctica), the other party may either cancel or set a reasonable price. [U.C.C. §2-305(3)]

e. Maximum-minimum price contracts [§135]

Contracts in which the price itself is not set, but both a floor and a ceiling on price are set ("not less than $750 nor more than $1,000") have met a mixed reception. Some courts hold them valid and enforceable against the seller at the maximum price, and against the buyer at the minimum. Others hold them void for indefiniteness. [**Dwight Bros. Paper Co. v. Ginzburg**, 238 Ill. App. 21 (1923)] Neither rule is entirely satisfactory, nor does the U.C.C. supply an answer.

(1) Note

Some authorities suggest that the most reasonable way to construe these contracts is to hold that they mean the buyer is to pay a reasonable price limited only to the maximum or minimum set. [16 Minn. L. Rev. 775]

(2) But note

Others construe such contracts as conferring on the *seller* the power to set the price somewhere between the maximum and minimum in a manner consistent with *good faith*. [**Oregon-Washington Vegetable & Fruit Growers Association v. Sunset Packing Co.**, 456 P.2d 1002 (Or. 1969)]

3. Open Quantity Arrangements [§136]

The quantity term is the one element the U.C.C. will not supply; the parties *must* set a quantity. If the contract is subject to the Statute of Frauds, quantity must be specifically set forth in writing (*supra*, §102). In any contract, this is the one term impossible for the courts to imply.

EXAM TIP	gilbert

This point is worth repeating. Although the U.C.C.'s gap-filling rules will provide many of the terms not covered by a contract, remember that if there is *no quantity term*, there is *no contract*.

---

a. "Requirements" and "output" contracts

(1) Requirements contracts [§137]

An agreement that specifies that the buyer will purchase from the seller *all* (or some percentage) of the buyer's *"needs" or "requirements"* for a given commodity during a given period is a valid contract. [U.C.C. §2-306(1)]

(a) Distinguish—illusory agreement

If, on the other hand, the contract is phrased in terms of the buyer's taking all buyer *"wants" or "desires,"* this obligation is deemed illusory, and the contract is void for want of mutuality of obligation. [**Bartlett Springs Co. v. Standard Box Co.**, 16 Cal. 671 (1911)]

EXAM TIP   gilbert

If you see a question that appears to involve a requirements contract, be sure to check the language of the contract very carefully. Words like *"desire" or "want"* are *not the same* as *"need" or "require."* If you see an exam question with a contract provision reading something like "Buyer agrees to buy and Seller agrees to sell all of the [specified goods] that Buyer *desires*," don't be fooled into thinking that this is a requirements contract—all the goods the buyer desires is not enough for a binding agreement, because he may not desire any!

---

(2) Output contracts [§138]

The counterpart of the requirements contract is the output contract, in which the buyer agrees to take *all* (or some percentage) of the *goods produced by a seller* from a specific production unit (*e.g.,* factory, farm, orchard) during a given period of time. Such contracts are clearly enforceable under the Code. [U.C.C. §2-306(1)]

(3) The changing quantity problem [§139]

It sometimes happens that the buyer's requirements or the seller's output balloons disproportionately to what the parties contemplated at the time of contracting.

---

e.g. Examples: Seller contracts to sell to Buyer all of Buyer's requirements of sugar over a three-year period. During the second year, the price of sugar suddenly soars and Buyer starts demanding 5,000% more than it demanded during the preceding year. Or Seller, who is operating a plant at 25% capacity, agrees to sell Buyer all of the refined pig iron produced during a three-year period. In the second year, the price of iron ore dips sharply and Seller suddenly finds it is economical to triple production and start demanding that Buyer take 300% more than was taken during the preceding year.

(a) Good faith limitations [§140]

The U.C.C. requires that the buyer or seller, as the case may be, act in *good faith* and limit the quantity that may be tendered by the seller (in output contracts) or demanded by the buyer (in requirements contracts) to an amount *not unreasonably disproportionate* to any stated estimate; or in the absence of a stated estimate, to any *normal or otherwise comparable* prior output or requirements. [U.C.C. §2-306(1)]

(4) The changing business problem [§141]

A similar problem arises where a buyer's needs, or a seller's output, radically decrease due to claimed financial reverses. Whether such decreases limit liability under a requirements or output contract is again basically a *good faith* issue. Under U.C.C. section 2-306(2), both parties must use *best efforts* to have output and requirements.

(a) Unmarketability of product—no breach [§142]

A firm may decide to discontinue a particular line of business, if it proves unmarketable over a prolonged period of time, without thereby breaching its duty of good faith under a requirements or output contract. [**Neofotistos v. Harvard Brewing Co.,** 171 N.E.2d 865 (Mass. 1961)]

---

e.g. **Example:** A buyer may be excused from any further purchases under a requirements contract if it decides to eliminate from its product line the particular product for which it was making purchases from seller. [**HML Corp. v. General Foods Corp.,** 365 F.2d 77 (3d Cir. 1966)—distributor could not profitably market salad dressing four months into 32-month requirements contract]

---

e.g. **Example:** Similarly, a seller may be excused from further supplying seller's "output" to the purchaser where seller has in *good faith* terminated production of the item in question. [**Feld v. Henry S. Levy & Sons,** 45 App. Div. 2d 720 (1974)—baker shut down manufacture of bread crumbs as uneconomical]

(b) Distinguish—contract becomes more expensive [§143]

Curtailment of output by a seller, or suspension of purchases by a buyer, merely because the *contract in question* is more expensive than that party wishes (thereby reducing profits or forcing operation at a loss) is *not* by itself sufficient to constitute "good faith." [U.C.C. §2-306, Official Comment 1]

4. Open Delivery Arrangements

a. Single vs. several lot deliveries [§144]

Unless otherwise specified by the parties, the U.C.C. requires parties to make delivery in *single lot* shipments. [U.C.C. §2-307] However, if "circumstances" (the contract or the situation as it evolves) give either party the right to make or demand delivery in lots, then such may be done. [U.C.C. §2-307]

b. Place of delivery [§145]

Where no place is specified for delivery of the goods, the place of delivery is the *seller's place of business,* or if there is none, the seller's residence. [U.C.C. §2-308(a)]

(1) Exception

If the parties contract with reference to *specific* goods in existence and identified at the time the contract is made, and *both parties know* that the goods are located somewhere *other than* the seller's business or residence, the place where the goods are located is the place of delivery, unless the parties agree otherwise. [U.C.C. §2-308(b)]

5. Open Time Arrangements [§146]

The general rule at common law has always been that if an agreement does not specify the time in which an act is to be performed, the law implies that it is to be performed within a *reasonable* time. The U.C.C. follows the common law rule. [U.C.C. §2-309(1)]

a. Contracts for indefinite duration

(1) Common law [§147]

At common law, a contract contemplating a continuing series of acts of performance for an indefinite time (*e.g.,* "to supply all of Buyer's requirements of crude oil") was deemed terminable *at will*, although some courts and writers have questioned whether such contracts are sufficiently "certain" to have any validity at all.

(2) U.C.C. rule [§148]

The U.C.C. dispels this doubt. Open duration agreements are *valid for a reasonable time.* [U.C.C. §2-309(2)]

(a) Notice required to terminate [§149]

The U.C.C. further modifies the common law rule—that such contracts are terminable at will—by providing that the power to terminate is conditioned on the terminating party giving to the other party *reasonable advance notice.* [U.C.C. §2-309(3); **Sinkoff Beverage Co. v. Schlitz Brewing Co.,** 51 Misc. 2d 446 (1966)] Indeed, the U.C.C. goes further and provides that the parties *cannot waive* in advance the notice requirement, if the failure to give notice would be "unconscionable." [U.C.C. §2-309(3)]

6. Open Payment Arrangements [§150]

Unless the parties have agreed otherwise, payment and delivery are *concurrent conditions.* [U.C.C. §2-310(a); *and see infra,* §§171 *et seq.*] This means that where the parties have not agreed that payment comes before delivery of the goods (or vice versa), neither party is in breach until the other side has tendered performance and the tender has been refused.

a. Place of payment [§151]

Payment is due at the time and place at which the buyer is to *receive* the goods. [U.C.C. §2-310(a)]

(1) "Receipt" [§152]

Section 2-103(1)(c) defines "receipt" as taking physical possession of the goods. Thus payment is due at *destination*, absent a contrary agreement.

(2) Document transactions [§153]

If delivery is authorized and made by a transaction involving shipping documents (*e.g.,* bills of lading or warehouse receipts, *see infra,* §§700 *et seq.*), then payment is due at the time and place the buyer is to receive *the documents*. [U.C.C. §2-310(c)]

b. Open credit [§154]

Where credit has been agreed upon, there is sometimes a question as to when the credit period commences to run. For example, Seller sells goods to Buyer on "30 days' credit." The goods are shipped on June 1 and (i) the invoice is dispatched to Buyer on the same day but not received until June 5; or (ii) the invoice is not sent to Buyer until June 5; or (iii) the invoice is sent to Buyer on June 1 but is postdated June 5. The issue is when does the 30-day credit period expire?

(1) General rule [§155]

The general rule is that the credit period begins to run from the *date of shipment*. [U.C.C. §2-310(d); **Dow Chemical Co. v. Detroit Chemical Works,** 175 N.W. 269 (Mich. 1919)]

(2) U.C.C. modification [§156]

The U.C.C. adds, however, that if dispatch of the invoice is delayed, the start of the credit period will be correspondingly delayed; and if the invoice is postdated, that too will delay the start of the credit period for the length of time elapsing between the date of shipment and the postdate affixed to the invoice. [U.C.C. §2-310(d)]

(3) Application

Thus, in the above example, if Seller ships the goods to Buyer on June 1, dates the invoice June 1, and dispatches it to Buyer on June 1, the 30-day credit period starts June 1 and ends June 30. If Seller does not send the invoice to Buyer until June 5, then the credit period starts June 5 and ends July 4. And, if Seller postdates the invoice June 5 and dispatches it on June 1, the credit period again starts June 5 and ends July 4.

7. Other Open Terms

a. Open assortment [§157]

Goods are sometimes purchased in mixed or bulk lots (*e.g.,* "100 tons of rock from quarry"), and have to be sorted out. Unless the parties agree to the contrary, the *buyer* is entitled to specify the assortment. [U.C.C. §2-311(1)]

b. Open shipping arrangements [§158]

The parties can, of course, agree that the goods will be shipped by a particular carrier (*e.g.,* "the good ship 'Peerless'") or that it will be incumbent upon one party to arrange for the means of shipment. If the parties do not so agree, then, under the U.C.C., the duty to make shipping arrangements falls on the *seller*. [U.C.C. §2-311(2); *and see infra, §§375 et seq.*]

8. One Party to Specify Missing Terms [§159]

Contracts sometimes provide that one party or the other is to specify details of performance at a later date (*e.g.,* buyer to specify date of delivery). Such contracts are enforced at common law, and the U.C.C. takes the same position. It provides simply that where details of performance are to be left to the specification of one party, that party is to make the specification in *good faith* and within the limits set by commercial reasonableness. [U.C.C. §2-311(1)]

9. Construction Terms [§160]

As discussed before (*see supra, §§16-20*), the usage of trade, course of dealing, and course of performance can also be used to fill in the gaps of the contract.

G. Revision of the Contract Terms

1. Modifications

a. New consideration not required [§161]

Under general contract law, an agreement once made is final and may **not** thereafter be modified unless the modification is supported by new consideration. However, under the U.C.C., such promises by the parties as to new and different terms (*i.e.,* modifications of a sales contract) are **valid even though unsupported by consideration.** [U.C.C. §2-209(1)]

Example: Suppose Buyer contracts to purchase 40 pairs of leather-lined boots from Seller. Thereafter, but before delivery, Buyer advises Seller that Buyer needs boots with fur linings, and Seller agrees to supply fur-lined boots. However, Seller proceeds to deliver leather-lined boots. Is Buyer obligated to pay for the leather-lined boots? Pursuant to the U.C.C., the modification of the contract is valid despite the lack of new consideration. Hence, Buyer would not have to purchase the leather-lined boots, and Seller would be in breach for not delivering the fur-lined ones.

---

(1) But note—good faith required [§162]

This does not mean that either party can "twist the other's arm" into changing the deal (*e.g.,* at the last minute, Seller refuses to deliver goods desperately needed by Buyer unless Buyer agrees to pay more). There is a basic obligation of *good faith* running throughout the U.C.C.; therefore, neither party can demand a modification without a *legitimate commercial reason.* [U.C.C. §§1-203, 2-209, Official Comment 2]

b. Whether writing required [§163]

Whether the modification must be in writing depends on whether the contract *as modified* falls within the Statute of Frauds. If the contract as modified involves the sale of goods for $500 or more, the modification must be in writing [U.C.C. §2-209(3)], even if the original contract did not require a writing. If the contract as modified is for the sale of goods for less than $500, no writing is required, even if the original contract was in writing.

---

e.g. Example: Buyer calls Seller and asks Seller to ship Buyer 200 widgets at $2 each. Seller agrees. There is a contract, and no writing is required. If Buyer subsequently calls Seller and asks Seller to change the order to 300 widgets, the modification is unenforceable because a writing is required under the Statute of Frauds because the contract amount is now over $500.

---

e.g. Example: Buyer and Seller agree in writing that Seller will sell Buyer 300 widgets at $2 a widget. Buyer then phones Seller and asks Seller to change the order to 200 widgets. The modification is enforceable without a writing since the contract as modified is for less than $500.

---

(1) Exception [§164]

The only exception is if the written contract *expressly requires* that any modification or rescission be by signed writing, in which event it cannot be modified orally, unless the court decides that the parties agreed to *waive* the "changes must be in writing" requirement. Furthermore, if the "changes must be in writing" clause is part of a boiler-plate form supplied by a merchant, any nonmerchant party must sign this provision separately to show that the signer was aware of it. [U.C.C. §2-209(2)]

2. Waivers [§165]

Even though an attempted modification proves ineffective as such, it may nevertheless be recognized as a waiver of contract rights. [U.C.C. §2-209(4)] For example, if the contract requires that all modifications be in writing, an attempted oral modification will be ineffective as a modification (*see* above), but it can still operate as a *waiver* of rights against the party who is seeking to avoid its application. Such a waiver will be found wherever the other party has *changed position in reliance* on the oral modification. [**Panno v. Russo,** 186 Cal. 408 (1947)]

a. Right to retract [§166]

However, a waiver is *retractable* by notice from the waiving party, *unless* the other party has in the interim materially changed position in reliance on the waiver. [U.C.C. §2-209(5)]

> **Example:** The original contract was for 400 pairs of boots and provided that "no modification shall be effective unless in writing." Later, the parties orally reduced (waived) the order to 100 pairs. Buyer later changes her mind and seeks to enforce the original contracts for the larger quantity. If Seller relied on the oral agreement in making other contracts for the 300 pairs of boots and has no other stock available, Buyer cannot retract her waiver. If Seller did not change position in reliance on the oral agreement, Buyer can retract the waiver and enforce the contract for the full quantity.

H. Assignment and Delegation of Contract

1. Delegation of Duties of Performance [§167]

Under normal circumstances, it should make no difference to the obligee under a sales contract whether the goods are delivered (or paid for) by the party with whom the obligee contracted or by some third party; provided, of course, that in the event of nonperformance, the obligee retains rights against the original contracting party. The U.C.C. accordingly provides that all duties are delegable, *unless* the parties otherwise agree or the obligee has a *"substantial interest"* in the *personal performance* by the original obligor (*e.g.*, installation of mosaic tiles by an artist). However, in no event will the delegation of performance relieve the delegating party of either the duty to perform (if the delegatee does not) or liability for breach. [U.C.C. §2-210(1)]

EXAM TIP gilbert

In exam questions addressing delegation of duties, be on the lookout for facts that deal with the *arts* or *highly skilled members of various professions* (*e.g.*, a celebrated chef). These scenarios will likely be deemed personal performance contracts, and thus *not be delegable*.

---

2. Assignment of Rights [§168]

Either the seller or the buyer can assign rights under the contract unless the assignment would (i) materially change the duty of the other party; (ii) increase materially the burden or risk imposed on that party by the contract; (iii) impair materially the chances of obtaining return performance; or (iv) violate a nonassignment provision in the contract. [U.C.C. §2-210(2)]

a. Note—payment rights always assignable [§169]

When the assignor has already performed, the assignor may *always assign* the payment rights under the contract—even in the face of a contractual nonassignment clause. The U.C.C. drafters felt that commerce depends on the ability to assign monies earned, so a provision in the contract forbidding this is simply void, and the money may nonetheless be assigned. [U.C.C. §2-210(2)]

b. **Meaning of clauses concerning assignments [§170]**

If the contract prohibits assignment, unless the circumstances indicate the contrary, the clause is read as prohibiting only a delegation of *duties* and not the assignment of the right to payment or other performance. An assignment of "the contract" or "all my rights under the contract" is presumptively also a delegation of duties to the assignee, acceptance of which by the assignee constitutes a promise to perform the delegated duties. This promise may be enforced by the assignor *or* the other original contracting party. [U.C.C. §2-210(4), (5)]

Chapter Three: Types of Sales

CONTENTS

Chapter Approach

Chapter Approach

Article 2 of the Uniform Commercial Code makes reference to several different types of sales contracts:

1. *Cash sales*, where payment must be made before the buyer has a right to receive the goods;

2. "*Sale or return*" and "*sale on approval*," each of which gives the buyer a right to return the goods; and

3. *Auction sales*.

To understand many U.C.C. provisions, you must become familiar with these sales categories. Be sure you understand the concepts and the distinct rules that apply to each type of sale.

A. Cash Sale Transactions

1. **Definition—Cash Sale [§171]**
   A "cash sale" is a bargain in which payment of the purchase price is a *condition precedent* to the buyer's *right to receive* the goods from the seller (*e.g.*, an over-the-counter sale in a retail store). [U.C.C. §2-507(2)] (If the buyer has somehow obtained possession without paying for the goods, the seller may *reclaim* the goods; *see* below.)

   a. **Distinguish—credit sale [§172]**
      In contrast, a sale on credit is one where the buyer has the right to possess, use, and dispose of the goods after delivery even though the buyer has not yet paid for them. The buyer's agreement is to pay *at a later date*, and if payment is not forthcoming, the seller merely has a *right of action* against the buyer for the *amount owed*, but this in no way limits the buyer's title or rights in the goods themselves.

   b. **Parties' terminology not conclusive [§173]**
      The fact that the parties denominate their agreement a "cash sale," or even use the provision "terms strictly cash," is not itself conclusive that a cash sale is intended. It may still be found (*e.g.*, through previous dealings or business usage) that such provisions merely mean that a buyer must pay for the goods promptly *after* receipt. In such a case, payment is not made a condition precedent to the right to possession and therefore it is a sale on credit, not a cash sale. [**Harris v. Merlino**, 61 A.2d 276 (N.J. 1948)]

2. **Cash Sale Presumed [§174]**

Under the U.C.C., all sales are cash sales, unless the parties specify otherwise. Thus, unless credit has been expressly agreed upon, **payment is due upon delivery** of the goods [U.C.C. §2-310(a)], and the right of the buyer to retain or dispose of the goods is conditioned upon such payment. [U.C.C. §2-507(2)]

3. **Waiver of Cash Sales Provision [§175]**

However, even though no credit was previously arranged, the seller may intentionally or unintentionally waive the cash sale requirement. Such a waiver will be found wherever it appears that the seller (having the right to demand cash) has nevertheless decided to rely on the buyer's credit to secure payment of the purchase price. Such waiver may be express, but more frequently it is implied from the seller's conduct.

a. **Waiver by accepting buyer's note [§176]**

The seller's acceptance of the buyer's promissory note for the price obviously shows the seller's intention to extend credit, and thus waives the requirement of cash payment. [**Capital Automobile Co. v. Ward,** 189 S.E. 713 (Ga. 1936)]

b. **Distinguish—bad check cases [§177]**

The seller's acceptance of the buyer's check, however, is **not** deemed a waiver. A check does not represent an extension of credit from the seller to the buyer. The check is treated as a **conditional** payment. Hence, if the seller delivers the goods to the buyer in return for the buyer's check, and the check bounces (*i.e.*, the bank refuses to pay because the buyer's funds are not sufficient), the condition has failed and the seller is entitled to **reclaim the goods** from the buyer. [U.C.C. §2-511(3); **Mansion Carpets, Inc. v. Marinoff,** 24 App. Div. 2d 947 (1965)]

(1) **Exception—certified check [§178]**

Payment by **certified check** is treated as a cash payment. If the bank subsequently refuses to pay, the seller must sue the bank on its certification; the seller cannot reclaim the goods from the buyer. [U.C.C. §3-802(1)(a)—original; U.C.C. §3-310(a)—revision]

c. **Failure to reclaim goods [§179]**

However, failure to reclaim the goods with reasonable promptness after the buyer fails to pay for them (*e.g.*, the check bounces) may result in a **waiver**.

(1) **Time period [§180]**

To comply with U.C.C. section 2-702 governing reclamation (*see infra*, §§552-566), demand for return of the goods generally must be made within **10 days** following the buyer's receipt of them. However, if the buyer has made a **written misstatement of solvency** in the three-month period before delivery, there is no 10-day limitation on the right to reclaim.

4. **Buyer's Resale to Innocent Third Party—Bad Check Cases [§181]**

Suppose the buyer issues a nonsufficient funds check in payment for goods in a cash sale transaction, and before the seller can reclaim the goods (having learned that the check is no good), the buyer sells the goods to an innocent purchaser. Can the seller recover the goods, or their price, *from* the innocent purchaser?

a. **Common law [§182]**

The common law gave primacy to the seller's ownership right and allowed the seller to reclaim the goods from the buyer or *any* subsequent party—even a good faith purchaser. The title of the buyer and all subsequent parties was deemed *void*. [*In re* **Perpall,** 256 F. 758 (2d Cir. 1919)]

b. **U.C.C. rule [§183]**

The U.C.C. emphasizes the free marketability of goods. Dishonor of the buyer's check renders the buyer's title "*voidable*" as against the seller. Nevertheless, the buyer may still *transfer full title to a good faith purchaser for value*. [U.C.C. §2-403(1)]

(1) **Note**

In protecting the good faith purchaser, the U.C.C. does not deny the seller all remedies; it simply demands that the seller take action against the party with whom the seller dealt (*i.e.,* the buyer).

(2) **And note**

The fact that the seller and the buyer specifically agree that the sale to the buyer is to be "strictly cash" does not change the above result so far as the third person is concerned. [U.C.C. §2-403(1)(c)]

(3) **Security interests—same rule [§184]**

Where the buyer has granted a *security interest* in the goods to an innocent creditor or lender, the same rule applies. The security interest cuts off the seller's right to reclaim the goods as against that creditor or lender. [*In re* **Samuels,** 526 F.2d 1238 (5th Cir. 1976)]

B. "Sale or Return" and "Sale on Approval" Transactions

1. **Definitions**

a. **"Sale or return" [§185]**

If a buyer ordered goods *primarily for resale*, and has the right to return them even though they conform to the contract, the transaction is a "sale or return." [U.C.C. §2-326(1)(b)]

Example: Dealer orders special goods from Wholesaler to fill a customer order; the terms of sale specify that Dealer may return the goods within 30 days if unsold.

b. **"Sale on approval" [§186]**

If a buyer ordered goods *primarily for buyer's own use*, and has the right to return them even though they conform to the contract, the transaction is a "sale on approval." [U.C.C. §2-326(1)(a)]

Example: Consumer bought a television set from Big Department Store, which has a sales policy of allowing the customer to return merchandise for a full refund within one week of purchase, even if there is nothing wrong with the goods. Such a sale is a "sale on approval."

2. **Sale or Return—Incidents of the Transaction**

a. **Writing required [§187]**

The right to return must be set forth *in writing* as part of the contract of sale. *Rationale:* Because the practice of returning goods is so much at odds with an ordinary contract of sale, where written agreements are involved the right to return must be contained in the written memorandum (*i.e.,* cannot be proved by parol evidence). [U.C.C. §2-326(4); *and see* **Harold Klein & Co. v. Lopardo**, 308 A.2d 538 (N.H. 1973)—refusing to allow proof of right to return as a "trade practice"]

b. **Time for return [§188]**

The contract often specifies the period of time within which the buyer must elect to return or keep the goods. If no time period is specified, the buyer must make the election within a *reasonable time*. In either event, the return must be made while the goods are substantially in their *original condition*. [U.C.C. §2-327(2)(a)]

(1) **Failure to return promptly [§189]**

If the goods are not returned to the seller within the time period allowed, the buyer is bound to keep and pay for the goods. [**Buckstaff v. Russell**, 79 F. 611 (8th Cir. 1897)]

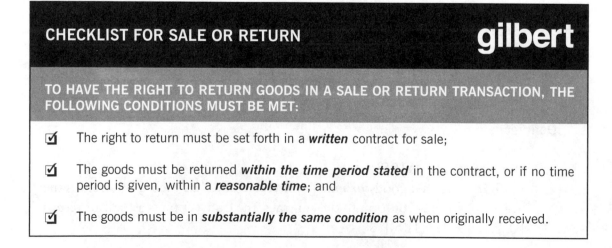

CHECKLIST FOR SALE OR RETURN — **gilbert**

TO HAVE THE RIGHT TO RETURN GOODS IN A SALE OR RETURN TRANSACTION, THE FOLLOWING CONDITIONS MUST BE MET:

- ☑ The right to return must be set forth in a *written* contract for sale;
- ☑ The goods must be returned *within the time period stated* in the contract, or if no time period is given, within a *reasonable time*; and
- ☑ The goods must be in *substantially the same condition* as when originally received.

c. **Status pending return [§190]**

Until the buyer elects to return the goods, there is a valid sale, and hence, the buyer has complete ownership rights in the goods. If the buyer properly exercises the right of return, title is revested in the seller.

(1) **Risk of loss [§191]**

The buyer bears the risk of loss until the seller actually receives the returned goods. Of course, if the property is damaged or destroyed (even through no fault of the buyer), the seller is not obligated to take the property back. [U.C.C. §2-327(2)(b); **Scrogin v. Wood,** 54 N.W. 437 (Iowa 1893)]

(2) **Expenses [§192]**

The buyer must also bear the expense of returning the goods to the seller. [U.C.C. §2-327(2)(b)]

3. **Sale on Approval—Incidents of the Transaction**

a. **What constitutes approval [§193]**

The buyer will be deemed to have manifested approval whenever the buyer either expressly or impliedly signifies *acceptance of the goods.* [U.C.C. §2-606(1)(a)] Alternatively, if the buyer *retains the goods* beyond the time stated in the contract (or if no time is stated, beyond a reasonable time) without giving notice of rejection, this too constitutes an acceptance. [U.C.C. §2-327(1)(b)]

b. **Trial use of goods [§194]**

A buyer may try out the goods in use or consumption without implying either approval or acceptance. [U.C.C. §2-327(1)(b)] It is a factual determination in each case as to whether the buyer's use or consumption is consistent with the purpose of the trial—*i.e.,* is it a mere sampling or is it evidence of the buyer's decision to approve?

EXAM TIP　　　　　　　　　　　　　　　　　**gilbert**

Remember that the distinction between simply sampling goods and approval of goods is determined by a *factual analysis*. Thus, on an exam you need to consider things such as the *length of time* the buyer used the goods and the *quantity consumed or used*.

c. **Status pending approval [§195]**

Until the buyer evidences approval, there is *no sale.* The buyer is merely a *bailee* in possession of the goods. The *seller* retains all the incidents of ownership.

(1) **Payment [§196]**

The buyer, therefore, is not obligated to pay the purchase price until the buyer accepts the goods. [U.C.C. §2-327(1)]

(2) **Risk of loss [§197]**

Furthermore, the *seller* must bear the risk of *accidental loss*, even though the goods are in the buyer's possession. However, the result is contra if the loss is caused by the buyer's *negligence*. [**B.F. Hirsch, Inc. v. C.T. Gustafson Co.,** 42 N.E.2d 123 (Ill. 1942)]

d. Return of goods [§198]

If a buyer elects to return goods held on approval, and gives the seller proper notice of this intent, the expense of return is on the *seller*. [U.C.C. §2-327(1)(c)]

(1) But note

A *merchant* buyer must follow all reasonable instructions of the seller in effectuating the return. [U.C.C. §2-327(1)(c)]

4. Rights of Creditors

a. Sale or return [§199]

While the buyer is in possession of goods being held on a sale or return basis, the buyer has *full ownership rights* to the goods (*see* above). Hence, the goods are subject to the claims of the *buyer's* creditors. [U.C.C. §2-326(2)]

b. Sale on approval [§200]

While the buyer is in possession of goods being held on a sale on approval basis, they are subject to the claims of the *seller's* creditors, and not to those of the buyer's creditors. Of course, once the buyer accepts the goods (or is deemed as a matter of law to have accepted them), the situation reverses—*i.e.*, the goods then become subject to the claims of the buyer's creditors. [U.C.C. §2-326(2)]

SALE OR RETURN VS. SALE ON APPROVAL		gilbert
	SALE OR RETURN	**SALE ON APPROVAL**
DEFINED	Buyer takes goods for resale but may return if unable to resell.	Buyer takes goods for trial period and may return them even though they conform to the contract.
RISK OF LOSS	**Buyer** bears risk of loss until goods are returned to Seller (risk remains on Buyer while goods are in transit).	**Seller** bears risk of loss until Buyer accepts goods (including failing to return them or to notify Seller of intention within the required time). If Buyer decides to return the goods, return is at Seller's risk.
CREDITOR'S RIGHTS	Goods are subject to the claims of **Buyer's** creditors while in Buyer's possession.	Goods are subject to claims of **Seller's** creditors until Buyer's acceptance; then goods become subject to claims of Buyer's creditors.

C. Auction Sales

1. **When Title Passes [§201]**
   Sale of goods at auction is complete when the auctioneer announces its completion by the fall of the hammer or in another customary manner. [U.C.C. §2-328(2)]

   a. **Bids are offers [§202]**
      Bids at an auction are deemed to be mere offers by the bidders. Thus, no contract is formed until the auctioneer accepts one of the bids by the fall of the hammer. Until that time, any bidder may withdraw the bid.

   b. **Acceptance [§203]**
      Once the hammer falls, however, the sale is complete, and neither bidders nor the auctioneer can unilaterally withdraw. [**Stanhope State Bank v. Peterson,** 218 N.W. 262 (Iowa 1928)]

      (1) **Note**
         If a bid is made while the hammer is falling, the auctioneer has complete discretion whether to reopen the bidding or declare the auction closed. [U.C.C. §2-328(2)]

   c. **Auction terms binding [§204]**
      Publicly announced terms and conditions of the auction are binding on all bidders. This is true whether or not a particular bidder has actual knowledge of the terms. [**Belanger & Sons v. United States,** 275 F.2d 372 (1st Cir. 1960)]

2. **Withdrawal of Goods by Auctioneer [§205]**
   Auctions can be held either "with reserve" or "without reserve." These terms relate to whether the seller is bound to accept any bids made at the auction, or whether, if the seller is dissatisfied with the bids, the goods may be taken off the bidding block and withdrawn from the sale.

   a. **Definitions [§206]**
      An auction sale "*with reserve*" means the seller has reserved the right to reject all bids and withdraw the goods from sale at any time and for any reason. At an auction "*without reserve,*" the right of withdrawal does not exist, and the seller is bound to accept the highest good faith bid received once the auction begins. [U.C.C. §2-328(3)]

   b. **U.C.C. presumption [§207]**
      Under the U.C.C., all auction sales are *presumed* to be *with reserve* unless expressly announced to the contrary. [U.C.C. §2-328(3)]

TYPES OF AUCTION SALES	gilbert
TYPE	**RIGHTS OF SELLER**
WITH RESERVE	Seller may *reject bids and withdraw* goods from auction at any time, for any reason
WITHOUT RESERVE	Seller is *bound to accept* the highest bid at auction, so long as it is made in *good faith*

3. Bids by Seller [§208]

At common law, it was fraud for a seller to bid unannounced (*e.g.*, by having a confederate in the crowd or having the auctioneer announce phony bids). Obviously, the seller is not really going to buy, so such a practice raises the price artificially. Thus, a seller may bid at an auction *only* if the seller expressly reserves the right to do so by *advance notice*. [U.C.C. §2-328(4)] If the seller does not give such notice and bids nonetheless, the successful buyer at the auction has an election: The winning buyer may either avoid the sale entirely, or may take the goods at the price of the last good faith bid made prior to the completion of the sale (which could give the buyer a very good buy). [U.C.C. §2-328(4)]

a. Distinguish—forced sales [§209]

The rule preventing secret bidding by the seller does not apply if the sale is a "forced sale" (*e.g.*, a judicial sale), where the involuntary seller is permitted to do whatever is possible to make the prevailing bid as high as possible. [U.C.C. §2-328(4)]

Chapter Four:
Warranties

CONTENTS

Chapter Approach

Chapter Approach

A large percentage of Sales problems that are actually litigated involve warranty disputes. This area is also a fertile source of exam questions; therefore, much of the information covered in this chapter is important to know.

When the word "warranty" comes up, most people think only of quality problems, but the U.C.C. divides warranties into two categories:

(i) *Warranty of title*—a warranty that the seller will convey good title and that transfer is rightful (this is not a major exam topic, but you should be familiar with its characteristics); and

(ii) *Warranties of quality*—express and implied warranties regarding the goods (this topic is very likely to appear on your exam).

A general approach to warranty questions is as follows:

1. *Was there an express warranty* made, *i.e.,* a statement of fact or promise relating to the goods and part of the basis of the bargain?

2. *Are any warranties implied* by law? Specifically look for:

   a. *Warranty of merchantability*—a merchant with respect to goods of the kind sold warrants that the goods are of "merchantable" quality; or

   b. *Fitness for a particular purpose*—any seller (merchant or nonmerchant) who has reason to know of the use contemplated by the buyer and that the buyer is relying on the seller's judgment warrants that the goods are fit for the use.

3. *Have any warranties been effectively disclaimed?* Remember that disclaimers are narrowly construed and that some have special requirements, especially:

   a. To disclaim the warranty of *merchantability,* the word "merchantability" must be *specifically mentioned*; the disclaimer may be oral or written, but if written, it must be *conspicuous.*

   b. To disclaim the warranty of *fitness for a particular purpose,* the disclaimer must be *in writing* and must be *conspicuous.*

   c. Remember that *"as is"* language may disclaim any *implied* warranties (including merchantability).

   d. And for *consumer goods,* recall that the Magnuson-Moss Act prohibits a disclaimer of the implied warranties (*e.g.,* merchantability or fitness for a particular purpose).

4. *Has any warranty been breached*, and, if so, what is the *effect* of the breach? If the goods have not lived up to the warranty, consider the U.C.C. requirements of proximate cause and notice, and the remedies available. Also, if the goods are *consumer goods*, think about the effects of any consumer protection legislation (which provide specific procedures to follow, additional remedies, etc.).

A. Background

1. Common Law [§210]

At early common law, breach of warranty was regarded as a tort. If the seller had used the magic words "warranty" or "guarantee," this was held to evidence an intention to be bound, and a breach was considered in the nature of fraud and hence tortious. Later, the common law cases recognized that the liability for breach of warranty was really *contractual* in nature, and as such, it was immaterial whether there was any actual fraud or bad faith. If the words used amounted to a warranty, the seller was bound even in the absence of proof that the seller intended to be bound. Also, the later cases rejected the requirement of "special words" of warranty and were willing to *imply* certain warranties into every sale, even where there were no express warranties.

2. U.C.C. [§211]

The concept of implied warranties has been embodied in the Code. Also, the Code divides warranties into two broad categories: warranties of title and warranties of quality, and first it is necessary to consider the warranty of title.

B. Warranty of Title

1. What Is Warranted by the Warranty of Title [§212]

The U.C.C. provides an automatic warranty that the seller will convey *good title* to the goods and that the transfer is *rightful*. [U.C.C. §2-312(1)(a)] The seller also warrants that the goods will be delivered *free of any claim* of the seller's creditors of which the buyer has no knowledge. [U.C.C. §2-312(1)(b)]

a. Note—not express or implied [§213]

Although this warranty arises automatically, as do implied warranties, technically it is not classified either as "express" or "implied." The reason for this is that the drafters did not want the warranty to be disclaimed by general language in the contract stating that there are "no warranties, express or implied." One thinks of such language as relating solely to quality warranties, and it is not sufficient to rid the seller of the warranty of title. [U.C.C. §2-312, Official Comment 6]

2. No Warranty of Quiet Possession [§214]

Note that the U.C.C. does *not* create a warranty as to "quiet possession" (*i.e.*, freedom from all lawsuits or threats thereof), even though such a warranty was part of the warranty of title under the Uniform Sales Act (which has been replaced by the U.C.C.) and common law rules. Instead, the warranty of title under the U.C.C. is breached only when someone makes a *nonfrivolous claim* to superior title. The seller is not responsible for colorless claims of superior title. [U.C.C. §2-312, Official Comment 1; **Jefferson v. Janes**, 408 A.2d 1036 (Md. 1979)]

Example: A thief steals a car from the true owner and sells it to a used car dealership. An innocent consumer purchases the car and is annoyed when the police show up and take the car away from her. The consumer can sue the used car dealership for breach of the warranty of title (and the dealership can use the same theory against the thief). It is no defense that the dealership acted in good faith, was nonnegligent, or thought it had good title.

Compare: On the other hand, if the consumer bought the car directly from the true owner, and an enemy of the true owner tried to cause trouble by bringing suit against the consumer, wrongfully claiming to be the owner of the car, the warranty of title is *not* breached and the consumer must defend the spurious claim without aid from the true owner of the car.

3. Warranty Against Infringement [§215]

The U.C.C. provides for a new warranty as part of the title warranty section. Where the seller is a *merchant*, the seller warrants that the goods shall be delivered free of the rightful claims of any third person by way of *patent or trademark* infringement or the like. [U.C.C. §2-312(3)]

a. Exception [§216]

Where the seller supplied goods according to *specifications furnished by buyer*, the buyer must hold the seller harmless from any infringement claim arising out of the seller's compliance with the specifications. [U.C.C. §2-312(3)]

> **EXAM TIP**   **gilbert**
>
> This is yet another rule that depends on the *seller's status as a merchant*. When answering exam questions, be sure to note whether the seller is a merchant and, if so, consider how that will impact your analysis.

4. Disclaiming the Title Warranty

a. Usage of trade [§217]

The title warranty does *not arise* in certain situations where the buyer should reasonably know that the seller makes no claim of title. For example, a judicial sale has always been caveat emptor ("let the buyer beware") as to title warranties (which is one of the reasons why such sales bring so little). Therefore, by usage of trade, no warranty of title is made in judicial sales. [U.C.C. §2-312(2), Official Comment 5]

b. Express disclaimer [§218]

While general language disclaiming warranty liability will not rid the contract of the warranty of title (*see supra*, §212), *specific* language in the contract that disclaims the warranty of title will be given effect. [U.C.C. §2-312(2)]

C. Express Warranties

1. Creation of Express Warranty [§219]

A statement of *fact or promise* made by the seller to the buyer in the course of negotiations that *relates to the goods* and is "*part of the basis of the bargain*" creates an express warranty that the goods will conform to the statement or promise made. [U.C.C. §2-313(1)(a)]

2. Statement of Fact or Promise [§220]

In addition to statements of fact and promises, descriptions of the goods, samples, and models may be sufficient to create an express warranty.

a. Form of warranty

(1) No technical words [§221]

Contrary to the early common law rule, no magic words of warranty need be used. *Any affirmation of fact* ("This is a new car"), *promise* made in connection with the sale ("If it doesn't work, I'll fix it"), *description* of the goods ("When it arrives, it will be painted orange"), or *sample or model* ("It will look just like this one over here") may be sufficient. It is not necessary that the seller use technical words such as "warranty" or "guarantee." [U.C.C. §2-313(1), (2)]

(2) Written or oral [§222]

In general, an express warranty may be written or oral. In appropriate cases, it may be expressed by conduct, rather than words. [**Rinkmasters v. City of Utica**, 75 Misc. 2d 941 (1973)—illustrations in sales catalogs create express warranties that goods will conform to pictures, even where verbal description accompanying pictures is more modest in its description; **Bemidji Sales Barn Inc. v. Chatfield**, 250 N.W.2d 185 (Minn. 1977)—statement made as part of sales pitch; **Drayton v. Jiffee Chemical**, 591 F.2d 352 (6th Cir. 1978)—television ad]

b. Seller's intent or culpability immaterial [§223]

No intent to warrant is required. If the words used amount to a warranty, it is immaterial that the seller did not intend them as such or did not intend to be bound thereby. Liability is predicated on breach of the contract created by the warranty, not fraud or negligence. Where the warranty is breached, the seller becomes *absolutely liable*. The fact that the warranty was given in good faith, or that the seller was innocent or nonnegligent in causing the breach, is irrelevant. [U.C.C. §2-313(2)]

c. Fact vs. opinion [§224]

In determining whether portions of a "sales pitch" constitute an express warranty, the U.C.C. provides: "[A]n affirmation *merely* of the value of the goods or a statement purporting to be *merely* the seller's opinion or commendation of the goods does not create a warranty." [U.C.C. §2-313(2)—emphasis added] In other words, the seller will be held liable only for statements of fact or promises—not for mere "puffing" or dealers' talk.

Example: A statement that "this is a 102 horsepower engine" is a positive representation of fact. But a statement that "this is a good engine" is merely one of opinion and thus not a warranty.

---

(1) Note—apparent trend

Many cases in this field are extremely difficult to classify (*e.g.*, "this engine has been thoroughly engineered"). There is a discernible judicial trend to narrow the scope of the permissible "puff," and thus expand the concept of warranty. Remarks that a generation ago would be called merely opinions are today called warranties. However, each case is still *sui generis*. The courts consider the words used in the light of the circumstances surrounding the sale.

(2) Application

One of the principal factors the courts consider is the *relative knowledge of the parties* concerning the goods. If the buyer has only limited knowledge of the seller's wares, then the seller's vague statements will more likely be held to be representations of fact rather than opinion; but the opposite result is reached where the buyer has almost as much—or as much—information as the seller.

EXAM TIP	gilbert

In determining whether a statement by a seller is *fact or puffing*, look for adjectives and superlatives. They will often indicate that the seller is giving an opinion rather than a warranty. Also, look at the facts to determine what the buyer knows about the goods—the more the buyer knows, the less likely the seller's statements will create a warranty.

---

3. Basis of the Bargain [§225]

Under the U.C.C., not only must the alleged warranty "relate to the goods" (an obvious enough requirement), but it also must go to the "basis of the bargain."

[U.C.C. §2-313(1)] What does this mean? It means that the statement must have been part of the deal, the sort of thing that *played some part in the buyer's decision to buy*.

a. Buyer's reliance [§226]

At common law and under the Uniform Sales Act (which the U.C.C. replaced), the *buyer* had the burden of proving that he *relied* on the warranty statement. The common law looked upon the buyer's reliance as the heart and soul of an express warranty. Without it, the buyer could not recover. The U.C.C., however, uses the much more vague phrase "basis of the bargain" and the Official Comment says that *reliance is no longer to be of prime significance*. All statements by the seller become "part of the basis of the bargain" *unless good reason* is shown to the contrary. [U.C.C. §2-313, Official Comments 3, 8]

(1) Analysis

What the U.C.C. has in effect done is to shift the burden of proof on the issue. Previously, the buyer was required to plead and prove reliance in making out a case. Under the Code, however, the buyer makes out a prima facie case that the questioned statement was part of the "basis of the bargain" simply by showing that the buyer made the purchase after the seller made the representation. The burden of proof then shifts, and it is the *seller* who must demonstrate that the buyer did *not* rely—*i.e.*, that the statement did not form "part of the basis of the bargain."

b. Time of warranting—statements made after sale [§227]

If a statement of fact is made *after* the sale contract is closed, will it be deemed an express warranty?

(1) Common law [§228]

The common law cases are almost unanimous in holding that it will not. [**M.C. Smith Co. v. Fisher Plastics Corp.**, 76 F. Supp. 641 (N.D. Ohio 1948)]

(2) U.C.C. rule [§229]

Under the U.C.C., however, if a post-transactional affirmation in fact becomes part of the "basis of the bargain," it can be deemed a *modification of the contract*, and will be effective even without any new consideration. [U.C.C. §2-209, *see supra*, §161]

Example: Farmer purchased a product that was advertised as allowing hay to be baled safely when freshly cut, rather than having to be stored and dried in the field. After the purchase of this product, the seller visited Farmer in order to promote more sales. He told Farmer that he could safely go ahead and bale his hay crop using this product. Farmer did so in reliance upon the seller's statements. However, the high moisture level in the baled hay caused spontaneous combustion which burned down Farmer's barn. Although the seller's statement postdated the sale, it was treated as part of the "basis of the bargain" because it was made to promote continued business. It was enforceable as a *modification* of the original contract. [**Bigelow v. Agway, Inc.,** 506 F.2d 551 (2d Cir. 1974)]

c. **Unread warranties [§230]**

If the seller makes an express warranty but the buyer does not learn of it until *after* the sale (*e.g.*, the buyer sees an old advertisement), can the buyer recover for breach of the warranty? The technical argument against this is that the unread warranty can hardly be "part of the basis of the bargain." However, the buyer might prevail by claiming to be a *third party beneficiary* of the express warranty made to those who did see the warranty and purchased as a result of it. Such parties would legitimately expect any purchaser hurt by breach of the warranty to be able to sue the warrantor for the breach.

4. **2003 Revision Adds Warranties to Remote Purchasers [§231]**

The revision has two new sections fleshing out an idea that the courts had mostly reached without statutory guidance under the original Code (*see* discussion of privity, *infra,* §§306-328)—express warranty liability to remote purchasers. The revision avoids the privity problem by creating express warranty liability in the manufacturer in these situations in two new sections. Sections 2R-313A ("Obligation to Remote Purchaser Created by Record Packaged with or Accompanying Goods") and 2R-313B ("Obligation to Remote Purchaser Created by Communication to the Public") give the remote purchaser of *new goods* the ability to sue for breach of express warranties in these situations, but allow the seller to limit remedies as part of these warranties, and particularly to avoid liability for the buyer's lost profits.

Example: The manufacturer of an automobile creates a television commercial that states the vehicle will get 50 miles per gallon and also states this claim in the warranty that accompanies the car when it is sold by the car dealer to the consumer. Since the manufacturer and consumer are not in privity (no direct sale between them), are such warranties part of the basis of the bargain? Under the 2003 revision to the U.C.C., the answer is yes.

D. Implied Warranties

1. **In General [§232]**

In addition to any express warranties that may be made in connection with the sale, the law may *imply* certain additional warranties simply because a sale of goods has been consummated. These are the implied warranties, which are created by law to promote higher standards and to discourage sharp dealings in business. They are imposed *irrespective of the seller's intentions*, and despite the fact that the seller has made *no representations or promises* whatsoever concerning the goods. Unless expressly negated by the parties or the circumstances, they arise by operation of law in *every sale of goods*, new or used, as part of the seller's cost of doing business.

2. Warranty of Merchantability [§233]

In every mercantile contract of sale where it is not expressly disclaimed, the law implies a warranty that the goods shall be of "merchantable" quality. [U.C.C. §2-314]

a. Who makes the warranty? [§234]

The U.C.C. imposes the implied warranty of merchantability only upon a seller who is a *"merchant with respect to goods of that kind."* [U.C.C. §2-314(1)]

(1) Application

Thus, basically, an implied warranty of merchantability arises in all sales transactions *except* sales by private individuals or "occasional" sales by professionals who normally deal in other markets. [**Samson v. Riesing**, 215 N.W.2d 662 (Wis. 1974)—no implied warranties as to food served at church picnic; servers were not "merchants"]

EXAM TIP   **gilbert**

On your exam, whenever you see the sale of goods that aren't as they should be, you should always consider the *warranty of merchantability*. The first thing to do is to see if the sale was by a *merchant*, and the second thing is to check that the merchant *deals in goods of that kind*. Thus, if Aunt Bea sells handmade potholders at a church picnic, and the potholders don't protect against hot pots and pans, there won't be a breach of warranty of merchantability because Aunt Bea is not a merchant. However, if Aunt Bea sells those potholders at her Mayberry Potholder Emporium, she is a merchant, and the warranty of merchantability may well have arisen. *But note:* If Aunt Bea sells her extra Potholder Emporium cash register to Floyd's Barber Shop, and it doesn't work, no warranty of merchantability has arisen because Aunt Bea is not a merchant with respect to cash registers.

---

(2) But note

There is still an obligation of *good faith* in every sale transaction, so that even a *nonmerchant* seller may be held liable for failure to disclose a *known* hidden defect in the goods. [U.C.C. §1-203]

b. Standard of merchantable quality [§235]

The U.C.C. establishes a six-part definition of merchantability. Goods must meet *at least all six standards* (and any others the courts add to the merchantability definition). The standards are:

(1) Contract description [§236]

The goods must be capable of passing without objection in the trade under the contract description. [U.C.C. §2-314(2)(a)] If the contract says that the object sold is a "car," it had better have an engine inside; everyone thinks of cars as having engines. The courts have said that the standard means that goods must be *readily saleable and useable*. [**McNeil & Higgins Co. v. Czarnikow-Reinda Co.,** 274 F. 397 (S.D.N.Y. 1921)]

(2) Fungible goods [§237]

"Fungible goods" are those that can be interchanged without comment (like grain commingled in a grain elevator); the owner does not care whether the original goods are returned as long as a like quantity is delivered. In the case of fungible goods, to be "merchantable," the goods must be of *"fair average quality"*; *i.e.,* the *bulk* (not the whole) of the goods must hover around the middle belt of quality. [U.C.C. §2-314(2)(b)]

(3) Fit for ordinary purpose [§238]

To be merchantable, goods must also be "fit for the ordinary purposes for which such goods are used." [U.C.C. §2-314(2)(c)] In other words, the goods must do *what is normally expected of such goods*. Actually, this is typically the only warranty that the buyer needs—a warranty that the goods will work.

EXAM TIP   **gilbert**

That the goods must be *fit for the ordinary purposes* of such goods is by far the most important standard of "merchantability," and the one you will most likely have to look for on an exam.

(a) Comment

Buyers would be more disturbed when the warranty of merchantability is disclaimed if they understood that by doing so the seller is disclaiming the most basic responsibility, *i.e.,* that the goods will work.

(4) Variations within normal limits [§239]

It is also required that the goods "run *within the variations permitted by the agreement*, of even kind, quality, and quantity within each unit and among all units involved." [U.C.C. §2-314(2)(d)—emphasis added] Thus merchants are required to adhere to established standards in multi-unit deliveries of merchandise.

(5) Adequately contained, packaged, and labeled [§240]

Goods must also be "adequately contained, packaged, and labeled as the agreement may require." [U.C.C. §2-314(2)(e)] Some items are expected to be labeled (*e.g.,* medicine); others are not (*e.g.,* bowling balls). Some items are expected to be packaged (*e.g.,* fine china); others are not (*e.g.,* automobiles). Section 2-314(2)(e) applies only where the nature of the goods and of the transaction require a certain type of container, package, or label. [U.C.C. §2-314(2)(e), Official Comment 10; *but see* **Shaffer v. Victoria Station,** 588 P.2d 233 (Wash. 1978)—wine served to a customer in a glass that shattered and injured the customer's hand was not adequately "contained"]

(6) Conforms to label [§241]

Finally, to be merchantable, goods must conform to the promises or affirmations of fact made on the *container or label*. [U.C.C. §2-314(2)(f)]

(a) Dealer liability [§242]

This changes pre-Code law, which generally held that a *dealer* was not bound by express warranties made by the *manufacturer* of goods, even where such warranties accompanied or were annexed to the goods (via containers or labels), unless the dealer had adopted the warranties as part of the sale. [**Moneta v. Hoinacki,** 67 N.E.2d 204 (Ill. 1946)] Under the U.C.C., however, the dealer becomes responsible for affirmations on the label or container via the implied warranty of merchantability, *unless* the dealer disclaims them.

(b) Inadequate labeling [§243]

Moreover, this facet of the merchantability definition also apparently means that the goods can be *safely* used in accordance with the labeling and packaging instructions. Consequently, if the labeling is incorrect or incomplete so that the goods cannot be safely used in reliance thereon, there is a breach of the implied warranty of merchantability.

(c) May be breach of express and implied warranties [§244]

Note that if the goods do not conform to the label or package, this failure may also be a breach of an *express* warranty. However, if the package is not delivered to the buyer until *after* the offer and acceptance process is closed, it may be that no express warranty arose since the statements thereon are no longer part of the "basis of the bargain" (*see supra*, §225). Even if no express warranty arose, the implied warranty of merchantability would be breached by the failure of the goods to conform to the package or label.

SUMMARY OF SIX STANDARDS OF MERCHANTABLE QUALITY — gilbert

GOODS MUST MEET *ALL* OF THE FOLLOWING SIX STANDARDS:

- ☑ The goods must be *fit for the ordinary purpose* of such goods, or do what is normally expected of the goods;

- ☑ The goods must be capable of passing without objection under the *contract description*;

- ☑ If fungible, the bulk of the goods must be of *fair average quality*;

- ☑ The goods must be of *even kind, quality, and quantity,* running within the variations permitted in the agreement;

- ☑ The goods must be *adequately packaged, contained, and labeled* as required by the agreement; and

- ☑ The goods must conform to the promises made *on the container or label*.

3. **Implied Warranty of Fitness for a Particular Purpose [§245]**
If a seller has *reason to know of the particular use* of goods contemplated by the buyer, and is also aware that the buyer is *relying on the seller's judgment* to select suitable goods, then an implied warranty of fitness for that particular use or purpose arises, unless specifically excluded by the seller. [U.C.C. §2-315]

a. **Objective test [§246]**
The seller must only have "reason to know" of the buyer's particular purpose and reliance on the seller. Actual knowledge is *not* required; thus, this is an objective test (*i.e.,* would a reasonable person in the seller's position have known?).

EXAM TIP   **gilbert**

Whenever the facts of a question talk about **what the buyer wants to do with particular goods**, consider the warranty of **fitness for the particular purpose**. Be sure to examine the facts carefully to see if the seller had reason to know about the buyer's proposed use of the goods. If this warranty is to apply, you will see some indication that the seller knew about this proposed use—usually by **being told** by the buyer himself.

---

b. **Meaning of "particular purpose"—distinguish merchantability [§247]**
Since the implied warranty of merchantability (*see supra,* §233) provides that the goods will fulfill their *ordinary* purpose, that coverage is not part of this warranty. Instead the implied warranty of fitness for a particular purpose means that the goods will do something *different* from their ordinary purpose.

Example: Buyer needed to paint the outside of her house. She went to the paint store and told this to Seller, who sold Buyer paint. The paint was for interior use only and easily washed off the outside of the house over the following winter. The paint was useful as interior paint (*i.e.,* was fit for its *ordinary* purpose), but since it did not fulfill Buyer's *particular* purpose (exterior paint), Seller breached the implied warranty that it would do so.

Compare: In the above example, the buyer told the seller of the particular purpose. If the buyer had not done so, but instead had merely asked the seller for paint, the sale of paint only suitable for interior use would not have led to seller liability.

---

c. **Merchant or nonmerchant seller [§248]**
Unlike the implied warranty of "merchantability" (*supra,* §233), which applies only to sales by merchants, the implied warranty of fitness for a particular purpose applies in *any* sale transaction, whether by a merchant or nonmerchant. (*But note:* The requirements of seller's knowledge and buyer's reliance are usually absent in sales by nonmerchants.)

d.   Buyer's reliance essential [§249]

The buyer must in fact rely on the seller's superior skill or judgment as part of the transaction for the warranty of fitness for a particular purpose to apply. [**Sylvia Coal Co. v. Mercury Coal & Coke Co.,** 156 S.E.2d 1 (W. Va. 1967)]

(1)   Sales by brand or trade name [§250]

Whenever goods are sold by their brand or trade name (*e.g.,* "one dozen Remington shotgun shells"), there is an issue as to whether the buyer was relying on the seller's selection, or rather on the manufacturer's brand name. Clearly if the buyer insisted upon a particular brand, the buyer cannot show the necessary reliance on the seller's judgment. However, in other cases, the mere designation by brand name will not by itself preclude reliance. It remains a question of fact in each case.

(2)   Sale according to buyer's specifications [§251]

If the sales contract is based on plans and specifications furnished by the buyer, there is *no reliance* on the seller's selection of the goods; hence, there is no implied warranty of their fitness for the buyer's purpose. [**Corporation of Presiding Bishop v. Cavanaugh,** 217 Cal. App. 2d 492 (1963)—no implied warranty of fitness in sale of heating system to church because the church had designed and set specifications for the system]

(3)   Distinguish—merchantability warranty [§252]

The buyer's reliance is *not* required for the implied warranty of merchantability (*see supra,* §235). Hence, even where the buyer clearly did not rely on the seller's skill or judgment in selecting goods for the buyer's *particular* use, the buyer can still enforce the seller's implied warranty that the goods sold were "merchantable"—*i.e.,* that they were fit for ordinary use. [**Ryan v. Progressive Grocery Stores,** 255 N.Y. 388 (1931)]

e.   Seller must select or furnish goods [§253]

The seller must either *select or furnish* the goods. Often the seller does both; but in situations such as those existing in supermarkets, the seller only furnishes the goods while it is the buyer who selects them. However, *either* selecting or furnishing will suffice.

f. Does warranty liability extend to abnormal reactions? [§254]

A frequent issue is whether the seller's warranties of *fitness and merchantability* cover even unique or abnormal reactions sustained by the buyer in use or consumption of the seller's product. For example, the seller markets a hair styling product; the buyer purchases some and after using it, the buyer's hair falls out. Evidence indicates that the buyer's scalp is unusually sensitive to a chemical contained in the product. Is the seller liable for breach of warranty of fitness for that product?

(1) Former law [§255]

Under the Sales Act, a seller warranted only that the product was "reasonably" fit for the purpose for which it was sold. Under this wording, it was repeatedly held that the seller was *not* responsible for injuries to the buyer that were caused by the buyer's peculiar sensitivity or allergy to the seller's product.

(2) U.C.C. rule [§256]

The word "reasonable" does not appear in U.C.C. section 2-315; it provides merely that the goods "shall be fit for such [particular] purpose," and the question has thus arisen whether the seller's warranty now extends even to unique and abnormal reactions.

(a) Majority rule

So far, most courts have continued to apply the pre-Code rule; *i.e.,* the warranty is *not breached* unless the buyer can show that the reaction is common to "an appreciable number of users." [**McNamara v. City of New Britain,** 214 A.2d 676 (Conn. 1965); **Harris v. Belton,** 258 Cal. App. 2d 595 (1968)]

(b) Minority rule

Other courts have solved the problem by placing the burden on the seller to establish that the buyer's injuries were abnormal and exotic, *i.e.,* by presuming that the buyer's reaction is normal until the seller proves to the contrary. [**Casagrande v. F.W. Woolworth Co.,** 165 N.E.2d 109 (Mass. 1960)]

4. Implied "Warranty of Wholesomeness" [§257]

When the goods sold are either foods or beverages, a special implied warranty arises that the goods are *fit for human consumption* or are "wholesome." Doctrinally, there is no such implied warranty as "fitness for human consumption" or "wholesomeness"; rather, the foodstuff cases are technically a subcategory of the "merchantability" and "fitness for particular purpose" warranties of U.C.C. sections 2-314 and 2-315, *supra.* The implied warranty of merchantability specifically covers goods to be consumed on the premises or elsewhere. [U.C.C. §2-314(1)]

a. **Retail grocer [§258]**

A retail grocer impliedly warrants the wholesomeness of the food sold. This warranty extends to all foods sold—both those selected by the grocer for the customer and those selected by the customer from the grocer's shelf (self-service selection).

(1) **Normal use only [§259]**

The warranty guarantees only the fitness for *normal* use. Thus, in a sale of meat, ordinarily the warranty is that it is suitable to eat when cooked, not that it is fit to eat raw. [**McSpedon v. Kunz,** 271 N.Y. 131 (1936)]

(2) **Sealed package doctrine [§260]**

The warranty of fitness for human consumption is implied even where the food comes to the dealer prepackaged in a sealed container. [**Chandler v. Anchor Serum Co.,** 426 P.2d 82 (Kan. 1967)] Although the grocer had no opportunity to examine or inspect the goods in the container, the grocer is still held to warrant their fitness for consumption. *Rationale:* The grocer is in a better position to ascertain their wholesomeness than the buyer, as the seller can choose to stock foods of reputable suppliers. [**Bonenberger v. Pittsburgh Mercantile Co.,** 28 A.2d 913 (Pa. 1942)]

(3) **Injury before checkout [§261]**

The "sale" is deemed to take place when the shopper takes the goods off the grocer's shelf. Thus warranty liability applies even where the injury takes place before the customer reaches the checkout stand (*e.g.,* canned goods explode in customer's hand). [**Sheeskin v. Giant Foods, Inc.,** 318 A.2d 874 (Md. 1974)]

(a) **Note**

It is an open question whether the same result would be reached if the injury was caused by goods that the customer had *not selected* (*e.g.,* where canned goods stacked in an aisle explode). Some cases hold that there is still a "sale," on the theory that the *expectation* of sales is enough to impose liability.

(b) **But note**

Even if there is no warranty liability, *strict liability in tort* could probably be imposed to protect the customer while shopping.

b. **Restaurants [§262]**

The Code clarifies uncertainties under previous law and specifically includes food sold for consumption. [U.C.C. §2-314(1)] It makes no difference whether the food is sold for consumption on the premises or to be taken out. It is still a sale, and the warranty of fitness is implied.

c. **"Wholesomeness" [§263]**

There remains the question of *how* fit food must be to be suitable for human consumption.

(1) Contamination [§264]
Of course if food is contaminated, it is unfit and recovery can be had against the restaurant owner.

(2) Indigenous vs. nonindigenous objects [§265]
If there is an object in the food, however, a strange distinction has been drawn by some of the courts. If the object is "indigenous" or "natural" to the food—such as a chicken bone in a chicken pie, or an oyster shell in an oyster stew—some courts hold that the warranty does *not* extend to injuries caused by ingesting such items. Only if the article is *alien* to the repast (*e.g.*, ground glass in chow mein) is recovery allowed.

(a) Rationale
This distinction is based on the *consumer's reasonable expectations* in consuming food or drink. Thus, where a restaurant patron broke a tooth on an olive pit served in his martini, his right to recover depends on whether the jury determines he acted reasonably in chewing the olive with the expectation that it contained no pit. [**Hochberg v. O'Donnell's Restaurant, Inc.**, 272 A.2d 846 (D.C. 1971)]

(3) "Reasonable expectation" test [§266]
This distinction between "indigenous" and "nonindigenous" objects is now being reexamined by many courts, and most reject it in favor of a test that asks whether the difficulty in the food was one that the buyer had a *reasonable expectation* of encountering. Thus the test is not whether the object is foreign or natural, but whether it is the sort of thing the buyer should have been being careful to avoid (*e.g.*, bones in fish, shells on nuts, etc.). [**Morrison's Cafeteria v. Haddox**, 431 So. 2d 975 (Ala. 1983)]

E. Disclaimer of Warranty

1. Disclaimers of Warranties—In General [§267]
The most troublesome area of warranty jurisprudence has been the extent to which the seller can lawfully exclude, modify, or disclaim express or implied warranties. The U.C.C. contains an elaborate section that addresses the subject [U.C.C. §2-316], but that still leaves certain questions unanswered. At the outset, it should be understood that courts everywhere have manifested extreme hostility to warranty disclaimers. The cases on the subject are buyer-oriented to a substantial degree, and the rules that have evolved must be gauged in the light of this prevalent judicial attitude.

a. Disclaiming express warranties [§268]
U.C.C. section 2-316 states:

gilbert

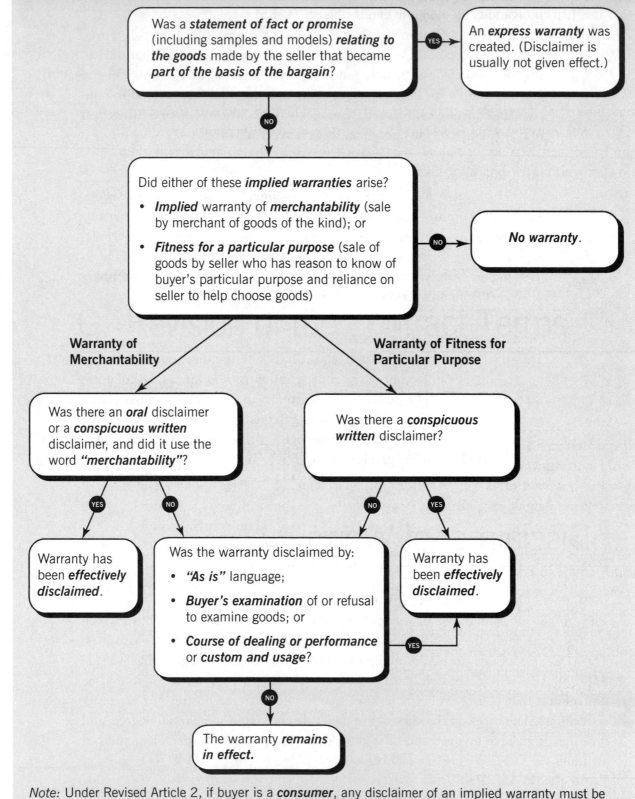

Was a **statement of fact or promise** (including samples and models) **relating to the goods** made by the seller that became **part of the basis of the bargain**?

— YES → An **express warranty** was created. (Disclaimer is usually not given effect.)

— NO ↓

Did either of these **implied warranties** arise?

- **Implied** warranty of **merchantability** (sale by merchant of goods of the kind); or

- **Fitness for a particular purpose** (sale of goods by seller who has reason to know of buyer's particular purpose and reliance on seller to help choose goods)

— NO → **No warranty**.

Warranty of Merchantability

Warranty of Fitness for Particular Purpose

Was there an **oral** disclaimer or a **conspicuous written** disclaimer, and did it use the word **"merchantability"**?

Was there a **conspicuous written** disclaimer?

— YES → Warranty has been **effectively disclaimed**.

— NO ↓

Was the warranty disclaimed by:

- **"As is"** language;

- **Buyer's examination** of or refusal to examine goods; or

- **Course of dealing or performance** or **custom and usage**?

— NO → Warranty has been **effectively disclaimed**.

— YES → Warranty has been **effectively disclaimed**.

— NO ↓

The warranty **remains in effect**.

Note: Under Revised Article 2, if buyer is a **consumer**, any disclaimer of an implied warranty must be conspicuous, in a writing, and contain specific warning language.

Words or conduct relevant to the creation of an express warranty and words or conduct tending to negate or limit warranty shall be construed wherever reasonable as *consistent* with each other; but subject to the provisions of this Article on parol or extrinsic evidence (section 2-202), *negation or limitation is inoperative* to the extent that such construction is unreasonable. [Emphasis added] In other words, the Code attempts to give effect to both the express warranty and the disclaimer where possible, but any inconsistency results in the *failure of the disclaimer.*

(1) All disclaimers narrowly construed [§269]

U.C.C. section 2-316 requires courts to construe disclaimers *narrowly* so as to preserve all express warranties made by the seller wherever reasonable. Thus, for example, an express provision imposing a time limit of 15 days "for discovery of defects" has been held not applicable to *latent* defects that could not reasonably be discovered within that period. [**Neville Chemical Co. v. Union Carbide Corp.,** 294 F. Supp. 649 (W.D. Pa. 1968)]

(2) Can express warranties be disclaimed at all? [§270]

Where the disclaimer otherwise *would* apply to some express warranty made by the seller, the U.C.C. provides that the disclaimer shall be *disregarded* ("inoperative") to the extent it is *unreasonable.* [U.C.C. §2-316(1)]

(a) Rationale

The Code drafters thought that it was basically inconsistent for a seller to make an express warranty part of the "basis of the bargain" and then to try and disclaim it (frequently in unread fine print). Thus, U.C.C. section 2-316(1) commands the court to try to read the entire contractual language about warranties and disclaimers as consistent, but if this is impossible (as it typically is), the warranty stands and the attempted disclaimer is void.

(b) Comment

The way to avoid liability for an express warranty is to *not make it in the first place.* Having made the warranty and created buyer reliance thereon, the seller must live with the liability.

(3) Admissibility of parol evidence [§271]

The usual fact pattern will have the express warranties made orally (typically as part of a sales pitch) and not included in the sales contract itself, and the contract will contain a broad disclaimer of any warranties not contained therein. Before the buyer can prove that the express warranty was made (and thus avoid the disclaimer), the buyer must figure a way around the parol evidence rule. [U.C.C. §2-202; *see supra*, §92] The courts have been sympathetic to this tactic and have let the evidence in under one of three routes:

(a) Unconscionability [§272]

Courts often hold it unconscionable to create an express warranty and then try to disclaim it by a writing. This argument is most appealing when the buyer is a consumer. (*See supra*, §21.)

(b) Fraud [§273]

The parol evidence rule does not bar evidence of fraud, so the buyer may argue that it is fraudulent to make an express warranty planning not to live up to it and to disclaim it in the writing. [**O'Neil v. International Harvester,** 575 P.2d 862 (Colo. 1978)]

(c) Lack of agreement to merger clause [§274]

The U.C.C.'s parol evidence rule applies only where *both* parties intend for the writing to reflect their agreement. If the buyer can convince the court that the buyer did not so intend, the parol evidence rule does not bar the introduction of evidence of the express warranty. [**Drier v. Perfection, Inc.,** 259 N.W.2d 496 (S.D. 1977)]

b. Disclaiming implied warranties [§275]

Because implied warranties arise apart from any agreement of the parties, the parties are given greater latitude to limit or disclaim liability arising therefrom. Subsections (2) and (3) of U.C.C. section 2-316 list four ways that implied (but not express) warranties can be disclaimed.

(1) By specific language [§276]

The seller may rely on clauses in the sales contract that disclaim liability for implied warranties. However, the U.C.C. imposes certain requirements for disclaiming the two basic implied warranties, merchantability and fitness for particular purpose.

(a) Disclaiming the implied warranty of merchantability [§277]

To be valid, a disclaimer of the implied warranty of merchantability must *specifically mention "merchantability."* It may be *oral*; but if in writing, it must be *conspicuous*. [U.C.C. §2-316(2)] The reason for requiring the clause to mention the word "merchantability" is that the drafters thought that it is such an important warranty that its disclaimer should be made obvious.

1) Specific language required [§278]

A clause stating that "any claim for defects is waived unless made within 10 days" does *not* avoid the warranty of merchantability because the word itself is not used. [**Wilson Trading Corp. v. David Ferguson, Ltd.,** 23 N.Y.2d 398 (1968)]

2) "Conspicuous" [§279]

Whether a disclaimer is conspicuous is a *question of law* for the court. A disclaimer is "conspicuous" only if it is so written that a reasonable person against whom it is to operate ought to have noticed it. A printed heading in capital letters is conspicuous, as is any language in the body of a document that is either in larger print or type or in contrasting color. [U.C.C. §1-201(10)]

a) Fine print—inconspicuous [§280]

Language in fine print, or on the back of the form, is often held insufficient. [**Matthews v. Ford Motor Co.,** 479 F.2d 399 (4th Cir. 1973)]

b) Mislabeling disclaimer—inconspicuous [§281]

Mislabeling the disclaimer as a "warranty" when it is really the warranty *disclaimer* makes the disclaimer inconspicuous and therefore ineffective. [**Hartman v. Jensen's Inc.,** 289 S.E.2d 648 (S.C. 1982)]

c) Actual knowledge of disclaimer [§282]

If a disclaimer is not "conspicuous," is it nonetheless effective if the buyer admits to having read it? The courts have split on the issue. Some hold that actual knowledge does make the disclaimer effective; but others hold that public policy is at stake, and that to inquire into this issue introduces a question of fact into what otherwise would be a question of law. [*See* Special Project on U.C.C. Warranties, 64 Corn. L. Rev. 30, 182-187 (1978)]

FACTORS TO CONSIDER IN DETERMINING WHETHER A DISCLAIMER IS CONSPICUOUS — gilbert		
	CONSPICUOUS	INCONSPICUOUS
SIZE	Larger print or capital letters	"Fine print"
COLOR	Contrasting colored type	Same type as body of text
FONT	Italics or boldface	Standard
LABEL	Labeled as "disclaimer"	Labeled as "warranty"
LOCATION	Front and center of form	Back of form

(b) Disclaiming the implied warranty of fitness for a particular purpose [§283]

An oral disclaimer (sufficient to disclaim merchantability, above) is *not* sufficient to exclude the implied warranty of fitness for a particular purpose. The particular purpose disclaimer must be *in writing*, and the writing must be "*conspicuous*" (*see* above).

1) Need not mention "fitness" [§284]

As to language, "fitness" need not be specifically mentioned. Thus, the words "there are no warranties which extend beyond the description on the face hereof" are sufficient. [U.C.C. §2-316(2)]

EXAM TIP   **gilbert**

Disclaimer of implied warranty questions are quite common on law school exams. Therefore, you must keep the rules straight in your mind:

- For *merchantability*—the disclaimer can be *oral or written*, but if written it has to be *conspicuous*. It *must mention merchantability*.

- For *fitness for a particular purpose*—the disclaimer *must be written and conspicuous,* but it does *not* need to mention fitness.

- Don't forget about disclaimers by *"as is"* language, *inspection*, *custom, and usage* (see *infra*).

(c) Disclaiming implied warranties to consumer buyers—2003 revision [§285]

The revision adds some requirements before a disclaimer of implied warranties is effective where the buyer is a *consumer*. Section 2R-316(2) requires that such disclaimers in consumer contracts be in a writing (which the revision calls a *"record"*), be *conspicuous*, and be accompanied by this *warning*: "The seller undertakes no responsibility for the quality of the goods except as otherwise provided in this contract." (For the implied warranty of fitness for a particular purpose the language is: "The seller assumes no responsibility that the goods will be fit for any particular purpose for which you may be buying these goods, except as otherwise provided in the contract.")

(d) Timing the disclaimer [§286]

The disclaiming language must be part of the offer and acceptance process to be effective. A disclaimer delivered *after* the contract is in existence comes too late to have any effect, unless the buyer agrees to the modification. [**Taterka v. Ford Motor Co.,** 271 N.W.2d 653 (Wis. 1978)]

Example: The offer and acceptance process ended for the car sale when the consumer shook hands with the saleswoman and said, "I'll buy." Two days later, the car was delivered and in the glove compartment was a warranty booklet. It made an express warranty, and then tried to disclaim all other warranties. This is ineffective as a disclaimer. [**Zoss v. Royal Chevrolet,** 11 U.C.C. Rep. Serv. 527 (Ind. 1972)]

---

1) **But note**

Warranties can be *added* after the sale is over. U.C.C. section 2-209(1) permits modification *by agreement* without any additional consideration. However, absent proof that the buyer agreed to the disclaimer, it will be ineffective if delivered after the contract has been formed.

2) **"Layered" contracts [§287]**

In recent years, a revolution in the law of contracts has allowed sellers to include limitations and disclaimers inside a packaged object as long as the remote buyer who objects to such new terms is given the opportunity to reject the contract if he wishes. [*See* **ProCD, Inc. v. Zeidenberg**, 86 F.3d 1447 (7th Cir. 1996)] Since the contract between the manufacturer and the remote purchaser is not formed until the buyer sees these terms and has a chance to return the goods (a "layered" or "rolling" contract), the theory is that the buyer is not harmed by allowing such late limitations or disclaimers. This idea is catching on and has sometimes been applied to disclaimers of warranties in the sale of goods. [**Rinaldi v. Iomega Corp.**, 41 U.C.C. Rep. Serv. 2d 1143 (Del. 1999)]

(2) **"As is" or similar language [§288]**

Another method of exclusion for implied (but not express) warranties is the "as is" disclaimer. If the goods are sold "*as is*" or "*with all faults*" (or similar language that in common understanding calls the buyer's attention to the fact that the goods are not warranted), *no implied warranties* of any kind arise. Such language is sufficient by itself to alert the buyer that the seller is assuming no risk and all implied warranties are excluded. [U.C.C. §3-316(3)(a)]

(a) **Must be conspicuous [§289]**

Nothing in section 2-316(3)(a) specifically requires an "as is" disclaimer to be "conspicuous." Even so, courts have held that a fine print "as is" clause is *not* effective. Any other result (permitting the seller to hide the "as is" clause and still disclaim all implied warranties) would make no sense. [**Osborne v. Genevie**, 289 So. 2d 21 (Fla. 1974); **Gindy Manufacturing Corp. v. Cardinale Trucking Corp.**, 268 A.2d 345 (N.J. 1970)]

EXAM TIP   **gilbert**

It may seem odd that there are specific disclaimer methods, with detailed requirements, and general disclaimer methods, requiring little formality. In actual practice, it is better to use the specific disclaimers because general disclaimers may be limited by the circumstances. However, on an exam an *"as is"* or *"with all faults"* disclaimer will generally be *as effective as a specific disclaimer*.

---

(3) Buyer's examination of the goods [§290]

If the buyer either examines the goods *or* the seller demands that the buyer examine the goods and the buyer does not do so, there are *no implied warranties* as to anything the buyer *should* have found. Thus, implied warranties with respect to *patent defects* may be waived by the buyer's inspection of the goods prior to sale.

(a) Express warranties and inspection [§291]

Note, however, that inspection in no way affects the existence of *express warranties.*

(b) What buyer *should* have found [§292]

What the buyer "should" have found depends on the individual buyer. For example, a professional car mechanic buying a used car is held to a higher standard than a bank cashier doing so. [U.C.C. §2-316, Official Comment 8; **Perry v. Lawson Ford Tractor Co.,** 613 P.2d 458 (Okla. 1980)]

(4) Custom or usage [§293]

The U.C.C. specifically recognizes that implied warranties may be excluded or modified by course of dealing or performance between the parties or by custom and usage in the trade generally. [U.C.C. §2-316(3)] Thus, if the parties understand (or should understand as a matter of their prior dealings or common sense) that no implied warranties are part of the transaction, none will arise. [**Country Club Inc. v. Allis Chalmers Manufacturing Co.,** 430 F.2d 1394 (6th Cir. 1970)]

c. Disclaiming by limiting the remedy [§294]

The U.C.C. authorizes the parties to specify what remedy shall be available in the event of breach of the warranty and to make such remedy "exclusive." [U.C.C. §2-719(1)(b); *and see infra,* §679] Consequently, a provision limiting a seller's liability to "repair or replacement of defective parts, *in lieu of* all other warranties, express or implied" is generally held effective as a disclaimer of any other fitness or merchantability warranty. [**Seeley v. White Motor Co.,** 63 Cal. 2d 9 (1965)]

(1) But note—may give rise to new promise

Such a warranty implies a promise to *repair or replace* defective goods. If the seller repeatedly fails to correct the defect as promised (*i.e.,* fails to "repair or replace"), the seller is liable for breach of *that* promise. [**Seeley v. White Motor Co.,** *supra*]

(2) Or may void disclaimer

Alternatively, courts may hold that the seller's failure to honor a parts and service warranty *voids the disclaimer* of other warranties, making the seller fully liable for the breach. [**Jones & McKnight Corp. v. Birdsboro Corp.,** 320 F. Supp. 39 (N.D. Ill. 1970); *and see infra,* §686]

gilbert

TYPE	HOW ARISES	MADE BY	DISCLAIMER
WARRANTY OF TITLE (title is good, transfer rightful, no liens or encumbrances)	By sale of goods	Any seller	By specific language or circumstances showing seller does not claim title
EXPRESS	By affirmation of fact, promise, description, model, or sample	Any seller	Extremely difficult to disclaim
IMPLIED			
WARRANTY OF MERCHANTABILITY (fit for ordinary purposes)	By sale of goods of the kind regularly sold by the merchant	Merchant only	By disclaimer mentioning "merchantability" (if written disclaimer, it must be conspicuous)*
WARRANTY OF FITNESS FOR PARTICULAR PURPOSE (fit for buyer's particular purpose)	By sale of goods where seller has reason to know of particular purpose and of buyer's reliance on seller to choose suitable goods	Any seller	By conspicuous *written* disclaimer*
WARRANTY OF WHOLESOMENESS (fit for human consumption)	By sale of food or beverages	Any seller (retail or restaurant)	Cannot be disclaimed

*These may also be disclaimed by language such as "as is"; by buyer's examination of goods (or refusal to examine); or by course of dealing or performance, or custom and usage of trade.

2. **Limitations on Warranty Disclaimers [§295]**

The effectiveness of any warranty disclaimer is limited as follows:

a. **Judicial constructions [§296]**

First, it is the policy of the U.C.C. to prevent the transfer of worthless goods and to provide some fair remedy for any breach. Hence, wherever possible, courts will construe warranty disclaimers *narrowly* in order to preserve an action for breach. [U.C.C. §2-719, Official Comment 1; **Admiral Oasis Hotel Corp. v. Home Gas Industries, Inc.,** 216 N.E.2d 282 (Ill. 1965)]

b. **Consumer protection statutes [§297]**

State and federal statutes have made further inroads into the enforceability of warranty disclaimers in consumer sales transactions (*see infra*, §344).

c. **Tort law [§298]**

A disclaimer is effective only as to the warranty (contract) claim, and does not bar an action for negligence or strict tort liability where a defective product has caused personal injury or property damage (including damage to the product itself). (*See* Products Liability in Torts Summary.)

F. Cumulation and Conflict of Warranties

1. **Background [§299]**

In many sales, there are both implied and express warranties, and while often all warranties mesh, sometimes they clash, and rules are needed to resolve the conflict. At common law, the general rule was that if a sales contract contained an express warranty, no warranties of any kind could be implied. [**Hall v. Duplex-Power Car Co.,** 135 N.W. 118 (Mich. 1912)] The Sales Act reversed this, providing that an express warranty does not negate an implied warranty unless *inconsistent* therewith. [Uniform Sales Act §15(6)]

2. **U.C.C. [§300]**

However, no integrated approach to the problem of cumulation of warranties existed until promulgation of the U.C.C. The Code basically provides that all warranties are to be construed whenever possible as *cumulative and consistent*, unless application of this rule produces unreasonable results. In such event, the *intent* of the parties determines which warranties dominate. [U.C.C. §2-317]

a. **Seller may be estopped from claiming inconsistency [§301]**

If the seller has led the buyer to believe that all warranties can be performed, the seller is estopped from using any inconsistency in the warranties as an "escape hatch."

b. **Rules for ascertaining intent [§302]**

Where there is no evidence to the contrary, the intent of the parties is to be determined from the following three rules set forth in U.C.C. section 2-317, which focus on the factors to which the parties probably paid the most attention in the first place.

(1) Effect of specifications [§303]

Exact or technical specifications prevail over an inconsistent sample or model or general language of description. [U.C.C. §2-317(a)]

(2) Effect of samples [§304]

A sample from an existing bulk prevails over inconsistent general language of description. [U.C.C. §2-317(b)]

(3) Effect of express warranties [§305]

Express warranties *displace* inconsistent implied warranties other than an implied warranty of fitness for a particular purpose. [U.C.C. §2-317(c); *and see* **Klimate-Pruf Paint & Varnish Co. v. Klein Corp.,** 161 S.E.2d 747 (N.C. 1968)]

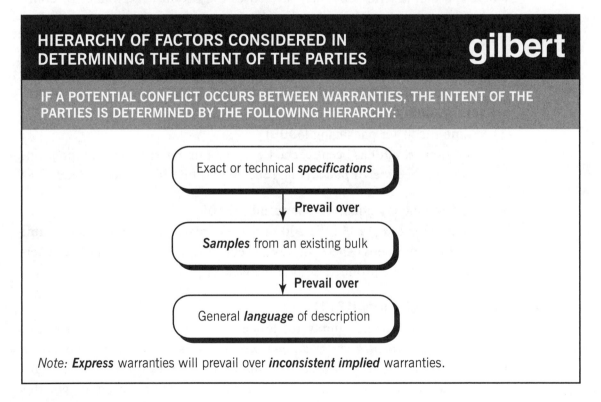

HIERARCHY OF FACTORS CONSIDERED IN DETERMINING THE INTENT OF THE PARTIES gilbert

IF A POTENTIAL CONFLICT OCCURS BETWEEN WARRANTIES, THE INTENT OF THE PARTIES IS DETERMINED BY THE FOLLOWING HIERARCHY:

Exact or technical *specifications*

Prevail over

Samples from an existing bulk

Prevail over

General *language* of description

Note: Express warranties will prevail over *inconsistent implied* warranties.

G. Privity

1. Early View [§306]

The traditional view was that no person could complain of a breach of warranty unless that person stood in "privity" of contract with the party who made the warranty.

"Privity" meant a sufficient legal connection that the law would accord that person a right of suit. Thus, if the buyer buys goods from the seller, and the buyer's son then used the goods with ensuing injuries, the son could not sue the seller for breach of warranty because he was not a party to the sale; *i.e.*, there was "no privity." Or, if the goods were originally produced by a manufacturer or wholesaler who supplied them to the seller, the buyer had no cause of action against the manufacturer or wholesaler because, again, there was no privity. [**Winterbottom v. Wright,** 152 Eng. Rep. 402 (1842)]

2. **Modern Law [§307]**

Privity is a dying doctrine. Under one rationale or another it is being abandoned by practically every state. It started to die in the foodstuff cases—*e.g.*, Wife buys tainted meat at the local grocer and Husband consumes it; since Husband was not the purchaser, the privity doctrine would bar his recovery. However, all courts today allow recovery in such cases, and most courts have gone considerably beyond the foodstuff cases. Some of the theories employed by the courts are as follows:

a. **Advertisements as express warranties to consumer [§308]**

Where the manufacturer publicly advertises the product, a number of courts (struggling with privity) hold that the advertisement constitutes an *express* warranty to the *entire public*, so that if any purchaser buys and uses the product in total or partial reliance on the advertisement, there is sufficient "privity" to hold the manufacturer liable. [**Hamon v. Digliani,** 174 A.2d 294 (Conn. 1961); **Inglis v. American Motors Corp.,** 209 N.E.2d 583 (Ohio 1965)]

(1) **Same result for packaging [§309]**

The same result has been reached where a purchaser relies on representations on the *label or packaging*. [**Seeley v. White Motor Co.,** *supra*, §294]

(2) **Revision clearly endorses this result [§310]**

As noted *supra* (§233), the 2003 revision creates express warranty liability for new goods where an advertisement is made to the public or enclosed with the product, despite the lack of privity.

b. **Abandonment of privity [§311]**

Later, a number of courts simply abandoned the privity requirement altogether when dealing with *inherently dangerous products* (particularly foodstuffs, medicines, firearms, etc.), so that the implied warranties run from the manufacturer and all subsequent sellers to the *ultimate user* of the product, whether or not the actual purchaser. [**Jacob E. Decker & Sons v. Capps,** 164 S.W.2d 838 (Tex. 1942)]

(1) **Creation of privity through legal fiction [§312]**

Other courts reached the same result by legal fiction, *e.g.*, that a warranty extended to the buyer and "family"; and then broadly defining "family" to include practically anyone who had any relationship with the buyer (*e.g.*, an employee or even a neighbor). [*See* **Miller v. Preitz,** 221 A.2d 320 (Pa. 1966)]

(2) Rejection of privity requirement outright [§313]

Recently, a few courts have simply rejected the privity requirement in any warranty action, ignoring the issue of whether the product is dangerous or nondangerous. [**Santor v. A. & M. Karagheusian, Inc.,** 207 A.2d 305 (N.J. 1964)—defective carpeting]

(3) Comment—in defense of privity requirement [§314]

Abandoning privity has been criticized as undermining the true nature (*i.e.*, contractual nature) of a warranty action. If a direct action is to be allowed by an injured consumer against the manufacturer, between whom no contractual relationship of any kind exists, it would seem that *tort* concepts (below) should be used.

EXAM TIP   **gilbert**

Although *privity has fallen out of favor* with the courts, it is still taught in the majority of law schools. You likely will be expected to master this topic for your exam.

---

c. Alternate tactic—negligence [§315]

Courts have also circumvented the privity requirement by imposing tort liability in appropriate cases. Wherever there is a *foreseeable risk of harm* in the use or consumption of a product, the manufacturer owes a *duty of reasonable care* in the design and manufacture thereof, and this duty is owed not only to the purchaser but to *all other persons within the foreseeable scope of use* of the product. Since this is a tort duty, the contractual "privity" requirement does not apply. [**MacPherson v. Buick Motor Co.,** 217 N.Y. 382 (1916); *and see* Torts Summary]

(1) Tort liability extends to dealers [§316]

Similar tort duties are imposed against any dealer or "middleman" in the marketing chain *if* that person has reason to know that the product is in a defective condition *and* fails to make it safe or warn the purchaser. [6 A.L.R.3d 1]

d. Modern trend—strict liability in tort [§317]

The modern trend goes beyond negligence concepts, imposing strict liability in tort against the manufacturer and all other sellers in the marketing chain for injuries to persons or property caused by defects in *unreasonably dangerous products*. No showing of negligence is required, and lack of privity between the injured party and the seller is immaterial. [Restatement (Second) of Torts §402A; **Greenman v. Yuba Power Products, Inc.,** 59 Cal. 2d 671 (1962); *and see* Torts Summary]

(1) Comment

This view gives explicit recognition to what other courts have been doing covertly in abandoning the privity requirement in warranty cases; *i.e.,* the contract basis for the action is rejected, and instead the *tort* nature of the obligation is being restored.

(2) Impact on warranty defenses

Moreover, this approach circumvents all of the traditional defenses to a warranty action—lack of privity, lack of notice of breach (*infra*), disclaimers, "no sale," etc.

(3) Significant distinctions between tort and warranty actions [§318]

Even so, there are still some significant differences between the strict tort liability action and the warranty action.

(a) Type of injury [§319]

First, the tort action is available in most states only for *physical harm* to person or property, whereas a warranty action allows recovery for such harms *and* for purely *economic* losses (*infra*). [**Seeley v. White Motor Co.,** *supra,* §309]

(b) Type of product [§320]

The strict tort liability action is available only where the product sold is "*inherently*" or "*unreasonably dangerous,*" whereas the warranty action is available as to *all* products.

(c) Statute of limitations [§321]

The tort action is usually subject to a rather short statute of limitations (often, one year), whereas the warranty action is governed by the four-year statute of U.C.C. section 2-725 (*infra,* §§690, 693). (This is offset in part by the fact that the warranty action begins to run at the time of delivery of the goods, whereas the tort action commences only on injury.)

(d) Wrongful death action [§322]

In the event of a death, a wrongful death action is available where the death was *tortiously* caused; but courts have held that a wrongful death action *cannot* be maintained on the basis of breach of warranty. [**Geohagan v. General Motors Corp.,** 279 So. 2d 436 (Ala. 1973)]

(4) Trend [§323]

Despite the distinctions noted above, the apparent trend is to emphasize the similarities and to collapse the distinctions between the tort and warranty actions, so as to come up with a single cause of action in products liability cases. For example, one leading decision has held that there is no justification for the differing limitations periods (*supra,* §321), and has adopted a single statute of limitations for all products liability claims. [**Heavner v. Uniroyal, Inc.,** 305 A.2d 412 (N.J. 1973)—rejecting the four-year statute of limitations of section 2-725, in favor of the shorter tort statute, although the action was for "breach of warranty"; *see infra,* §693]

3. Effect of U.C.C. [§324]

In connection with the privity requirement, the U.C.C. has little or no utility. This is one area where the provisions of the U.C.C. were simply outmoded even before they were adopted. The Code speaks to the issue by addressing which potential plaintiffs are "third party beneficiaries" of the warranties made to the buyer. The seller is not allowed to restrict the protection granted by U.C.C. section 2-318.

a. Original section 2-318 [§325]

As originally promulgated (and as adopted in most states), U.C.C. section 2-318 merely provided that the seller's warranty—express or implied—extended not only to the actual purchaser of the goods, but also "to any natural person who was a *member of his household or family, or a guest* in his home," wherever it was reasonable to expect that the other persons might use or come into contact with the goods, and who in fact sustained *personal* injuries by breach of such warranty. Being so restrictive, it was rejected entirely in several states.

(1) Horizontal and vertical privity [§326]

As written, section 2-318 speaks only to the issue of "horizontal privity," which answers the question "who, other than the buyer, can sue the seller for breach of warranty?" However, the section is neutral as to the claims of the buyer against others in the distributive chain (the issue of "vertical privity"). Thus, the question "can the buyer's daughter sue the *retailer* for breach of warranty?" (an issue of horizontal privity) is answered "yes" by the Code. The question "can the buyer sue the original manufacturer?" is not addressed. [U.C.C. §2-318, Official Comment 3]

b. 1966 amendments [§327]

Because of widespread criticism on this account, the Commissioners adopted two alternative provisions (in addition to the above, which was retained as "Alternative A") in 1966:

(1) "*Alternative B*" extends the seller's warranty liability to "any *natural person* who may reasonably be expected to use, consume or *be affected by* the goods" (*i.e.,* the innocent bystander injured by the defective car), but only for *personal injury.*

(2) "*Alternative C*" goes even further and extends warranty liability for *property* damage as well. (To parallel the position of Restatement (Second) of Torts §402A; *see* above.) Further, "Alternative C" is not limited to the protection of "natural" persons, so that *corporate* plaintiffs, for example, could sue as third party beneficiaries of the warranty.

c. Judicial interpretations [§328]

The courts have construed the above sections *very broadly*. For example, Alternative B, which extends liability to any person "affected by" the product, has been held to cover a claim against an auto manufacturer by a bicyclist who ran his bike into a parked car, shattering a light on the car, which in turn caused injury to the bicyclist's leg. The court reasoned that all persons using public highways were "affected by" the automobile and thus the U.C.C. privity requirement was satisfied. [**Nacci v. Volkswagen, Inc.**, 325 A.2d 617 (Del. 1974)]

H. Action for Breach of Warranty— Requirements

1. Breach of Warranty Must Be Proximate Cause of Injury [§329]

In an action for breach of warranty, the buyer must always show that the breach was the proximate cause of the loss sustained. [U.C.C. §2-715(2)(a)(b)] It is not sufficient that the buyer demonstrate that the defendant's breach of warranty could have been one of several possible causes of the damage; rather, the buyer must *prove* that the breach of warranty is *the proximate cause* of the injury. [**Davis v. Firestone Tire & Rubber Co.**, 196 F. Supp. 407 (N.D. Cal. 1961)]

2. Notice Requirement [§330]

To recover for a breach of warranty, the buyer must *plead* and *prove* that the seller was given notice of the breach within a *reasonable time* after the breach should have been discovered. If no notice is given, the buyer's right to recover against the seller in a warranty action will be entirely *barred*. Failure to give notice deprives the buyer of any rights under the Uniform Commercial Code. [U.C.C. §2-607(3)(a)]

a. Rationale

The purpose of this technical requirement is to protect the *seller's* rights. The seller has a right to inspect the goods before they deteriorate further [U.C.C. §2-515], to *cure* the defect in certain situations (*see infra*, §424), and to propose settlement of the dispute. All of these rights are prejudiced by failure to receive timely notice.

b. Form of notice immaterial [§331]

No particular form of notice is required. It can be written or oral (although, for evidentiary reasons, it is smarter to put it in writing).

c. Content of notice [§332]

According to the U.C.C. drafters, the notice need *not* contain any claim of damages or threat of litigation. It is sufficient merely to inform the seller that the transaction is troublesome and bears watching.

(1) But note
Some courts require precision in identifying the existence and nature of the claimed breach, and state that the notice must at least impliedly *threaten legal action*. The idea here is that the other side must be alerted to the seriousness of the claim. [**Eastern Airlines, Inc. v. McDonnell Douglas Corp.,** 532 F.2d 957 (5th Cir. 1976)]

d. Filing of suit as notice [§333]
The courts have disagreed as to whether the filing of the lawsuit itself can serve as a notice satisfying the U.C.C. requirements. While some courts have upheld this practice [**Pace v. Sagebrush Sales,** 560 P.2d 789 (Ariz. 1977)], others have not allowed the lawsuit to serve as proper notice, observing that it hardly fulfills the function of encouraging settlement [**Armco Steel v. Isaacson Structural Steel,** 611 P.2d 507 (Alaska 1980)].

3. "Vouching In" [§334]
The U.C.C. provides that where the *buyer* is sued by *any third party* on any claim for which the buyer would have a cause of action as against the seller (*e.g.,* buyer has resold goods and is now sued for breach of warranty), the buyer can notify the seller to come in and defend against the third party's claim or be bound by the facts determined therein. Such a request is called a "vouching in" notice. If the seller refuses to defend in the buyer's subsequent action against the seller for breach of warranty, the seller is bound by any determination of fact common to the two litigations. [U.C.C. §2-607(5)(a)]

I. Remedies for Breach of Warranty

1. Before Acceptance [§335]
If a breach of warranty occurs prior to acceptance of the goods, the breach is treated like any other failure to perform the contract. The buyer may *reject* the goods for this reason (*see infra,* §465), demand *specific performance* (*see infra,* §648), *cover* (*see infra,* §611), or measure *damages* according to various U.C.C. formulas (*see infra,* §653).

2. After Acceptance [§336]
Once the buyer has accepted the goods, the U.C.C. provides that the buyer may recover any *loss in value* of the goods because of the breach [U.C.C. §2-714(1)] plus *consequential and incidental* damages where proper [U.C.C. §2-714(3)]. In appropriate circumstances, the buyer may revoke acceptance and recover damages (*see infra,* §483).

a. Loss in value of goods [§337]
The standard measure of value in goods in a breach of warranty suit is the difference, at the time and place of acceptance, between the *value of the goods*

accepted and the value they *would have had if they had been as warranted*. [U.C.C. §2-714(1)]

(1) Note

The *price* of the goods has nothing to do with fixing damages (except that where there is no open market in the goods, the price may be *evidence* of their value). Thus, where the market price has fluctuated upward or downward from the price at which the buyer bought, and the buyer still elects to accept the goods and sue for breach of warranty, the buyer gets the *benefit of the bargain* under the contract: the difference between what was promised and what was received.

b. Consequential damages [§338]

Often the loss of value of goods will represent only a part of the buyer's loss. Thus the U.C.C. follows the rule of **Hadley v. Baxendale,** 156 Eng. Rep. 145 (1854) (*see* Contracts Summary) and imposes liability where the seller at the time of contract *had reason to know* of additional loss that would result from a failure to meet the buyer's needs or requirements. [U.C.C. §2-715(2)(a)]

Example: Seller sells Buyer 200 lbs. of what Seller expressly warrants to be "bearded barley seed." The seed is in fact beardless barley seed. There is a difference in value: 100 lbs. of beardless barley seed sells for $10, while the same amount of bearded barley seed sells for $11. Under the standard measure of damages, Buyer is entitled to $2. However, Buyer does not know, at the time of delivery, of the breach of warranty and plants and cultivates the crop produced from the seed. By the time of harvest, Buyer learns of the error, but it is then too late. A crop of beardless barley is worth only $3,000, whereas a crop of bearded barley would be worth $7,000, and Seller had reason to know this when the seed was sold. Buyer can recover $4,000 consequential damages from Seller, in addition to the $2 standard damages.

---

(1) May include any economic loss [§339]

In appropriate cases, consequential damages may include any of the following: *loss of profits* from expected resale of goods; loss of operating profits due to disruption of business; and damage to goodwill or business reputation. [**AM/PM Franchise Association v. Atlantic Richfield Co.,** 584 A.2d 915 (Pa. 1990)]

(a) Note

A retailer who is held liable to a customer for breach of warranty of merchantability will normally have the same cause of action against the wholesaler or manufacturer who supplied the product. Whatever damages the retailer is forced to pay its customer are recoverable as consequential damages in an action against the wholesaler or manufacturer. [**Kelly v. Hanscom Bros.,** 331 A.2d 737 (Pa. 1974); *and see supra,* §334]

(2) May include noneconomic losses [§340]

Even noneconomic losses may be recoverable as consequential damages under appropriate circumstances. For example, the purchaser of a defective "big game" rifle was allowed to recover as consequential damages his safari expenses, plus $10,000 for the "loss of prestige in killing a Bengal tiger." [**Thomas v. Olin Mathieson Chemical Corp.,** 255 Cal. App. 2d 806 (1967)]

(a) Personal injury or property damage [§341]

Of course, where there is a foreseeable risk of harm to person or property through use or consumption of the seller's product, the buyer may recover consequential damages for personal injuries or property damage resulting from breach of warranty. [U.C.C. §2-715(2)(b)] In personal injury cases, this may include medical bills and damages for pain and suffering (just as in a negligence case). Some courts even allow recovery for loss of consortium in a warranty action.

1) And note

For injury to *person or property* (as opposed to mere economic loss, like lost profits), foreseeability (**Hadley v. Baxendale**) is *not* required. [U.C.C. §2-715(2)(b)]

(3) Limitation—concept of "cover" [§342]

Where consequential damages are claimed on account of the *nonavailability* of the goods bargained for (rather than on account of injuries or losses sustained through their use), then to whatever extent the damages could have been prevented by "covering" with goods from another source, damages are limited to the cost of "cover" (*see infra*, §661).

c. Incidental damages [§343]

Finally, the buyer may also recover any cost or expense reasonably incurred incidental to the seller's delay or delivery of defective goods, *e.g.*, storage or inspection charges, return freight, costs of cover, etc. [U.C.C. §2-715(1)]

d. Other damages

For further discussion of buyer's damages generally, *see infra*, §§653-669.

REMEDIES FOR BREACH OF WARRANTY	**gilbert**
BEFORE ACCEPTANCE OF GOODS:	**AFTER ACCEPTANCE OF GOODS:**
☑ Reject goods;	☑ Recover loss in value of goods;
☑ Demand specific performance;	☑ Consequential damages; and
☑ Cover; or	☑ Incidental damages.
☑ Damages.	

J. Expansion of Warranty Liability— Consumer Protection Statutes

1. In General [§344]

The implied warranties of merchantability and fitness for particular purpose have been expanded by statute, insofar as they apply to sales of *"consumer goods"*—*i.e.*, those purchased primarily for personal, family, or household purposes (including major purchases such as automobiles and motor homes).

2. Federal Warranty Act [§345]

The leading federal statute is the Magnuson-Moss Warranty Act [15 U.S.C. §§2301-2312], which is supplemented by regulations promulgated by the Federal Trade Commission ("FTC") [*see* 12 C.F.R. §§700 *et seq.*]. The statute does *not* require a seller to give any warranty on consumer products. However, if any written warranty is given on consumer products costing more than $10, it must be *conspicuously designated* as either a *"full warranty"* (statement of duration, *e.g.,* "one year") or as a *"limited warranty."* (This rule applies to advertisements or "service policies" as well as to warranty cards accompanying the product.) [15 U.S.C. §2303]

a. Full warranty [§346]

A "full warranty" must meet certain standards: *e.g.,* the seller must provide reasonable service and repair facilities; must allow the purchaser to obtain a refund or replacement if the product proves defective and cannot be repaired after a reasonable number of attempts by the seller; and there can be *no limitation or disclaimers* on implied warranty liability. [15 U.S.C. §2304]

b. Limited warranty [§347]

A "limited warranty" is anything less than a "full warranty." Even with a "limited warranty," however, no total disclaimer of implied warranty liability is allowed. However, a limitation on the *duration* of liability to a reasonable period of time is permitted *if conscionable in length* and *conspicuously disclosed.* [15 U.S.C. §2308]

c. Disclaimers void [§348]

The most important feature of the federal statute is the prohibition on disclaimers of the implied warranties that arise under state law (*e.g.,* merchantability and fitness for a particular purpose). If the warrantor decides to give a *written warranty* (and remember, doing so is never required), the warrantor *may not disclaim* the implied warranties given by state law. Any attempt to do so is *void*. This means that consumer warranties will have teeth in them. However, as above (*see supra,* §347), if the warrantor offers only a "limited warranty," the warrantor is allowed to limit the duration of the implied warranties in some situations. This is not true of "full warranties." If a full warranty is given, the duration of implied warranties cannot be limited; they last for a reasonable time (a question of fact).

d. FTC rules [§349]

The Federal Act also authorizes the FTC to promulgate rules requiring sellers to make *presale disclosure* of the availability of written warranty terms (*e.g.*, products and persons covered by the warranty, procedure for obtaining repairs, etc.); and to provide *informal procedures for settlement* of warranty disputes. [15 U.S.C. §§2302, 2310] The FTC has promulgated rules specifying what information is to be contained in the text of the warranties and what methods of presale disclosure are acceptable. [*See* 16 C.F.R. §§701 - 703]

e. Scope of the Act

(1) "Suppliers" [§350]

Suppliers of consumer products and others who give written warranties on such products are the targets of the law. "Suppliers" are any persons engaged in the business of making a consumer product directly or indirectly available to consumers. [15 U.S.C. §2301(4), (5)]

(2) "Consumers" [§351]

A "consumer" is a buyer of any consumer product (but not a purchaser for resale), or any other person receiving such a product for the duration of the warranty or service contract. [15 U.S.C. §2301(3)]

(3) "Warranty" [§352]

Under the Act, a "written warranty" is a written statement about the nature or quality of the product and its condition, or what the warrantor will do if anything goes wrong with the product. [15 U.S.C. §2301(6)]

(4) Deceptive warranties [§353]

In addition to the general obligations of the law regarding disclosure, designation, and standards for warranties, federal government enforcement is authorized to prevent use of deceptive warranties. Deceptive warranties are those that contain "false or fraudulent affirmation, promise, description, or representation, or which, in light of all the circumstances, would mislead a reasonable individual exercising due care." [15 U.S.C. §2310(c)]

f. Attorney's fees [§354]

The successful plaintiff in a Magnuson-Moss warranty suit may get legal and equitable relief and is entitled to costs and a reasonable attorney's fee. [15 U.S.C. §2310(d)]

3. State Legislation [§355]

The Federal Warranty Act sets minimum standards with respect to consumer goods transactions. It does not preempt the field, however, and several states have statutes that go beyond the federal law. [15 U.S.C. §2311(e)(i)—preserves any "right or remedy of any consumer under state law"]

a. Common legislation [§356]

Examples of provisions found in various state consumer protection legislation are the following:

(i) *Manufacturer's warranties* are made to run directly to the purchaser of the goods (dispensing with "privity" problems);

(ii) *Disclaimers* of the implied warranties of merchantability and fitness for particular purposes are prohibited, except where merchandise is sold "as is" or "with all faults," with a conspicuous notice in writing attached to the goods and explaining the legal impact of these terms;

(iii) *Duration of warranties* is regulated to a reasonable period (*e.g.*, not less than 60 days nor more than one year following the sale);

(iv) *Adequate service and repair facilities* must be provided for goods covered by express warranties; and

(v) *Remedies are expanded* so that, for example, attorney's fees may be recovered in any action, and treble damages may be awarded for a willful breach of express warranties.

[*See also* Cal. Civ. Code §§1790 - 1795; Mass. Ann. Laws Ch. 106, §2-316]

Chapter Five:
Passage of Title

CONTENTS

Chapter Approach

Passage of title issues are not a major source of Sales test questions because passage of title has little significance, under the U.C.C., to Sales issues. But sometimes such a question does appear on a Sales exam, usually "disguised" as a problem asking who owns goods for purposes of insurance or taxation. In fact, the only reason the U.C.C. deals with passage of title questions at all is to resolve those non-Sales issues.

If you need to determine whether title has passed (for purposes of insurance, for example), ask yourself:

1. Have the goods been "*identified*"? Title cannot pass unless the goods have been identified to the contract. Also, consider the *effects* of identification (*e.g.*, buyer can insure the goods, etc.).

2. When did the parties *intend* for title to pass? Remember that if they have not provided for passage of title, the U.C.C. *presumes* that title passes when the seller has completed performance.

A. Concept of Title

1. Background [§357]

Under the Uniform Sales Act, "title" to the goods was of utmost importance. Whether title had passed was determinative of many questions—*e.g.*, whether the seller or the buyer bore the risk of loss, whether the buyer could sue the seller for the price, and whether a party's creditors had any rights in the goods.

2. U.C.C.—Title Insignificant [§358]

The U.C.C. scheme, however, is built on rules that in no way depend on who has title to goods. The U.C.C. does have a general rule with respect to passage of title: Unless the parties agree otherwise, title passes when the seller completes performance with respect to *physical delivery of* the goods (that is, *title follows possession*). But, unlike the Sales Act, no consequences flow from the fact that title has or has not passed. Thus, to determine who bears the risk of loss, one does not determine who has title but rather looks to the rules of the U.C.C. "risk of loss" sections. Similarly, if one wants to know what remedies are available to the buyer, one looks to the buyer's remedies sections of the Code, and not to the question of whether title has passed.

B. Requirement of Identification

1. Identification of Goods Required [§359]

Before title to goods can pass, the goods must be identified. [U.C.C. §2-401(1)] This is a requirement more of logic than law.

2. "Identification" Defined [§360]

"Identified" goods are those to which the contract refers. All that identification requires is that the goods that are the subject matter of the contract have somehow been singled out from all the goods of that type in the world. [U.C.C. §2-501]

Example: Seller agrees to sell 100 clocks to Buyer. At this point, the goods are unidentified. Any 100 clocks existing anywhere in the world could conceivably be the clocks Seller will deliver to Buyer. Later, Seller takes 100 clocks from stock on hand and packages them in cartons addressed to Buyer. The goods that are the subject matter of the contract have now been identified.

3. Methods of Identifying Goods

a. Identified by making of contract [§361]

Some goods can be identified simply by the making of the contract. The first requisite is that the goods be *in existence*, and the second is that it is clear what chattels the parties mean. For example, Seller agrees to sell to Buyer a certain Chevrolet, which Seller describes by serial and engine number. The goods are identified at the time the contract is made. [U.C.C. §2-501(1)(a)]

b. Identified by subsequent action [§362]

Other goods cannot be identified at the time the contract is made, and subsequent actions by the parties are necessary to identify them. For example, Seller contracts to sell 10 radios to Buyer. Later, Seller segregates 10 radios from stock and packages them in cartons addressed to Buyer. At that point, the goods are identified. [U.C.C. §2-501(1)(b)]

4. Seller's Right to Substitute Goods After Identification [§363]

Even though goods have been identified to the contract, the seller may thereafter substitute other goods for those identified (provided the seller and not the buyer made the original identification) unless and until one of three events occurs: (i) the seller *defaults* on the contract, (ii) the seller becomes *insolvent*, or (iii) the seller *notifies* the buyer that the identification is final. [U.C.C. §2-501(2)]

C. After Identification, Title Passes When Parties Intend

1. Where Parties Have Expressed Intent [§364]

Once goods are identified, title thereto passes from the seller to the buyer at whatever time the parties *intend* that it should pass. Such intent may be determined from the provisions of the sales *contract* or the parties' *conduct* in reference thereto. [U.C.C. §2-401(2)]

a. Question of fact [§365]

The question of the parties' intent is always a factual one, to be determined under the particular circumstances of each case. [**Aiello v. Sliskovich,** 72 Cal. App. 2d 39 (1945)]

b. Future goods [§366]

Regardless of the parties' express intent, however, title cannot pass until goods are *in existence*. Thus, even though future goods are described (*e.g.,* "the crops to be grown on your farm for the next five years"), title to the goods cannot pass because they do not yet exist.

2. Parties' Intent Presumed [§367]

Where the parties have not specifically provided for the passage of title and there is no other evidence as to their intent on this matter, the U.C.C. adopts the presumption that title passes when the *seller has completed whatever performance* is required with respect to delivering the goods to the buyer. [U.C.C. §2-401(2)]

a. Where goods are to be shipped [§368]

If goods under a contract must be shipped (*e.g.,* Buyer mails Seller an order for 100 radios), the place of delivery depends on whether the contract merely authorizes shipment (*i.e.,* a *shipment contract*) or requires delivery at a specific destination (*i.e.,* a *destination contract*). For a detailed discussion of shipping terms, *see infra,* §§375-401.

(1) Contracts authorizing shipment [§369]

If the contract authorizes the seller to ship the goods to the buyer but does not require the seller to deliver the goods at a specific destination, delivery occurs and title passes when the seller turns the goods over *to a carrier*. [U.C.C. §2-401(2)(a)]

(2) Contracts requiring delivery [§370]

Conversely, if the contract requires delivery at a destination, title passes only when the goods are tendered *at that destination*. [U.C.C. §2-401(2)(b)]

b. Delivery without movement [§371]

In those cases where delivery is to be made without moving the goods (*e.g.*, pile of ore, mobile home, etc.), title passes at the time and place where the *documents of title* are delivered; or, if no documents of title are involved, at the time of contracting. [U.C.C. §2-401(3)]

DETERMINING WHETHER TITLE HAS PASSED— A CHECKLIST — gilbert

WHEN ANALYZING A FACT PATTERN TO DETERMINE WHETHER TITLE HAS PASSED AT A SPECIFIC POINT IN TIME, ASK YOURSELF THE FOLLOWING QUESTIONS:

☑ Have the goods been *identified* either:

- In the drafting of the contract or

- By subsequent action?

☑ Did the parties *intend* for title to pass at this time?

D. Other Effects of Identification of Goods—Insurable Interests

1. As to Buyer [§372]

Once goods are identified to the contract, the U.C.C. affords the buyer "a special property and an insurable interest" in the goods. [U.C.C. §2-501(1)] Under insurance law, the buyer must have some sort of property interest in the goods before there is any right to obtain insurance thereon. If the buyer were to procure insurance without a property interest, the buyer would not be deemed to have an insurable interest in the goods and therefore could not collect on the insurance if the goods should be destroyed. For that reason, the U.C.C. provides the buyer with both a "special property" and an "insurable" interest in the goods.

a. Rationale

The U.C.C. rationale here is that as soon as the buyer knows or could determine what goods are about to be received, expectancies are created that the buyer may want to protect by insurance.

b. Note

The buyer's special property and insurable interest arises even if the identified goods are *nonconforming*, and even though the buyer may have an option to return or reject them. [U.C.C. §2-501(1)]

c. **Attachment of security interest [§373]**

Since the buyer gets a property interest in the goods at the moment of identification, the buyer at that moment also has sufficient rights in the goods that any existing security interest of buyer's creditors would attach to the goods on identification, thus giving buyer's creditors an interest in the goods. [U.C.C. §9-203(1)(c), *and see* Secured Transactions Summary]

2. As to Seller [§374]

Identification of the goods to the contract does not divest the seller of an insurable interest therein *until* title passes to the buyer *and* any security interest that the seller may have in the goods (to secure payment of the price) is preserved. [U.C.C. §2-501(2)]

Chapter Six: Performance of the Contract

CONTENTS

Chapter Approach

Chapter Approach

Performance of a sales contract generally means that the seller delivers the goods to the buyer, who accepts and pays for them. But "performance" is never that simple—at least not on Sales examinations. Exam questions on performance will cover situations where things have not gone exactly as planned (*e.g.,* where the seller's delivery deviates from the contract) or where the parties have not actually made a plan (*e.g.,* how delivery may be made to a buyer at a distant location). Your approach to these problems should be as follows:

1. **Parties' Agreement**

   Determine whether the parties have reached an agreement on the particular point (*e.g.,* have they provided for a procedure to handle the seller's failure to deliver conforming goods). Obviously if there is an agreement, you have to apply the terms of that agreement to the extent possible.

2. **U.C.C. Rules**

   If the parties have failed to reach an agreement on the particular point, look to the U.C.C. gap-filling rules, especially for problems such as those listed below:

   a. **Seller's duties**

      (1) **Shipment**

          If the problem involves the seller's shipment of the goods, be aware that often the answer depends on the *type* of contract involved:

          (i) A *shipment* contract (the most common type) requires the seller to deliver goods to the *carrier*; therefore, if the goods are damaged in transit, the buyer usually bears the loss;

          (ii) A *destination* contract requires the seller to deliver to the buyer's set destination; thus, the seller is liable for damages in transit.

          In commercial contracts, watch for the "shorthand" terms ("F.O.B.," "C.I.F.," etc.) because your answer will vary depending on which term is used.

      (2) **Tender**

          Keep in mind that the seller need only tender the goods to the buyer; the seller need not actually deliver them if the buyer refuses to accept. Look to all the facts to determine whether the seller has "tendered" the goods; don't forget that tender may be "constructive" or may involve a bailee. Probably the most likely tender problem involves the common law "*perfect tender*" rule. Remember that the U.C.C. has mitigated this rule to allow *cure* of defective tender in some circumstances, and in certain circumstances, *substantial performance* will suffice.

b. **Buyer's duties**

(1) Inspection

The buyer has the right to inspect *before* payment, although that right may be given up in the contract. Remember that inspection may include testing or sampling the goods.

(2) Acceptance and payment

The buyer's duty is to accept and pay for the goods. Consider all the facts to determine whether the buyer will be *deemed to have "accepted,"* e.g., by holding the goods for an unreasonable time. Remember that the buyer must pay when the goods are received, unless the contract specifies otherwise.

(3) Rejection

If the goods are *nonconforming*, the buyer may reject them, but be sure that the buyer follows the U.C.C. procedures as to timely *notice*, proper *handling* of the rejected goods, etc.

(4) Revocation of acceptance

Finally, note that after "acceptance" the buyer *cannot reject* but may, under certain circumstances, *revoke acceptance* as long as there is substantial impairment of the contract.

A. Performance by Seller

1. Shipment by Seller

a. Types of contracts—shipment or destination [§375]

Sales contracts frequently require the seller to ship goods by carrier to the buyer. The seller's obligations with respect to the shipment depend on whether the contract involved is a "shipment contract" or a "destination contract." A *shipment contract* is one that requires the seller to deliver the goods *to a carrier* at the place of shipment, after which the seller's responsibility with respect to the goods ceases. (The buyer bears the risk of damage in transit.) A *destination contract*, on the other hand, obligates the seller to deliver the goods *to a particular destination* before the seller will be deemed to have discharged all contractual obligations (and thus, the seller bears the risk of damage in transit to the destination).

(1) Basic presumption [§376]

The U.C.C. establishes a basic presumption that all contracts are *shipment*

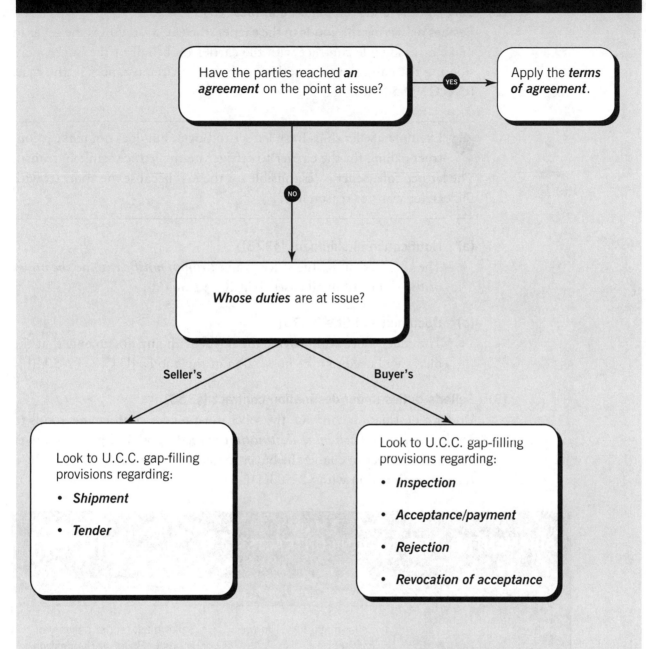

Have the parties reached **an agreement** on the point at issue? — YES → Apply the **terms of agreement**.

NO ↓

Whose duties are at issue?

Seller's ↙   Buyer's ↘

Look to U.C.C. gap-filling provisions regarding:
- **Shipment**
- **Tender**

Look to U.C.C. gap-filling provisions regarding:
- **Inspection**
- **Acceptance/payment**
- **Rejection**
- **Revocation of acceptance**

contracts unless the parties *expressly* agree to the contrary. [U.C.C. §2-503, Official Comments]

(2) Seller's duty under shipment contract [§377]

Besides delivering the goods to the carrier, the U.C.C. requires the seller to make a reasonable contract with the carrier on behalf of the buyer, considering the nature of the goods and the other circumstances of the case. [U.C.C. §2-504(a)]

---

e.g. Example: Seller ships fresh lettuce to Buyer, but does not make a contract calling for the carrier to refrigerate the lettuce while in transit. The lettuce rots. Seller is responsible for the loss because the contract with the carrier was not reasonable.

(a) Notification of shipment [§378]

The U.C.C. requires the seller to give *prompt notification to the buyer* of the shipment in all cases. [U.C.C. §2-504(c)]

(b) Documents of title [§379]

The seller must also provide the buyer with any documents that the buyer will need to take possession of the goods. [U.C.C. §2-504(b)]

(3) Seller's duties under destination contract [§380]

Under a destination contract, the seller must tender conforming goods to the buyer *at the particular destination* agreed upon and give the buyer reasonable *notice* to enable the buyer to take delivery. [U.C.C. §2-503(3), read in conjunction with §2-503(1)]

SHIPMENT VS. DESTINATION CONTRACTS	gilbert	
	SHIPMENT CONTRACT	**DESTINATION**
PLACE OF DELIVERY	Seller must deliver *to the carrier*	Seller must tender delivery of goods to Buyer *at the destination*
WHEN DOES RISK OF LOSS SHIFT FROM SELLER TO BUYER?	When goods are delivered *to the carrier*	When Seller tenders delivery of goods to Buyer *at the destination*

b. Commercial shipment terms and abbreviations [§381]

Commercial contracts are often made in abbreviated terms indicated by mercantile symbols. This is particularly true in the area of shipment, where certain terms—F.O.B., F.A.S., or C.I.F.—are widely used by those in the business to indicate whether they intend a particular contract to be a shipment contract or a destination contract.

(1) F.O.B. [§382]

The letters "F.O.B." stand for *"free on board."* [U.C.C. §2-319(1)]

(a) F.O.B. point of shipment [§383]

If the term is merely F.O.B. point of shipment (*e.g.,* "F.O.B. seller's factory"), then the seller is required only to bear the risk and expense of putting the goods into the possession of the carrier; the seller does *not* bear the expense or risks of loading. [U.C.C. §2-319(1)(a)]

(b) F.O.B. vehicle of transportation [§384]

If, however, the contract term is "F.O.B. Car 4029, Union R.R. Depot, Los Angeles," or a similar term having reference to the vehicle of transportation, then the seller is clearly obligated to bear the expense and risk of having the goods loaded *on board*. [U.C.C. §2-319(1)(c)]

(c) F.O.B. point of destination [§385]

If the contract provides that the seller is to ship the goods F.O.B. destination (*e.g.,* buyer's showroom), this means that the seller must arrange to transport the goods *to the point of destination* at the seller's own expense and risk. [U.C.C. §2-319(1)(b)]

(2) F.A.S. [§386]

The letters "F.A.S." mean *"free alongside"* and are generally used in *maritime* shipping contracts. They are intended to denote that the seller is to deliver the goods free of expense to the buyer alongside (on the dock next to) the vessel on which they are to be loaded and is to obtain a receipt therefor, in exchange for which the carrier is obligated to issue a bill of lading. The buyer bears the expense and risk of loading onto the vessel. [U.C.C. §2-319(2)]

(3) C.I.F. and C. & F. [§387]

The letters "C.I.F." stand for *"cost, insurance, and freight."* The letters "C. & F." stand for *"cost and freight."* Both are almost *exclusively maritime* shipment terms. Under a "C.I.F." contract, the price agreed to be paid by the buyer includes (i) the cost of the goods, (ii) all freight charges to the named destination, and (iii) appropriate insurance of safe delivery for the shipment. Under a "C. & F." contract, the price does not include the insurance, but it does include the freight. [U.C.C. §2-320(1)] "C.I.F."

and "C. & F." always indicate *shipment contracts*, with the buyer having the risk of transit damage, and this is true even though the delivery term is used in connection with the destination (*e.g.*, "C.I.F. Buyer's warehouse" is a *shipment contract*). [U.C.C. §2-320(2)]

(a) Seller's obligations [§388]

Under a C.I.F. contract, the seller is to bear the expense and risk of putting the goods into the possession of a carrier at the port of shipment; obtain negotiable bills of lading covering their transportation to their destination; have the goods loaded; pay the cost of loading; obtain a receipt from the carrier showing that the freight has been paid or provided for; obtain an appropriate certificate of insurance; prepare an invoice and other necessary documents; and forward and tender the documents to the buyer with any indorsement necessary to perfect the buyer's rights. [U.C.C. §2-320(2)] A "C. & F." term imposes the same obligations except those relating to insurance. [U.C.C. §2-320(3)]

(b) Tender of documents [§389]

Upon tender of the proper documents, the buyer is obligated to pay the full purchase price. [U.C.C. §2-320(4)] This obligation is irrespective of whether the goods themselves arrived or ever will arrive. [**Smith Co. v. Marano**, 110 A. 94 (Pa. 1920)] Indeed, tender of the goods without tender of the enumerated documents is *not* full performance by the seller, and the buyer is not obligated to accept or pay for the goods. [U.C.C. §§2-320(4), 2-601]

1) Note

The same rules regarding tender of documents are true when the shipment term is "F.O.B. Vessel" or "F.A.S." [U.C.C. §2-319(4)]

(4) Ex ship [§390]

When a seller agrees to deliver "ex ship," the commercial understanding of the term is that no particular ship is intended. [**Harrison v. Fortlage**, 161 U.S. 57 (1896)] Rather, it means that the seller is to bear *full risk and expense* until the goods "leave the ship's tackle" (*i.e.*, are unloaded). [U.C.C. §2-322(1), (2)(b)] The seller is required to discharge all liens arising out of the carriage and furnish the buyer with such documents as are required to enable the buyer to take possession of the goods. [U.C.C. §2-322(2)(a)]

(5) No arrival, no sale [§391]

The term "no arrival, no sale" is used to keep the risk of loss during carriage on the seller, and yet absolve the seller from liability to the buyer for damages if for some reason, *not due to the seller's fault*, the goods either do not arrive or arrive in such a damaged or deteriorated condition that they no longer conform to the contract standard. [**Salmon v. Berg**, 37 N.Y.S.2d 985 (1942)]

(a) Seller must ship goods [§392]

Use of this term does not mean that the seller has the option not to ship. [**Haber v. S.A. Jacobson Co.**, 185 App. Div. 650 (1918)] The seller must ship goods, and they must conform to the contract at the time of dispatch. [U.C.C. §2-324(a)]

(b) Arrival/nonarrival of goods [§393]

If the goods arrive, the seller must tender them to the buyer. If they do not arrive, and their nonarrival has not been caused by the seller, the seller is under no further obligation to the buyer. [U.C.C. §2-324(a)]

(c) Damaged goods [§394]

If the goods arrive in a damaged or deteriorated condition without fault on the part of the seller, the buyer may either treat the contract as avoided or accept the goods with due allowance from the contract price for the deterioration but without further rights against the seller. [U.C.C. §2-324(b)—read in conjunction with §2-613(b)]

COMMONLY USED SHIPMENT ABBREVIATIONS — gilbert

TERM	STANDS FOR	RISK AND EXPENSE ON SELLER UNTIL:
F.O.B.	Free on board	F.O.B. point of shipment—Goods in *carrier's possession*
		F.O.B. vehicle of transportation—Goods loaded *on board*
		F.O.B. point of destination—Goods *reach destination*
F.A.S.	Free alongside	Goods *alongside the vessel* on which they are to be loaded
C.I.F.	Cost, insurance, and freight	Goods in *carrier's possession* (Seller also must obtain negotiable bills of lading, have goods loaded and pay for loading, obtain a receipt and appropriate certificate of insurance, prepare and tender invoice and other necessary documents to Buyer.)
C. & F.	Cost and freight	Goods in *carrier's possession* (Seller has same obligations as under C.I.F. *except for insurance*.)
EX SHIP	(No particular ship intended)	Goods *are unloaded* from carrier. (Seller must discharge all liens and provide necessary documents to Buyer.)
NO ARRIVAL, NO SALE	(Seller not liable if loss or damage is not Seller's fault)	Goods *reach destination*, but if they *don't arrive or are damaged, not due to Seller's fault*, Seller is not liable

c. Shipment under reservation [§395]

A "shipment under reservation" is one where the seller retains control over the goods in transit by *consigning them to himself* on a negotiable bill of lading (*see* detailed discussion *infra*, §§702 *et seq.*). A shipment under reservation reserves in the seller a *security interest* in the goods quite apart from title to the goods. The seller, rather than the buyer, is entitled to possession of the goods. [U.C.C. §2-505(1)]

(1) Purpose [§396]

This practice is widely used to ensure that the buyer will not obtain control of the goods unless they are paid for on arrival. The buyer has no right to obtain physical possession of the goods from the carrier unless the buyer presents the bill of lading, and the seller will, of course, not indorse it over to buyer until payment is made.

(2) Seller's duty regarding delivery of documents [§397]

It is customary in shipments under reservation for the seller to take the bill of lading, an invoice, and other appropriate documents to the seller's bank and have the bank transmit them to the buyer's bank. The buyer then pays the required price to the bank, which releases the bill of lading so that the buyer can collect the goods.

(a) Procedure [§398]

Delivery of documents through banking channels is specifically sanctioned by the U.C.C. [*See* U.C.C. §§2-308(c), 2-503(5)(b)] The seller must tender all such documents in correct form and properly indorsed so that the buyer can obtain the goods from the carrier. [U.C.C. §2-503(5)(a)]

(b) Draft [§399]

Frequently, in a documentary transaction, the documents will be accompanied by a draft. A draft is very similar in form to an ordinary check. In substance, it will provide "Pay to the order of [my bank] the price on such and such a date, signed Seller," and will be addressed to the buyer. For the buyer to procure the documents entitling the buyer to possession of the goods, the buyer will "accept" the draft by writing "Accepted" on it. This obligates the buyer to pay it. Drafts are used to enable collection of the price of goods against documents to be handled through banking channels.

1) Refusal to accept draft [§400]

If the buyer refuses to "accept" a draft, this constitutes rejection of the goods and sets in motion the chain of seller's remedies. [U.C.C. §2-503(5)(b); *see infra*, §§593-607]

2) Acceptance of draft [§401]

If the buyer accepts the draft, whether the documents are turned over immediately or later depends on the *payment date specified in the draft*:

a)   If the payment date is *more than three days* after the draft is presented to the buyer for acceptance, the buyer is entitled to get the documents upon acceptance, without making payment at that time; in other words, it is a *sale on credit*. [U.C.C. §2-514]

b)   On the other hand, if the payment date specified is *less than three days from* the date on which the draft is presented to the buyer for acceptance, the buyer cannot get the documents (absent contrary agreement) until the draft is paid, even though the buyer accepts it immediately. [U.C.C. §2-514]

2. Tender of Delivery [§402]

In cases where the goods have been shipped by the seller to the buyer, as well as in cases where delivery is to be made directly to the buyer by the seller without the need for carrier transportation, the seller must *offer* ("tender") the goods to the buyer to discharge the seller's duties under the sales contract. Of course, the seller need not make actual delivery where the buyer is unwilling to take the goods; the seller need only tender the goods, not force them on the buyer.

EXAM TIP   **gilbert**

Don't forget that the seller need only *tender* the goods to the buyer—*actual delivery is not required*. Be on the lookout for fact patterns involving a *bailee* or *constructive tender* in particular, as these scenarios frequently result in tender without actual delivery. (See *infra*, §§410-413.)

---

a. Effect of tender—shifts performance to buyer [§403]

Not only must the seller make a proper tender of conforming goods to discharge his duties under the sales contract, but until such a tender is made, the buyer is under no duty to accept or pay for the goods. [U.C.C. §2-507(1)] The principal effect of a valid tender, therefore, is to shift the obligation of performance to the buyer.

b. What constitutes tender of delivery

(1) By manual transfer of possession [§404]

Wherever the contract requires a manual transfer of possession from the seller to the buyer, tender of delivery requires that the seller put and hold conforming goods at the buyer's disposition, and give the buyer any documents and such notification as is reasonably necessary to enable the buyer to take delivery. [U.C.C. §2-503(1)]

(a) Time of delivery [§405]

Tender of delivery must be made at a *reasonable* hour. [U.C.C. §2-503(1)(a)] What is "reasonable" is, of course, a question of fact.

(b) Place of delivery [§406]

As already discussed, the place where delivery is to be made—in the absence of contrary agreement—is the *seller's* (not the buyer's) place of business or residence. [U.C.C. §2-308]

(c) Tender must be maintained a reasonable period of time [§407]

Where delivery is to be made at the seller's place of business and the seller has notified the buyer that the goods are ready, the seller must hold the goods for a period of time reasonably necessary for the buyer to take possession of the goods. Thereafter, the seller may resort to the various remedies afforded when the buyer breaches (*see infra*, §§593-603).

1) Same rule for tender at buyer's place of business [§408]

Similarly, if the contract requires the seller to transfer possession at the buyer's place of business, the tender must be maintained for a reasonable period of time. This means that the seller must give the buyer reasonable notice that the goods are available and attempt delivery in a reasonable manner and at a reasonable time, in order to discharge the delivery obligation and place the buyer in breach.

2) "Reasonable" period [§409]

What is a "reasonable" period for holding the goods depends on the facts of the case. The period is very short if the goods are perishable or threaten to decline speedily in value.

a) But note

If the sales contract specifies a delivery date, the goods do not have to be held beyond that date.

(2) By "constructive" tender [§410]

Sometimes goods are tendered by the seller to the buyer without an actual offer to transfer physical possession of the goods themselves.

---

e.g. **Example:** Seller sells a pile of lumber located at a railroad siding to Buyer. The pile is extremely bulky. Seller says to Buyer, "The lumber is yours." This is a sufficient tender of delivery if Buyer has agreed to transport the lumber.

---

(3) Goods in possession of bailee [§411]

A tender of delivery can also occur without an offer of manual transfer of the goods when the goods are in the hands of a bailee. One method of tendering goods under such circumstances is for the seller to procure an acknowledgment from the bailee that the goods are henceforth being held for the buyer. [U.C.C. §2-503(4)(a)]

(a) Negotiable document of title [§412]
Such a tender is also sufficient where the seller gives the buyer a negotiable document of title covering the goods. The possession of such a document of title entitles the possessor to compel the bailee to deliver the goods. [U.C.C. §§2-503(4)(a), 7-403(3)]

(b) Nonnegotiable document of title [§413]
Moreover, tender of a nonnegotiable document of title or a written direction to the bailee to deliver the goods is sufficient *unless the buyer reasonably objects*. However, risk of loss to the goods and the risk that the bailee will refuse to honor the nonnegotiable document of title or the direction to deliver remains on the seller until the buyer has had a reasonable time to present the document or direction to the bailee. If the bailee refuses to honor the document or obey the direction, the tender of delivery is defeated and risk of loss never shifts. [U.C.C. §2-503(4)(b)]

c. What constitutes sufficient tender?

(1) Common law—perfect tender rule [§414]
At common law, there evolved a rigid rule requiring the seller to make a delivery of goods that *conformed in every respect* to the contract requirements: quality, quantity, and place and time of shipment. This was called the "perfect tender rule."

Example: Seller agreed to sell pig iron to Buyer "shipment from Glasgow, Scotland." When the time came for shipment, no ships were available at Glasgow. Buyer's factory was equidistant from Glasgow and Leeds, and since vessels were available at Leeds, Seller sent the iron to Leeds for shipment. On arrival Buyer rejected. *Held:* Buyer was privileged to do so; a contract calling for shipment from Glasgow is not fulfilled by a shipment from Leeds. [**Filley v. Pope**, 115 U.S. 213 (1885)]

(a) Comment
Ultimately, application of this rule led to the famous statement by Judge Learned Hand that "there is no room in commercial contracts for the doctrine of substantial performance." [**Mitsubishi v. Aron,** 16 F.2d 185 (2d Cir. 1926)]

(2) U.C.C. rule [§415]

Although the perfect tender rule for years has been under fire from commentators on the grounds that it creates an inhuman standard of performance, the U.C.C. retains it in part.

(a) Basic rule [§416]

The basic rule of perfect tender is set forth in U.C.C. section 2-601, which provides that "if the goods or the tender of delivery *fail in any respect* to conform to the contract, the buyer *may reject* the whole, accept the whole, or accept part and reject part."

(b) Rule mitigated [§417]

However, much of the force of the perfect tender rule is mitigated by other U.C.C. provisions. Most important is the provision allowing *cure of a defective tender* (*see* detailed discussion below). Also, special rules allow *substantial performance* of a sales contract in the following two instances:

1) Installment sales—substantial performance sufficient [§418]

Contrary to Learned Hand's famous dictum, above, U.C.C. section 2-612 establishes a rule of substantial performance in installment sales contracts. (Section 2-612(1) defines an installment sales contract as any contract "which requires or *authorizes the delivery of goods in separate lots* to be separately accepted.")

a) Limiting buyer's right to reject installment [§419]

Thus, when the seller is to make deliveries in installments to the buyer, the buyer is privileged to reject an installment only if the defect in tender "*substantially* impairs the value of that installment." [U.C.C. §2-612(2)]

b) Limiting buyer's right to cancel contract [§420]

Similarly, only if nonconformity of one or more installments "substantially impairs the value of the *whole contract*" is there a breach of the entire contract by the seller. [U.C.C. §2-612(3)] Whether the breach is this serious (*i.e.*, "substantially impairs") is a question of fact.

---

e.g. **Example:** A mere showing of delays in delivery and quality control problems do not justify a buyer's canceling an installment sales contract. The buyer must also prove that the defects and delays "substantially impaired the value of the *whole contract*," and the longer the contract, the harder this is to prove. [**Holiday Manufacturing Co. v. BASF Systems, Inc.,** 380 F. Supp. 1096 (D. Neb. 1974)]

> c) **Seller may recover for performance [§421]**
> Note that the U.C.C. is very supportive of installment sales contracts and permits the seller under such a contract to recover for performance rendered, even where the deficiencies in seller's performance are such as would clearly be a breach in any other kind of sales contract.

2) Shipping arrangements—substantial performance sufficient [§422]
Another mitigating provision of the U.C.C. is section 2-504, which provides that even if the seller does not adhere rigidly to the contract insofar as shipping arrangements are concerned, the buyer is not privileged to reject unless *material* delay or loss ensues.

> a) **Note**
> If without the fault of either party the agreed type of carrier becomes unavailable or the agreed manner of delivery otherwise becomes commercially impracticable, but a *commercially reasonable* substitute is available, the substitute means of performance *must* be tendered and accepted. [U.C.C. §2-614(1)]

> **e.g.** **Example:** In the shipment from Glasgow example (*supra,* §414), Buyer would not have been privileged to reject, because shipment from Glasgow at that time was impossible and shipment from Leeds was a commercially reasonable substitute. [*See* U.C.C. §2-614(1)] Indeed, if Seller could have shipped from Glasgow but carelessly dispatched the goods from Leeds, Buyer still would not be permitted to reject unless, under U.C.C. section 2-504, Buyer could show material prejudice by a shipment from Leeds rather than Glasgow.

d. Curing improper tender

(1) Common law [§423]
As indicated above, at common law, the seller either made a perfect tender of delivery the first time, or the seller was in breach of contract (unless, of course, the buyer was willing to waive rigid adherence to the contract).

(2) U.C.C. rule [§424]
The U.C.C. gives the seller somewhat more leeway. If the seller's original tender of delivery is rejected because it is nonconforming *and the time for performance has not yet expired*, the seller may promptly notify the buyer

of an intention to "cure," and then within the contract time for performance, the seller may tender a conforming delivery. If the seller does so, it constitutes sufficient performance, removing any breach resulting from the original improper delivery. [U.C.C. §2-508(1); **Tiger Motor Co. v. McMurtry,** 224 So. 2d 638 (Ala. 1969)]

(a) Notice required [§425]

For the seller to cure, the buyer must be notified of the seller's intention to attempt a second conforming delivery. [**Beco, Inc. v. Minnechaug Golf Course,** 256 A.2d 522 (Conn. 1968)] Notice must be given "seasonably," which means if no time has been agreed upon, *a reasonable time.* [U.C.C. §1-204(3)] The notice need not be in any particular form, although it should state the approximate date (*within* the permitted contract period) by which the substitution will be accomplished.

(b) Surprise rejections [§426]

There may be cases where the seller's tender was nonconforming but the seller nevertheless had *reasonable grounds* to believe that it would be acceptable (with or without an allowance from the price). This is frequently the case where merchants have been dealing with each other for a period of time. Occasionally, the buyer who has been accepting imperfect tenders in the past may want to get out of a contract without breaching, and therefore, without warning to the seller, will suddenly reject a tender of delivery as being imperfect. Under such circumstances, the surprised seller may, *if* the buyer is given seasonable notification, have a further reasonable time in which to substitute a conforming tender. [U.C.C. §2-508(2)]

1) Effect

Under these limited circumstances, the seller gets additional time to cure *even if the time for performance has expired* under the terms of the contract.

---

e.g. **Example:** Buyer phoned a department store and asked to be shipped a pocket calculator, Model AA. The store clerk agreed to do so (and bill Buyer), but discovered that Model AA had recently been replaced by Model BB, which was a newer version of Model AA and which was cheaper even though it had four additional features. If Buyer rejects the calculator because it is not the one ordered, this also is the kind of "surprise rejection" giving rise to the right of the store to have a further reasonable time in which to try to produce a Model AA.

(c) Variation—2003 revision [§427]

Cure under the revision is even easier, being allowed in all cases where the seller has made an improper tender but behaved in *good faith* and in circumstances where cure is *"appropriate."* [U.C.C. §2R-508(2)] This vague language should allow the courts much leeway in policing the validity of a seller's attempted cure whenever the buyer has rejected goods or revoked acceptance, but where the substitution of conforming goods is the best solution to the difficulty.

PERFECT TENDER RULE UNDER THE U.C.C.   **gilbert**

BASIC RULE:

If the goods or tender do not conform to the contract in any respect, Buyer may *reject the whole*, *accept the whole*, or *accept part and reject part*. [U.C.C. §2-601]

U.C.C. PROVISIONS THAT MITIGATE BASIC RULE:

☑ *Substantial performance* is sufficient:

- *Installment sales*—Buyer can reject an installment only if the nonconformity *substantially impairs the value of that installment* (and even then the contract is not breached unless the nonconformity of one or more installments substantially impairs the whole contract). [U.C.C. §2-612]

- *Shipping arrangements*—Buyer cannot reject unless the deviation in shipping procedures causes *material delay or loss*. [U.C.C. §2-504]

☑ *Cure of a nonconforming tender* is available if:

- The *time for performance has not yet expired*;

- Seller *"seasonably" notifies* Buyer of an intention to cure; and

- Seller tenders *conforming delivery within contract time for performance* (additional reasonable time allowed for surprise rejections).

[U.C.C. §2-508(1)]

B. Performance by Buyer

---

1. **Facilitating Receipt of Goods [§428]**
   The buyer's first duty is to furnish facilities reasonably suited for receipt of the goods. [U.C.C. §2-503(1)(b)]

2. **Right to Inspection of Goods [§429]**
   Unless the parties agree otherwise, the buyer has the right to inspect the goods *before payment or acceptance*. [U.C.C. §2-513(1)]

a. Exercising right of inspection

(1) Time of inspection [§430]

Inspection must be made *within a reasonable time after receipt* of the goods, or the right is lost. What is reasonable depends on all of the circumstances of the transaction, including the nature of the goods, marketability, usage of trade, and the like. Inspection must be made at a reasonable hour. [U.C.C. §2-513(1)]

(2) Place of inspection [§431]

Under the U.C.C., the buyer is permitted to make the inspection at *any* reasonable place. [U.C.C. §2-513(1)] Furthermore, if the parties by contract fix a place for inspection, it is presumed to be exclusive; but if for some reason the goods cannot be inspected there, inspection can be had at any reasonable place unless the place fixed was *clearly* intended as an *indispensable* condition, failure of which avoids the contract. [U.C.C. §2-513(4)]

(3) Right to test and sample [§432]

If visual inspection is not sufficient to determine whether the goods conform, the buyer has the right to test a reasonable amount of the goods, and to use and consume the same in such tests, as long as these actions are reasonable. [U.C.C. §2-513(1)]

EXAM TIP	gilbert

Don't automatically assume that when a buyer begins to use or consume the goods that he has accepted them. Remember that such use or consumption may just be *sampling*, so pay particular attention to the *quantity* and *duration* to distinguish sampling from true acceptance.

(4) Expense [§433]

Under the U.C.C., expenses of inspection must be borne by the *buyer*, but may be recovered from the seller if the goods do not conform and are rejected (*see infra*, §662). [U.C.C. §2-513(2)]

b. Loss of right to inspect by contractual provision [§434]

Provisions in the sales contract may be inconsistent with the buyer's right to inspect the goods prior to payment of the purchase price. For example:

(1) Payment against documents [§435]

Provisions calling for the buyer to pay against shipping documents before receipt of the goods *override* the right to inspect before payment. [U.C.C. §2-513(3)(b)]

(2) Payment C.O.D. [§436]

Similarly, where the contract calls for payment "C.O.D.," there is *no right of inspection* unless the agreement provides otherwise. [U.C.C. §2-513(3)(a)]

(3) Effect on duty to pay [§437]

Note that in such contracts not only is the buyer deprived of any right to inspect the goods before acceptance, but the buyer also *must make full payment before* getting possession of the goods (in a C.O.D. case) or the documents of title (in a payment against documents situation). [U.C.C. §2-512]

(a) Payment in such cases not an acceptance [§438]

It is important to note, however, that payment under such circumstances does *not constitute an acceptance* of the goods (*see* below), nor does it waive any of the buyer's remedies against the seller if the goods are nonconforming. Thus, although the buyer may have paid for the goods before receipt, there is still a right to inspect them upon receipt, and thereafter the buyer may reject nonconforming goods and recover any payment made to the seller, plus damages. [U.C.C. §2-512(2)]

3. Acceptance of Goods [§439]

The buyer's basic duty is to "accept and pay for" the goods. [U.C.C. §2-301]

a. What constitutes acceptance [§440]

Acceptance may occur by words or conduct of the buyer signifying approval of the goods delivered.

(1) Acceptance after reasonable opportunity to inspect [§441]

The most obvious acceptance occurs when the buyer, after having had a *reasonable opportunity* to inspect the goods, indicates to the seller either that (i) the goods are conforming or (ii) the buyer will take them in spite of their nonconformity. [U.C.C. §2-606(1)(a)]

(2) Failure to make valid rejection [§442]

Another method of acceptance is for the buyer simply to hold the goods for an unreasonable length of time without notifying the seller of rejection. [U.C.C. §2-606(1)(b)—read in conjunction with §2-602(1)]

(a) Trial use period [§443]

Acceptance by inaction cannot occur, however, until the buyer has had a reasonable opportunity to inspect. *Note well: Possession* is *not* the same thing as "acceptance"; the buyer is entitled to a reasonable "trial use period." [U.C.C. §2-606(1)(b)]

(b) Length of period [§444]

How long does the trial use period last? It varies with the nature of the goods, *e.g.*, being quite short if the goods are ice, and somewhat longer if they are bricks.

(3) Performance of acts inconsistent with seller's ownership [§445]

A third method of acceptance is for the buyer to do any act inconsistent with the seller's ownership—*e.g.*, consuming the goods or selling them to others can constitute acceptance of the goods. [U.C.C. §2-606(1)(c); **Carlo Bianchi & Co. v. Builders' Equipment & Supplies Co.**, 199 N.E.2d 519 (Mass. 1964)]

(a) But note

There are circumstances, however, where the goods are perishable or threaten to decline speedily in value, in which the buyer can resell *without* accepting (*see infra*, §§472-482).

ACCEPTANCE BY BUYER—A CHECKLIST   **gilbert**

UNDER THE U.C.C., BUYER MAY ACCEPT BY *WORDS OR CONDUCT* SIGNIFYING APPROVAL IN THE FOLLOWING MANNER:

☑ Indicating that the goods are *conforming*;

☑ Indicating that although the goods are *nonconforming*, she *will accept* them;

☑ *Failing to make a valid rejection* within a *reasonable* period of time; or

☑ Acting in any way *inconsistent with the seller's continued ownership*, such as by selling the goods.

b. Right to make partial acceptance [§446]

If the seller makes a tender that in any way fails to conform to the contract (*e.g.*, part of the shipment is defective), the buyer may accept *any commercial unit* or units and reject the rest. [U.C.C. §2-601(c)] If the buyer accepts part of any commercial unit, the entire commercial unit is deemed accepted. [U.C.C. §2-606(2)]

(1) "Commercial unit" [§447]

A "commercial unit" is one that by commercial usage is treated as a single whole for the purpose of sale, and division of which materially impairs its character or value on the market or in use. A commercial unit may be a single article (*e.g.,* a machine), or a set of articles (*e.g.,* a suite of furniture or an assortment of sizes), or a quantity (*e.g.,* a bale, gross, or carload), or any other unit treated in use or in the relevant market as a single whole. [U.C.C. §2-105(6)]

c. Effect of complete acceptance [§448]

Once the buyer accepts the goods, payment is due at the contract rate. The buyer cannot thereafter reject the goods as nonconforming. [U.C.C. §2-607(1), (2)]

(1) Exception [§449]

Under certain limited circumstances, a buyer may be entitled to *revoke* the acceptance and *rescind the sale.* [U.C.C. §2-608; *see infra,* §483]

(2) Claim for damages possible [§450]

In any event, the buyer's acceptance does *not* bar a claim for *damages.* Thus, where the seller is late in delivery or delivers nonconforming goods, the buyer may keep and use the goods, and still sue the seller for damages, or assert the claim for damages as a setoff to any action brought by the seller to recover the purchase price. To preserve this right to damages, the buyer need only be sure to give notice of the seller's breach within a reasonable time after the buyer should have discovered it. [U.C.C. §§2-714, 2-717; *see supra,* §336; *and see infra,* §617]

EXAM TIP   gilbert

This is an important point to remember—acceptance bars *rejection*, but it does *not bar an action for money damages.* So if you see facts that show that the buyer has accepted the goods, don't state that buyer has no remedy for nonconforming goods. Remember to discuss the possibility of damages.

---

4. Payment [§451]

The second part of the buyer's basic duty under any sales contract is to pay for the goods. [U.C.C. §2-301]

a. Time of payment [§452]

Unless credit has been arranged, the buyer must tender payment as a condition *concurrent* to the seller's obligation to tender delivery of the goods to the buyer. Thus, payment is due at the time of delivery. [U.C.C. §2-310; *see supra,* §174]

(1) Documents of title [§453]

If the sale involves the transfer of documents of title, then (unless credit is agreed upon) payment is due at the time the buyer is to *receive the documents* (regardless of when the goods themselves are to be received). [U.C.C. §2-310(c); *see supra,* §153]

b. Manner of payment [§454]

Payment is sufficient when made in *any manner reasonable* in the ordinary course of business, unless the seller demands payment in legal tender *and* gives the buyer an extension of time necessary to procure the legal tender. This means that, in the usual case, payment by check is sufficient. [U.C.C. §2-511(3)]

c. Method of payment [§455]

Payment normally is in money, but this is not essential. The parties can agree on any form of consideration.

(1) Other goods [§456]

The price may be made payable in *commodities*, in which event, each party is a seller of the goods transferred and a buyer of the goods received. [U.C.C. §2-304(1)]

(2) Real estate [§457]

Even though the U.C.C. does not cover real estate transactions, the fact that a seller takes payment in the form of an interest in real estate does not affect the buyer's right or the seller's obligations as set forth in the U.C.C. with respect to the goods involved in the exchange. [U.C.C. §2-304(2)]

(3) Payment by letter of credit [§458]

Letters of credit are payment devices that substitute the liability of a bank for that of the buyer. In a letter of credit transaction, the buyer obtains a local bank's written *guarantee* to a seller that the goods will be paid for by the bank upon tender of a draft drawn on the bank (which may or may not be accompanied by a document of title, typically a bill of lading). In effect, the bank becomes the buyer, and sellers are thus more certain of getting payment.

(a) Independence principle [§459]

By issuing the letter of credit, the buyer's bank obligates itself to pay the amount specified in the letter of credit (the price) upon receipt of proper documents. Under what is called the *independence principle*, the bank's letter of credit obligation is separate from the performance of the underlying sales transaction. [U.C.C. §5-103(d)] As long as the seller complies with the terms of the letter of credit, the bank is obligated to pay, even if it knows or suspects that goods being delivered by the seller do not conform to the contract. [U.C.C. §5-108(f)(1); **Maurice O'Meara Co. v. National Park Bank,** 239 N.Y. 386 (1925)]

Only if the buyer obtains a court order *enjoining* the bank from making payment is the bank privileged not to honor the letter of credit. [U.C.C. §5-109(b); *and see* U.C.C. §2-512(1)(b)]

(b) Documents must conform [§460]

The *documents* must strictly conform to the terms stated in the letter of credit, or the bank is not required to honor the letter. [U.C.C. §5-108(a)]

1) Exception—minor deviation [§461]

It has been held that if the documents and other papers demanded by the terms of the letter of credit do not strictly conform to the credit, the bank must still pay if the deviation is so minor that there is *no chance* that the bank can suffer harm from the nonconformity. [*See* discussion in Official Comment 1 to U.C.C. §5-108]

EXAM TIP   **gilbert**

Remember to distinguish between the rules for shipment and tender and those regarding payment. The more relaxed "substantial performance" rule does **not apply** to payment by a **letter of credit**. The credit documents must strictly conform to the terms.

(c) Whether credit irrevocable [§462]

A letter of credit can be drawn so as to be revocable by the bank at any time prior to the presentation of the documents to it; or it may be drawn to be irrevocable. Where a sales contract calls simply for a letter of credit, a *presumption* arises that it means an *irrevocable* letter of credit unless it is expressly agreed otherwise. [U.C.C. §§2-325(3), 5-106(a)]

(d) Effect of furnishing letter of credit [§463]

Where the contract calls for payment by a letter of credit and the buyer has furnished a proper letter of credit, the buyer's *obligation to pay it is suspended.* [U.C.C. §2-325(2)] If the seller complies with the terms of the letter of credit, the issuing bank is under a *duty to pay*, and must respond in damages if it does not. [U.C.C. §§5-108(a), 5-111]

(4) Substitute method of payment [§464]

If the agreed means or method of payment fails because of a domestic or foreign government regulation (*e.g.,* devaluation of currency), the seller may withhold or stop delivery unless the buyer provides a means of payment that is commercially a substantial equivalent. [U.C.C. §2-614(2)]

5. Rejection [§465]

If the goods that the seller delivers do not conform to the contract, the buyer is entitled to *reject* them if the buyer follows certain formalities. [U.C.C. §2-601] (*Note:*

The following discussion deals with a *rightful* rejection of goods by the buyer. If the buyer does not have the right to reject, but does so anyway, then of course the rejection is wrongful, and entitles the seller to invoke the remedies discussed *infra*, §§593 *et seq.*)

a. Notice of rejection [§466]

To make an effective rejection of goods, the buyer must *notify* the seller of the rejection within a *reasonable time* after receiving the goods. Again, this period of time varies with the goods as to how long the "trial use period" lasts. [U.C.C. §2-602(1); *and see supra*, §§443-444]

(1) What constitutes reasonable time [§467]

"Reasonable" time contemplates due allowance for the right of inspection, the nature and size of shipment, etc. [**Trailmobile Division of Pullman, Inc. v. Jones**, 164 S.E.2d 346 (Ga. 1968)]

(2) Notice required even if defects known to seller [§468]

The notice must be given by the buyer even if the seller has *knowingly* shipped nonconforming goods. *Rationale:* Because the buyer might choose to accept the nonconforming goods, the notice is necessary to give the seller the opportunity of "curing" the defect (*supra*, §424).

(3) General rejection sufficient [§469]

The general rule is that the buyer need *not* specify the particular defects that are asserted as grounds for rejection; *i.e.*, a general notice of rejection for "nonconforming goods" is sufficient.

(a) Exception—two cases in which buyer must specify defect [§470]

If a defect is ascertainable upon reasonable inspection (*i.e.*, the buyer knew or should have known of it when rejecting) but the buyer does not specifically mention the defect to the seller on rejecting the goods (rejecting on other grounds), then the buyer will be precluded from later relying on the unstated defect to justify the rejection or establish breach in the following two situations: (i) whenever the seller *could have cured* the defect if stated seasonably by the buyer; and (ii) when both parties are *merchants* and the *seller has made a request* in writing for a full and final written statement of all defects on which the buyer proposes to rely. [U.C.C. §2-605]

1) Rationale

The policy here is to preserve the contract by encouraging cure where possible, and also the practical realization that a party who fails or refuses to state known defects is probably acting in bad faith.

b. Effect of rejection [§471]

Where the seller has shipped defective or nonconforming goods, and the buyer has made an effective rejection thereof, the buyer's *duty to pay never arises.* The goods remain the property of the seller, and the risk of loss also remains with the seller. [U.C.C. §2-510(1); *and see infra,* §538]

c.   **Duties with respect to rejected goods**

   (1)   **No exercise of dominion [§472]**
   Once goods have been rejected, the buyer is under a duty *not* to exercise dominion over the goods. This means that the buyer must not behave as if the buyer (and not the seller) is the owner of the goods.

   (a)   **Effect of exercise of dominion—acceptance [§473]**
   If the buyer does exercise ownership—*e.g.,* by using or reselling the goods—most courts hold that the buyer has made an "acceptance," like it or not, and that it is too late for the buyer to *reject* the goods. [U.C.C. §2-602(2)(a); **Wadsworth Plumbing & Heating v. Tallycraft Corp.,** 560 P.2d 1080 (Or. 1977)—continued use is an "act inconsistent with the seller's ownership"; *but see* **McCullough v. Bill Swad, Inc.,** 449 N.E.2d 1289 (Ohio 1983)—continued use of car allowed where "reasonable"]

   (b)   **Unavoidable use [§474]**
   All courts will excuse postrejection use of the goods where unavoidable. In **Garfinkel v. Lehman Floor Covering Co.,** 60 Misc. 2d 72 (1969), the item rejected was a car dealership's carpeting. The seller refused to remove it from the showroom, so the court excused the buyer's continued use of it.

   (c)   **Mobile homes [§475]**
   The courts have been generous to mobile home buyers who reject the home and continue to live in it for a reasonable period of time while they try to find new living accommodations. The courts sometimes state that the continued use here benefited the seller by providing a caretaker for the mobile home. [**Keen v. Modern Trailer Sales,** 578 P.2d 668 (Colo. 1978)]

   (d)   **Variation—2003 revision [§476]**
   The revision provides that following either rejection or revocation of acceptance *any reasonable use* of the goods by the buyer is allowed, but in appropriate cases the buyer is obligated to the seller for the *value* derived from this use. [U.C.C. §2R-608(4)(b)]

   (2)   **Duty to hold, return, or resell**

   (a)   **Storage [§477]**
   If the buyer has rejected goods but still has physical possession of

them, the buyer must hold the goods with *reasonable care* at the seller's disposition for a time sufficient to enable the seller to remove them. [U.C.C. §2-602(2)(b), (c)]

(b)   Seller may instruct buyer to resell goods [§478]

In addition to holding the goods, the buyer is *required* to follow the seller's *reasonable instructions* with respect to disposing of the goods if the following three factors are present: (i) the seller has no agent or place of business at the market of rejection; (ii) the buyer is a "merchant"; and (iii) the buyer has possession or control of the goods. [U.C.C. §2-603(1)]

1)   Note

Instructions are not "reasonable" if they do not include *indemnity for expenses*, where requested by the buyer. [U.C.C. §2-603(1); **Graybar Electric Co. v. Shook**, 193 S.E.2d 392 (N.C. 1973)]

(c)   Absence of instructions from seller [§479]

If the seller fails to give instructions within a reasonable time after the buyer has notified the seller of the rejection, or fails to indemnify the buyer on demand for expenses incurred in disposing of the goods per the seller's instructions, the buyer may (i) *store* the goods for the seller's account, (ii) *reship* them to the seller, or (iii) *resell* them for the seller's account. [U.C.C. §§2-604, 2-603(1)]

(d)   Perishables [§480]

However, if the goods are perishable or threaten to decline speedily in value (*e.g.,* baby chicks), the buyer is required to make *reasonable efforts* to sell the goods for the seller's account, whether or not instructions are forthcoming. [U.C.C. §2-603(1)]

CHECKLIST OF BUYER'S DUTIES UPON REJECTION OF GOODS — gilbert

AFTER BUYER HAS NOTIFIED SELLER OF THE REJECTION OF THE GOODS, BUYER HAS THE FOLLOWING DUTIES:

☑ *Store* the goods with reasonable care for a reasonable time pending the seller's removal

☑ Follow the *seller's reasonable instructions to resell* the goods (but only if the buyer is a *merchant* still *in possession* of the goods)

☑ If the seller gives no instructions within a reasonable time, buyer may:
- *Store* the goods for the seller's account;
- *Reship* the goods to the seller; or
- *Resell* them for the seller's account (especially perishable goods)

(e) Expenses [§481]

If the buyer does sell the goods—either because they are perishables or because the seller has given instructions under circumstances that require the buyer to follow the instruction—the buyer is entitled to *reasonable expenses* from the seller for caring and disposing of goods, including a selling *commission*. [U.C.C. §2-603(2)]

1) Note

The buyer is given a *security interest* in rejected goods to secure the recovery of expenses and/or any part of the purchase price already paid. The buyer need not surrender the goods to the seller until the expense/price is refunded. If the refund is not forthcoming, the buyer may resell the goods (using the mechanism described in U.C.C. section 2-706; *see infra,* §593) and sue the seller for any amount still due. [U.C.C. §2-711(3)]

(3) Resale not acceptance or conversion [§482]

If after a rightful rejection, the buyer sells the goods because they are perishable or because the buyer has received no instruction from the seller, the buyer will *not* be deemed to have accepted or converted the goods, as long as the buyer has acted in *good faith*. [U.C.C. §§2-603(3), 2-604]

6. Revocation of Acceptance [§483]

Once the buyer has made a technical "acceptance" of the goods, it is too late to *reject* them, although the buyer may sue for damages caused by the breach. Suppose, however, that after acceptance, the buyer discovers something seriously wrong with the goods. May the buyer rescind the contract and get back any payment made? Yes, but the remedy is now called "revocation of acceptance." [U.C.C. §2-608]

a. Common law [§484]

The common law called this remedy "rescission," but the U.C.C. has abandoned that term (and all the technical rules that went with it) in favor of "revocation of acceptance."

b. Defect must be substantial [§485]

If the buyer were "rejecting" the goods, in theory at least, this could be done for any breach of contract, even trivial ones (*see supra,* §414 for a discussion of the perfect tender rule). However, to *revoke acceptance* the buyer must find a breach of contract that *substantially impairs* the value of the goods to the buyer.

c. Buyer must justify acceptance [§486]

Furthermore, if the buyer is to prevail, the buyer's reason for accepting the goods when they contain a substantial defect must be explained. The U.C.C. gives two permissible reasons:

(1) Cure assumed [§487]

One is that the buyer knew of the nonconformity at the time of acceptance, but reasonably assumed that the seller would cure the difficulty (and the seller has failed to do so).

---

e.g. **Example:** When Buyer was test driving a car, the windshield wipers failed to work. Buyer nonetheless purchased the car, but if Seller is unable to fix the windshield wipers, Buyer may revoke acceptance and recover the money paid for the car.

---

(2) Difficulty of discovery or deception [§488]

The buyer may also revoke acceptance if either the defect was not discoverable prior to acceptance or the buyer was deceived by the seller's assurances that no problem existed.

d. Notice [§489]

As with rejection, revocation of acceptance is accomplished by notice to the seller of the revocation *within a reasonable* time after the buyer *should have discovered* the defect. [U.C.C. §2-608(2)]

e. Effect of change in goods [§490]

If, prior to revocation, the goods have substantially changed for some reason *other than because of the defect*, it is too late to revoke acceptance, and an action for money damages caused by the breach is the only available remedy.

---

e.g. **Example:** After buying a race car, Buyer painted it an outrageous shade of orange, on top of which were placed decals of dragons. Buyer then discovered that the car stalled at speeds over 50 m.p.h. and could not be fixed. The alterations in the vehicle prohibit a revocation of acceptance. Buyer must use the damages formula specified in U.C.C. section 2-714 (*see supra*, §336).

---

cf. **Compare:** Buyer bought a new sofa and was considerably annoyed when the fabric began unravelling bit by bit. Buyer gave immediate notice of the problem to Seller, who ignored Buyer. Two weeks later, the sofa was an unupholstered frame and a pile of yarn. Here the deterioration is due to the reason for revoking acceptance, and thus the change in condition does *not* prevent the buyer from revoking acceptance.

---

f. After revocation [§491]

Following the revocation, the buyer must behave in the same manner as if the goods had been rejected in the first place. Thus, the rules are the same as for following a rejection. The buyer must stop using the goods, must take reasonable care of them, may claim a possessory security interest in them for expenses, etc. (*see supra*, §§472-482).

g. **Revocation against manufacturer [§492]**

The courts have split on the issue of whether the buyer can recover the payment directly from the manufacturer in a revocation suit, or whether the buyer is permitted to revoke only against the immediate retail seller. This issue may become relevant if the retailer has become bankrupt. [*Compare* **Dunfree v. Rod Baxter Imports,** 262 N.W.2d 349 (Minn. 1977)—permitting revocation against the manufacturer, *with* **Seekings v. Jimmy GMC of Tucson,** 638 P.2d 210 (Ariz. 1982)—not allowing revocation against parties other than the actual seller]

h. **Damages [§493]**

On rightful revocation of acceptance, the buyer is entitled to all of the purchase price paid, plus consequential damages not preventable by cover. [U.C.C. §§2-711, 2-715]

REJECTION VS. REVOCATION				gilbert
	WHEN	**HOW**	**DUTIES**	**EFFECT**
REJECTION	Theoretically for *any breach* of contract (perfect tender rule)	Notice within reasonable time	To store, return, resell

No exercise of dominion | No duty to pay |
| **REVOCATION** | Only for breach that *substantially impairs value* of goods to buyer | Notice within reasonable time | Same as above | Damages—purchase price paid plus consequential damages not preventable by cover |

Chapter Seven: Breakdown of the Bargain

CONTENTS

Chapter Approach

Chapter Approach

Besides the performance problems discussed in the last chapter, other breakdowns in the bargain can occur. Look for the following situations on your exam:

1. When it seems as if one party to the contract is *not going to perform*, ask yourself: Is this *anticipatory repudiation* or should the other party *demand assurance of performance*?

   a. If the party *unconditionally repudiates* the contract, this is anticipatory repudiation, and it creates an *immediate* right of action. However, the repudiating party can retract the repudiation *if* the other party's position has *not* been materially altered.

   b. If the party is merely *equivocating*, think in terms of a demand for assurance. There must be *reasonable grounds for insecurity* before a demand can be made (look especially for insolvency of the equivocating party). Be sure that the demanding party follows the proper U.C.C. procedure.

2. When the question involves circumstances that make *performance impossible or impractical*, think of *excuse*. For the seller to be excused from performance, there must be some event the nonoccurrence of which was a *basic presumption* on which the contract was made, or there must be a statute or regulation passed *after* the contract was made that makes the seller unable to perform.

3. Finally, if your question involves *damaged or destroyed goods*, think about *risk of loss* problems. As mentioned in chapter five, in sales contracts this does *not* depend on the passage of title, but rather on the U.C.C. rules. The Code provides that (i) risk of loss passes when the parties *agree* that it passes or (ii) if there is no agreement, the risk generally falls on the *party in control* of the goods. It is important to keep in mind that the goods must have been injured without the fault of either party for these rules to apply.

A. Anticipatory Breach

1. Repudiation—In General [§494]

An unconditional repudiation by either party of some future performance due under the contract, other than the mere payment of money, is a breach of contract. It creates an *immediate* right of action by the other party, even if it takes place long before the time prescribed for the promised performance and before conditions specified in the promise have ever occurred. (*See* Contracts Summary.)

> **e.g.** **Example:** Under the terms of a sales contract for 10,000 #10 widgets, Seller
> agrees to deliver the widgets to Buyer on July 1, at which time Buyer will pay
> for them. On May 15, Buyer tells Seller, "I've decided to discontinue production of
> my product line that requires #10 widgets. So, don't send them—I have no use for
> them." This is an unconditional and unequivocal repudiation of the contract, which
> gives Seller an immediate right of action. Seller does not have to wait until July 1,
> tender the widgets, and then sue if Buyer refuses them.

EXAM TIP **gilbert**

Remember that anticipatory repudiation must be *unequivocal and unconditional*. If not,
no immediate right of action will arise in the other party. Thus, if the party says, "I'm not
sure I'll be able to perform," or "unless demand increases, I may not perform," there is no
anticipatory repudiation and no right of action at this time. (*See* "demand for assurance,"
infra.)

---

2. Rights of Aggrieved Party [§495]

When there is an anticipatory repudiation, the aggrieved party, of course, is under
no obligation to consent to the repudiation of the sales contract.

a. Common law [§496]

At common law, the aggrieved party could always ignore the repudiation and
await performance as agreed.

b. U.C.C. rule [§497]

Under the U.C.C., the aggrieved party may remain inactive only for a *commercially reasonable period of time* and then must take action in *mitigation*. If the
aggrieved party fails to do so, damages are measured as if some mitigation action
had been taken following a commercially reasonable length of time. [U.C.C. §2-610(a)]

c. Remedies for breach [§498]

The aggrieved party is entitled to resort to *any remedy* for breach, and this is
true even if the aggrieved party has notified the repudiating party that the aggrieved party would await the repudiator's performance and has urged retraction of the repudiation. [U.C.C. §2-610(b)]

(1) Seller in process of manufacture [§499]

If the aggrieved party is the seller and is manufacturing goods to the buyer's
order when the buyer repudiates, the seller need not suspend performance.
Rather, the manufacturing process may be completed and the goods may
be *identified* to the contract, *or* the seller may cease manufacture and
resell the product in its current state for scrap or salvage value. [U.C.C.
§2-610(c)—read in conjunction with §2-704(2); *see infra*, §§587-592]

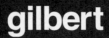

ANTICIPATORY REPUDIATION—RIGHTS OF AGGRIEVED PARTY

gilbert

WHEN THE OTHER PARTY'S WORDS OR ACTIONS OR THE CIRCUMSTANCES MAKE IT CLEAR THAT HE WILL NOT PERFORM, THE AGGRIEVED PARTY MAY:

☑ *Await performance* for a *commercially reasonable time*;

☑ Seek *any remedy for breach*, even if the aggrieved party urged the other to perform; or

☑ *Suspend performance*.

3. Retracting Repudiation [§500]

The repudiating party is free to retract the repudiation and perform the contract as originally agreed, unless the nonrepudiating party has **materially altered** his position in reliance on the repudiation (*e.g.*, by entering into another contract to acquire or dispose of the goods). [U.C.C. §2-611(1)]

a. Method of retraction [§501]

Where retraction is proper, it may be effected by **any method** that clearly indicates to the aggrieved party that the repudiating party now intends to perform as originally promised. [U.C.C. §2-611(2)]

B. Demand for Assurance of Performance

1. Grounds [§502]

Under the U.C.C., **either party** is entitled to demand adequate assurance that performance will be forthcoming when due, if there are **"reasonable grounds" for insecurity** with respect to the other party's performance. [U.C.C. §2-609(1)] Whether a party has reasonable grounds for insecurity is a question of fact.

 Example: Buyer's husband was arrested by a drug task force while in Buyer's automobile, which was briefly impounded and released to Seller with a warning that, if the car were seized again, the task force could not assure Seller that its lien on the car would be protected. Seller refused to release the car to Buyer unless Buyer provided additional security. There was no reason to believe that Buyer's car would be seized again, Seller had done no investigation into Buyer's ability to continue making payments, and Buyer was current on her payments. Therefore, the court held that Seller had no reasonable grounds to retain Buyer's automobile and demand additional assurance of performance from her. [**Ford Motor Credit Co. v. Ellison**, 974 S.W.2d 464 (Ark. 1998)]

a. Insolvency [§503]

This provision is most widely used where one party appears to be tottering on the brink of insolvency. If the "failing party" is the seller, the buyer is not required to wait and hope that needed materials will be delivered—*i.e.*, that the seller will not fail—but rather may demand assurances of performance. Conversely, if it appears that the buyer is about to fail, the seller is under no obligation to deliver goods unless the seller receives reasonable assurance of payment.

b. Distinguish—anticipatory repudiation [§504]

The rules discussed above concerning repudiation are available only where a party has made a *definite repudiation* ("I'm breaching"). Where, however, one party is merely equivocating about whether performance will be forthcoming as agreed ("I'm not sure if we'll be able to meet the deadline"), no *repudiation* occurs. Such language, however, does create reasonable grounds for insecurity (a question of fact) and *triggers the right to demand assurances* under section 2-609.

EXAM TIP   **gilbert**

Be sure that you understand the difference between circumstances giving rise to a right to demand assurances and those constituting anticipatory repudiation. The right to demand assurances arises when there are *reasonable grounds for insecurity*—something makes a party nervous that the other will not perform. Anticipatory repudiation requires much more than nervousness; there must be a *clear indication* that the other party is unwilling or unable to perform. Thus, for example, "I'm not going to perform" is an anticipatory repudiation, but "I'm not sure if I can perform" most likely is only a reason to demand assurances.

---

c. Other grounds [§505]

Request for assurance need not be limited to financial conditions or performance dates. Thus, a buyer might request assurance that the goods will *conform* to the contract if there are reasonable grounds for uncertainty in this regard.

2. Procedure

a. Written demand [§506]

Adequate assurance of due performance *must* be demanded in writing.

b. Adequate assurance [§507]

Upon receipt of the written demand (provided that the necessary grounds are present), the recipient must furnish adequate assurances of due performance within a reasonable time not exceeding 30 days. [U.C.C. §2-609(4)]

c. Right to suspend further performance [§508]

Until assurance is received, the aggrieved party is entitled to suspend any performance for which that party has not already received the agreed return performance. [U.C.C. §2-609(1)] At the end of the "reasonable time" period, failure to supply assurance is a *repudiation* of the contract, and the rules on repudiation (above) then apply. [U.C.C. §2-609(4)]

3. Standards [§509]

If the deal is between *merchants*—and it is in this context that the section is used almost exclusively—the reasonableness of grounds for insecurity and the adequacy of any assurance offered are to be determined in accordance with commercial standards. [U.C.C. §2-609(2)] In other words, the courts do not test grounds or assurances by what they deem is a proper legal standard, but rather, they make the resolution on the basis of factual testimony as to what is *customary in the trade*.

4. Effect of Acceptance or Payment [§510]

Acceptance of any improper delivery or payment does *not* prejudice the aggrieved party's right to demand adequate assurance as to *future* performance. [U.C.C. §2-609(3)]

C. Unforeseen Circumstances—Excuse

1. Doctrine of Commercial Impracticability [§511]

U.C.C. section 2-615 brings into the codified law of Sales the general body of contract law most frequently called *impossibility of performance* or *frustration of purpose*—*i.e.*, for one reason or another, the conditions under which both parties assumed the contract was to be performed fail, and it becomes either impossible or impracticable to perform the contract as contemplated.

2. Requirements [§512]

A seller is entitled to claim excuse by failure of presupposed conditions when:

(i)   *A contingency has occurred*, the *nonoccurrence* of which was a *basic presumption* on which the contract was made; or

(ii) The seller complies in good faith with a foreign or domestic government *regulation* that was promulgated *after the contract was formed*, and the seller is unable to provide a commercially reasonable substitute for the agreed-upon performance.

[U.C.C. §2-615(a)—read in conjunction with §2-614(1)]

EXAM TIP	gilbert

For performance under a contract to be excused, the unforeseen circumstances must have been unforeseen *at the time the contract was made*. If the change was reasonably foreseeable (*e.g.,* a price increase), it will not excuse performance.

3. Application [§513]

There is no definition of "commercial impracticability" in the U.C.C. It is essentially a *question of fact* in each case. So far, the cases have applied the doctrine conservatively.

a. Strikes [§514]

Whether a labor strike justifies nonperformance depends on the expectations of the bargaining parties at the time the contract was entered into, *i.e.*, whether they would have expected the contract to be performed even in the face of such labor difficulties. [**Mishara Construction Co. v. Transit-Mixed Cement Corp.**, 310 N.E.2d 363 (Mass. 1974)]

b. Higher costs [§515]

Mere inflation or skyrocketing costs of performance do *not* justify nonperformance *unless* the variation is so great that no reasonable person would have foreseen such a risk at the time the contract was entered into. [**Transatlantic Financing Corp. v. United States,** 363 F.2d 312 (D.C. Cir. 1966); **Maple Farms, Inc. v. City of Elmira,** 76 Misc. 2d 1080 (1974)—milk supply contract enforced even though supplier's costs, which had never varied by more than 4%, suddenly jumped 23%]

4. No Discharge If Part Performance Possible [§516]

If the seller is able to perform in part, this is required. The seller must *allocate* production and deliveries among all customers in any *fair and reasonable manner* and may also, at the seller's option, include regular customers not then under contract as well as the seller's own requirements for further manufacture. [U.C.C. §2-615(b)]

---

e.g. Example: Due to the energy shortage in the 1970s, Seller lacked sufficient fuel supplies to fill all contracts. This constituted an "unforeseen difficulty excusing Seller from full performance"; *i.e.*, Seller was entitled to prorate the available supply among all regular customers, even those not currently under contract. [**Mansfield Propane Gas Co. v. Folger Gas Co.**, 204 S.E.2d 625 (Ga. 1974)]

---

5. Procedure on Claiming Excuse [§517]

The seller must *notify* the buyer—orally or in writing—that there will be a delay or nondelivery; if there is going to be part performance via an allocation of production, the seller must also advise of the estimated quantity that will be forthcoming. [U.C.C. §2-615(c)]

6. Buyer's Alternatives [§518]

Upon receiving notice of excuse, the buyer may:

(i) *Terminate the contract* as to any *delivery* concerned, and may terminate the *entire contract* where the prospective deficiency "substantially impairs the value of the whole contract" [U.C.C. §2-616(1)(a)]; or

(ii) *Accept a modification* of the contract by agreeing to take any available quota in substitution for the amount originally called for under the contract [U.C.C. §2-616(1)(b)].

a. Note—failure to respond [§519]

If the buyer fails to respond within a reasonable time (not exceeding 30 days), the contract will *automatically lapse* with respect to any deliveries that the seller has indicated will not be made. [U.C.C. §2-616(2)]

7. No Waiver of Rights [§520]

The U.C.C. prohibits any contract clause made in advance that would purportedly "waive" the buyer's rights to terminate, etc. If the seller claims excuse, the buyer cannot be required to stand ready to perform. [U.C.C. §2-616(3)]

a. But note

The seller, however, can effectively waive the right to claim excuse. Thus, for example, if the seller has agreed in advance to fulfill the contract "despite any unforeseen contingencies," the seller is bound no matter what happens. [U.C.C. §2-615]

D. Damage or Destruction of Goods— Risk of Loss

1. Background [§521]

Where the goods are damaged or destroyed prior to delivery *without fault of either party* (*e.g.*, by act of God or some third party's negligence or wrongful act), who bears the loss? Under the Sales Act and the common law, the risk of loss from accidental damage or destruction of the goods was borne by whichever party had *title* to the goods (*see supra,* §357). This proved to be a source of uncertainty and litigation; consequently, this rule has been rejected by the U.C.C. As shown below, the U.C.C. rules as to risk of loss have nothing whatsoever to do with ownership or title to the goods. As a generalization, the U.C.C. rules follow *possession* of the goods, which means that the risk of loss passes from the seller to the buyer *later* than under prior law.

a. Note

The rules in this area presuppose that the damage to the goods was without fault of either party. If a party is at fault in causing damage or destruction, the occurrence has *no effect* on that party's obligations under the contract.

b. And note

Recall that if the contract is for specific existing goods at the time the contract is made and the goods have already been destroyed, there is no contract. (*See supra,* §45.)

2. U.C.C. Rules [§522]

The following are the rules as to when the risk of loss (from *accidental* damage or destruction of the goods) passes from the seller to the buyer.

a. **Risk of loss shifts when parties agree [§523]**

Obviously, if the parties' agreement specifies at what point the risk of loss shifts from the seller to the buyer, it controls. [U.C.C. §2-509(4)] Sometimes the parties' intent will be *implied* from the *nature of the transaction*:

(1) **Sale or return [§524]**

In a sale or return contract, the seller gives the buyer possession of the goods for the purpose of resale. Under this arrangement, the buyer may satisfy the contract either by making payment for the goods or by returning them to the seller. Until they are returned, risk of loss is with the *buyer*, who is in possession. [U.C.C. §2-327(2); *see supra*, §191]

(2) **Sale on approval [§525]**

In a "sale on approval" contract, the seller gives the buyer possession of the goods for a temporary period during which the buyer will decide whether or not to keep them. Under this arrangement, the risk of loss remains with the *seller* until the buyer signals acceptance of the goods. (Obviously, the result is contra where loss is the buyer's fault.) [U.C.C. §2-327(1); *see supra*, §§195-197]

b. **When parties have not agreed [§526]**

In absence of agreement, the following rules apply, basically turning on who has *control* of the goods:

(1) **Where goods are shipped via carrier [§527]**

If the contract authorizes or requires the seller to ship the goods to the buyer via common carrier (as opposed to delivering them in the seller's own trucks), the rule depends on whether the contract is a "shipment" or "destination" contract.

(a) **"Shipment contracts" [§528]**

If the contract is a "shipment contract" (*i.e.*, merely requires the seller to place the goods in the hands of a carrier and not to deliver them at any particular destination), the risk of loss passes to the buyer *on delivery of conforming goods to the carrier*. [U.C.C. §2-509(1)(a)]

1) **Application**

This covers the following types of contracts: F.O.B. origin, F.A.S. vessel, C.I.F., and C. & F. (*see supra*, §§381-389).

2) **Note**

It is immaterial who pays the freight charges; it is also immaterial that seller shipped under reservation (retaining title to insure payment of purchase price; *see supra*, §395).

(b) **"Destination contracts" [§529]**

On the other hand, if the contract is a "destination contract" (*i.e.*, requires the seller to deliver the goods to a particular destination), the risk of loss passes to the buyer only when the goods *arrive* at the destination *and* are duly *tendered* to the buyer in a manner sufficient to enable the buyer to take delivery. [U.C.C. §2-509(1)(b)]

1) Application

This covers F.O.B. *destination* contracts (*see supra*, §385). For example, if the contract's delivery term says that the price is "$5,000 F.O.B. buyer's warehouse," the parties have agreed upon a *destination* contract, and the price mentioned includes the cost *and risk* of getting the goods to the buyer.

(c) Construction in favor of "shipment contracts" [§530]

In practice, contracts calling for shipment of goods via carrier are usually "shipment contracts"; destination contracts are unusual. Unless the contract *expressly* contains an "F.O.B. destination" delivery term or the equivalent, it will be construed as a *shipment contract*, so that the seller's risk ends on delivery to the carrier. [**Eberhard Manufacturing Co. v. Brown,** 232 N.W.2d 378 (Mich. 1975)]

(2) Where goods held by bailee [§531]

Where goods are held by a bailee, when risk of loss passes depends on the document of title.

(a) Negotiable document of title [§532]

If, at the time of the sales contract, the goods are in the hands of a bailee (*e.g.*, a carrier or warehouser), are covered by a negotiable document of title (*e.g.*, a negotiable warehouse receipt), and are to be sold without being moved, then risk of loss passes to the buyer only on *receipt of the negotiable document of title* covering the goods. [U.C.C. §2-509(2)(a)]

(b) Nonnegotiable document of title [§533]

If the goods are in the possession of a bailee and are covered by a nonnegotiable document of title, then risk of loss passes to the buyer on receipt of the nonnegotiable document of title *or other written directions* from the seller to the bailee authorizing delivery of the goods to the buyer. [U.C.C. §2-509(2)(c)]

(c) No document of title [§534]

If the goods are in the possession of a bailee but are not covered by any document of title, negotiable or otherwise, then risk of loss passes from the seller to the buyer when the bailee *tenders* the goods *or otherwise acknowledges* that the buyer is entitled to immediate possession of the goods. [U.C.C. §2-509(2)(b)]

RISK OF LOSS IF GOODS HELD BY BAILEE	gilbert

DOCUMENT OF TITLE	WHEN RISK OF LOSS PASSES
NEGOTIABLE DOCUMENT OF TITLE	***On Buyer's receipt*** of the negotiable document of title
NONNEGOTIABLE DOCUMENT OF TITLE	***On Buyer's receipt*** of the nonnegotiable document of title or ***other written directions*** from Seller authorizing delivery
NO DOCUMENT OF TITLE	When bailee ***tenders the goods*** or otherwise ***acknowledges*** Buyer's right to immediate possession

(3) In all other nonbreach situations ("catch-all rule") [§535]

Innumerable situations may arise in which neither of the foregoing rules applies (*e.g.*, where the seller is to deliver possession directly to the buyer without a third-party carrier). Generally, risk of loss in such cases depends on whether the seller is a "merchant." If the seller is a merchant, risk of loss passes to the buyer only when the buyer actually ***receives*** (takes physical possession of) the goods. If the seller is *not* a merchant, risk of loss passes to the buyer on mere ***tender of delivery*** by the seller. [U.C.C. §2-509(3)]

Example: Seller is engaged in the business of selling used industrial machinery (*i.e.*, Seller is a "merchant"). Buyer orders a lathe from Seller, to be picked up by Buyer at Seller's warehouse. The night before Buyer is able to collect the lathe, a fire destroys Seller's warehouse. The risk of loss remained on Seller: Seller is a merchant, and Buyer has not yet received the goods. [**Ellis v. Bell Aerospace Corp.,** 315 F. Supp. 221 (D. Or. 1970)]

Compare: Seller and Buyer are both accountants. Seller agreed to sell Buyer his Chevrolet. Seller gives Buyer the keys and tells her that the Chevrolet is in Seller's garage and can be picked up by Buyer at any time. That night, before Buyer can collect the car, a fire destroys the garage and the car along with it. The risk of loss is on Buyer since Seller is not a merchant and has tendered delivery.

(a) Rationale

The reason for the difference in treatment between merchant and nonmerchant sellers is that merchants are more likely to carry ***insurance*** (and hence they should bear risk longer). [U.C.C. §2-509, Official Comment 3]

(b) 2003 revision—no distinction for merchants [§536]

The revision drops any distinction between merchant sellers and non-merchant ones, and provides a default rule that in all cases risk of loss passes to the buyer *on receipt* of the goods.

(4) Different rules apply where party in breach [§537]

The rules above presuppose that neither party was in breach at the time of the accidental damage or destruction of the goods. The results are different if the seller or the buyer was in *default* at such time.

(a) Seller's shipment of nonconforming goods [§538]

If the goods shipped by the seller so fail to conform to the contract as to give the buyer the right to reject them, the risk of loss remains with the *seller* until cure or acceptance. [U.C.C. §2-510(1)]

1) Buyer rejects [§539]

As discussed earlier, in single-delivery contracts, *any* defect justifies buyer's rejection; whereas in installment contracts, there is no right to reject unless the defect *substantially impairs* the value of the goods tendered. [U.C.C. §§2-601, 2-612; *see supra*, §§465-482] The risk of loss remains with the seller only if the goods have been properly rejected.

2) Buyer revokes acceptance [§540]

A similar rule applies where the buyer discovered the defects in the goods only after accepting them, and the defect is so substantial that it justifies the buyer's *revocation of acceptance* (*see supra*, §483). In such a case, the risk of loss is treated as having been *on the seller from the beginning* (to the extent that it is not otherwise covered by the buyer's insurance). [U.C.C. §2-510(2)]

(b) Buyer's repudiation [§541]

Where the seller has shipped *conforming* goods (*i.e.*, is not in breach), but the buyer has *wrongfully repudiated* (or otherwise breached before the risk of loss has passed to the buyer) and the goods are damaged and not covered by the seller's insurance, the seller may treat the risk of loss as resting on the *buyer* "for a commercially reasonable period of time." [U.C.C. §2-510(3)]

 Example: Buyer orders goods to be manufactured by Seller and shipped to Buyer. Just prior to shipment, Buyer repudiates. The goods are destroyed by lightning the following day. The loss falls on Buyer since the repudiation prevented the shipment that would have shifted the loss per the contract.

---

1) Note—only applicable to uninsured sellers [§542]

The above rule applies only where the seller is *uninsured* and has otherwise acted in a *commercially reasonable manner*. Thus, in the example above, if Buyer had repudiated and Seller had retained the goods for an indefinite period of time, Seller could not claim protection hereunder. At the end of a commercially reasonable period of time, a seller still in possession of the goods *regains* the risk of loss even though completely uninsured.

3. Right to Sue Third Parties for Damage to Goods [§543]

Third parties—carriers and warehousers, for instance—sometimes are responsible for loss of or damage to goods. The question then arises whether the buyer or seller (or both) have the right to sue for such loss or damage.

a. Prior law [§544]

At common law and under the Sales Act, the right to sue followed title. If title was in the seller, the seller could sue; if title had passed to the buyer, only the buyer could maintain the action.

b. U.C.C. rule [§545]

The U.C.C. provides that until the goods are *identified* to the contract, only the *seller* has the right to sue third parties for injuries to them. However, once identification occurs, the buyer gets a "special property" or "insurable interest" in the goods (*see supra*, §372), and thus obtains a right of action against third parties. The seller who reserves a "security interest" in goods to secure the buyer's performance (*see supra*, §395) may also maintain such an action, even though the seller no longer has possession. [U.C.C. §2-722(a)]

(1) Consent [§546]

Either party may, with the consent of the other, sue for the benefit of whomever it may concern. [U.C.C. §2-722(c)]

(2) Right to recovery [§547]

The *party who bears the risk of loss* has the primary right to sue and retain whatever is recovered, since obviously the loss is that person's—any recoveries to offset the loss should belong to that person as well. However, if the plaintiff in the suit against the third party is not the party who bears the risk of loss, and the plaintiff has not made specific arrangements with the other party with respect to splitting the recovery, then anything obtained by way of judgment or settlement in excess of the plaintiff's own interest must be held for the benefit of the other party. [U.C.C. §2-722(b)]

Chapter Eight: Remedies

CONTENTS

Chapter Approach

Whenever a breach occurs, either the buyer or the seller (whoever is the aggrieved party) will take remedial action. Therefore, whenever your question involves a breach of contract, you need to consider the remedies available to the injured party. Some of the remedies available have been covered in other chapters (*e.g.,* the buyer's right of rejection or revocation of acceptance; *see supra,* §§465, 483), but the bulk of the remedial rules are contained in this chapter.

To begin your analysis, ask yourself:

1. **Who Is the Injured Party?**
   The U.C.C. divides the law of remedies according to whether the seller or the buyer is the injured party.

2. **Have the Goods Been Accepted?**
   The Code further subdivides remedies depending on whether the goods have been "accepted" (*see supra,* §§440 *et seq.*). Once the goods have been accepted, the seller sues for the price; the buyer sues for damages for loss of the bargain. If the goods have not been accepted, the seller can resell the goods and the buyer can "cover" by making a substitute purchase.

3. **Can the Parties Take Action Prior to Litigation?**
   The seller can reclaim the goods, stop their delivery, or cease their manufacture. The buyer can reject or revoke acceptance, or set off damages when making payment.

A. Seller's Prelitigation Remedies

1. **U.C.C. Provides Remedies for Sellers [§548]**
   Various remedies are provided under the U.C.C. to protect a seller who, although under an obligation to deliver goods to the buyer, has either not been paid or has good reason to believe that there will be no payment.

2. **Right to Withhold Delivery or Demand Cash Payment [§549]**
   At common law (and under the Sales Act), the seller was deemed to have an implied-in-law "lien" on the goods as security for the unpaid purchase price. The U.C.C. abandons any such notion, and instead simply provides that, under appropriate circumstances, a seller is entitled to *withhold delivery* of the goods [U.C.C. §2-703(a)] or *demand cash payment* for them notwithstanding an earlier agreement for credit [U.C.C. §2-702(1)].

a. **Circumstances authorizing demand of cash [§550]**

If the buyer becomes *insolvent* and the seller *learns* of the insolvency, then irrespective of any credit term in the contract, the seller is privileged to demand payment in cash. This includes payment for goods previously delivered *and* for goods delivered thereafter, and the seller may withhold future deliveries until cash payment is forthcoming. [U.C.C. §2-702(1)]

b. **Circumstances authorizing withholding of delivery [§551]**

In addition, an unpaid seller who is still in possession of the goods may withhold delivery when the buyer (i) wrongfully *rejects*, (ii) *rescinds* (*i.e.*, revokes acceptance), (iii) *fails to make a payment* when due, or (iv) *anticipatorily breaches* the contract. [U.C.C. §2-703(a); **Portal Galleries, Inc. v. Tomar Products Inc.,** 60 Misc. 2d 523 (1969)]

(1) **Note—seller must have possession**

The seller loses the right to withhold delivery once the buyer gets possession of the goods. However, the seller then acquires another right—reclamation, which is also of great significance (*see* below).

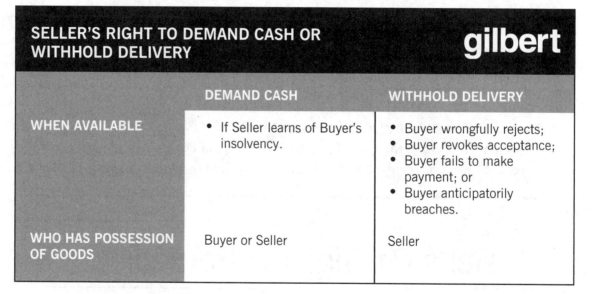

SELLER'S RIGHT TO DEMAND CASH OR WITHHOLD DELIVERY		**gilbert**
	DEMAND CASH	**WITHHOLD DELIVERY**
WHEN AVAILABLE	• If Seller learns of Buyer's insolvency.	• Buyer wrongfully rejects; • Buyer revokes acceptance; • Buyer fails to make payment; or • Buyer anticipatorily breaches.
WHO HAS POSSESSION OF GOODS	Buyer or Seller	Seller

3. **Reclamation of Goods**

a. **Prior law [§552]**

At common law and under the Sales Act, where the buyer obtained possession of the goods by defrauding or deceiving the seller (*e.g.*, by misrepresenting ability to pay), the unpaid seller's lien (discussed above) could be asserted against the buyer and any successor in interest of the buyer, except a bona fide purchaser. [**Ogden v. Cudworth,** 154 N.E. 755 (Mass. 1927)]

b. **U.C.C. rule [§553]**

Building on the above scheme, the U.C.C. recognizes an unpaid seller's right to reclaim goods in two situations: (i) *cash sales*—where the buyer pays by check at the time of delivery, but the check is returned for insufficient funds [U.C.C.

§2-507(2), *see supra*, §171]; and (ii) *credit sales*—where, after delivery of the goods to the buyer, the seller discovers that the buyer is *insolvent* [U.C.C. §2-702(2)]. In a cash sale, the seller may reclaim the goods regardless of whether the buyer is insolvent. In either situation, the seller may reclaim the goods by *demanding their return within 10 days* after the buyer receives them. [U.C.C. §2-702(2)]

(1) Buyer's insolvency [§554]

The seller's right to reclaim exists in all cases where the buyer is *in fact insolvent* at the time goods are *received*. This is true regardless of whether the buyer knew or should have known of the insolvency, or whether the buyer made any representations at all to the seller with respect to financial condition.

(a) Effect of misrepresentation as to solvency [§555]

If the buyer misrepresents solvency to the *particular* seller, *in writing*, within three months prior to the delivery in question, then the 10-day limit on demand for reclamation (above) does not apply. The seller has a *reasonable time* in which to demand reclamation. [U.C.C. §2-702(2)]

1) Note

Some courts hold that the buyer's check satisfies the requirement of a written representation of solvency.

2) 2003 revision variation—no misrepresentation required [§556]

Under the revision there is no 10-day rule, but instead the seller can demand return within a *reasonable time* after the buyer's receipt of the goods. The revision also drops any special rule about misrepresentation of solvency (thus bringing the Code into conformity with a similar provision in the Bankruptcy Code, which also lacks this exception). [U.C.C. §2R-702(2); 11 U.S.C. §546(c)]

(b) "Insolvency" defined [§557]

A person is insolvent within the U.C.C. meaning of the word if that person has ceased to pay debts in the ordinary course of business, cannot pay debts as they become due, *or* is insolvent within the meaning of the Federal Bankruptcy Act. [U.C.C. §1-201(23)] (A person is insolvent under the Federal Bankruptcy Act whenever liabilities exceed assets.) [11 U.S.C. §101(32)]

(c) Cash sales—no requirement of insolvency [§558]

Remember that where a cash sale is involved, if the buyer pays by check and the check bounces, the seller can reclaim the goods *regardless of the buyer's solvency*. [U.C.C. §2-507(2), *supra*, §177]

(2) Enforcement of right [§559]

The right of reclamation is exercised by a *written demand* for return of the goods. If the buyer refuses to honor the demand, then *an action for possession* of personal property—replevin or claim and delivery—will lie to recover it.

(a) No self-help [§560]

"Self-help" is not authorized. Unless the buyer voluntarily turns the goods over to the seller, the seller must institute appropriate legal actions or proceedings.

(b) Need not obtain goods within ten days [§561]

The seller need only make written *demand* within the 10-day period. He does not lose the right to reclaim merely by failing to obtain the goods within the specified time.

(3) Reclamation as election of remedies [§562]

Successful reclamation of goods *excludes all other remedies*. [U.C.C. §2-702(3)] The seller cannot thereafter sue for loss of profits on the sale. The theory here is that whenever the buyer is insolvent, the seller is lucky to get the goods back.

EXAM TIP   gilbert

This bears repeating: If the seller successfully exercises the right of reclamation, he *cannot* sue for damages. Thus, on an exam, remember that once the seller reclaims the goods, he has *no further options* against the buyer.

---

(4) Rights of third parties

(a) Bona fide purchasers [§563]

Transfer to a bona fide purchaser ("BFP") *cuts off* the seller's right of reclamation. Thus, if the buyer has transferred possession of the goods to a purchaser for value without notice of the seller's rights, the BFP prevails over the seller as to possession of the goods. [U.C.C. §2-702(3)]

(b) Secured creditors [§564]

A secured creditor who advanced money in the past and obtained a *perfected security interest* covering the debtor's *after-acquired* goods is generally treated as a "good faith purchaser" under U.C.C. section 2-702(3), and therefore prevails against the unpaid seller of the goods who attempts to reclaim them. [*In re* **Samuels**, *supra*, §184]

1) Effect [§565]

The seller's right of reclamation simply is not worth very much where the buyer of the goods is engaged in financing the acquisition of inventory. Lenders routinely require that inventory loans cover present *and future* inventory, and hence they will prevail against the supplier of the inventory, even in a supposedly "cash" sale (where an insufficient funds check is given). [*In re* **Samuels,** *supra*]

(c) Trustee in bankruptcy—not a BFP [§566]

The trustee in bankruptcy of the buyer is *not* given the status of a BFP of the goods, and hence cannot cut off the seller's right of reclamation under section 2-702. The Bankruptcy Code gives explicit relief to the reclaiming seller. It provides for reclamation of goods sold to an insolvent buyer if the seller makes a *written demand* therefor *within 45 days* of delivery, and this right *prevails* even over the trustee in bankruptcy of the buyer. [11 U.S.C. §546(c)]

THIRD PARTY'S RIGHTS VS. SELLER'S RIGHT OF RECLAMATION

gilbert

THIRD PARTIES	WILL THEY PREVAIL OVER A SELLER'S RIGHT OF RECLAMATION?
BONA FIDE PURCHASERS	Yes.
SECURED CREDITORS	Yes, if the secured party has a *perfected* security interest that covers *after-acquired* goods.
TRUSTEE IN BANKRUPTCY	No, as long as the seller's *written demand* is made within *45 days* of delivery of the goods at issue.

---

4. Stoppage in Transit

a. Nature of right [§567]

Once the goods have been delivered to a carrier for shipment to the buyer, the unpaid seller cannot withhold delivery. However, a seller in such a position may have the right to stop the goods while they are in transit and resume possession thereof. This puts the seller back in the position he was in before the goods were delivered to the carrier, *i.e.,* having the right to withhold delivery, to demand payment, etc. (*see* above).

b. Grounds for exercising right

(1) Buyer's insolvency discovered after shipment [§568]

The most frequently encountered situation occurs when the seller ships goods to the buyer on credit, and then, while the goods are still "in transit," the seller discovers that the buyer is or has become insolvent. [U.C.C. §2-705(1)]

(a) **Distinguish**

If the seller had learned of the buyer's insolvency *prior to shipment*, the seller would have had the right to refuse shipment and demand cash payment. [U.C.C. §2-702(1)—*see* above] Having only learned of the buyer's insolvency after shipment, but before arrival of the goods, the seller is still afforded protection by the right of stoppage in transit.

(b) **But note**

Of course, if the seller *knew* of the buyer's insolvency prior to shipment, and still shipped the goods to the buyer on credit, the seller would thereby *waive* any right to demand cash or to stop the goods once shipped.

(2) **Buyer's repudiation of large order [§569]**

Another ground for exercising the right of stoppage occurs when truckloads, planeloads, or larger shipments of express or freight are involved (in short, *big shipments*) and the buyer repudiates the contract, fails to make a payment due, or where for any other reason the seller would have had the right to withhold or reclaim the goods. [U.C.C. §2-705(1)]

(a) **Note—buyer's solvency not at issue [§570]**

In these cases, the right to stoppage in transit may be exercised regardless of buyer's solvency.

(b) **2003 revision—abandons requirement of big shipment [§571]**

The revision drops this big shipment requirement, and allows stoppage in transit in *all* cases where the buyer is insolvent, fails to make payment, or where for any reason the seller has a right to withhold or reclaim the goods. [U.C.C. §2R-705(1)]

c. **Goods must be "in transit" [§572]**

For the seller to exercise the right to stop delivery, the goods must be "in transit." This means that the seller may stop delivery until transit ends in one of the following ways:

(1) **Transit ends on buyer's receipt of goods [§573]**

Goods are in transit from the time they are delivered to a carrier for the purpose of transmission to the buyer until the buyer is in "receipt" of them. [U.C.C. §2-705(2)] "Receipt" means taking *physical possession*. [U.C.C. §2-103(1)(c)]

Example—delivery of goods: Where goods have arrived at their destination but have *not yet been delivered* by the carrier to the buyer, they are still in transit. [*In re* **Growe Construction Co.**, 256 F. 907 (N.D.N.Y. 1919)]

> **e.g.** **Example—rejection of goods:** If the goods have been *rejected* by the buyer and the carrier retains possession of them, the goods are still in transit.

(2) Transit ends on bailee's acknowledgment [§574]

Transit ends whenever, *after* the goods arrive at their appointed destination, a bailee acknowledges holding the goods *on behalf* of the buyer. [U.C.C. §2-705(2)(b)]

(a) Contrast "carrier" and "bailee" [§575]

The U.C.C. distinguishes between carriers and bailees in determining transit. Thus, as long as the carrier holds the goods *as a carrier*, they are still in transit; but if the carrier is holding the goods as a warehouser, and acknowledges holding them for the buyer, then transit ceases.

> **e.g.** **Example:** If the goods are to arrive at New York and the carrier has them at a New York terminal and advises Buyer that the goods are being held for Buyer, the goods are still in transit. However, if the carrier maintains a warehouse in New York and stores the goods as a warehouser after advising Buyer that the goods are being held for Buyer, this terminates transit under the U.C.C. [U.C.C. §2-705(2)]

(3) Transit ends when carrier becomes agent of buyer [§576]

Where the buyer contacts the carrier and orders the goods rerouted *after* they have arrived at the destination to which they were shipped by the seller, and the carrier does so, the seller can no longer exercise the right of stoppage in transit. Under the U.C.C., the carrier in this position is called a "carrier by reshipment," and becomes the agent of the *buyer* rather than the agent of the seller. [U.C.C. §2-705(2)(c)]

(4) Other scenarios [§577]

The U.C.C. also provides that transit ceases at any time that a *negotiable document of title* covering the goods is negotiated to the buyer. [U.C.C. §2-705(2)(d)] Also, transit ends if the carrier *wrongfully refuses to deliver* the goods to the buyer (*i.e.,* the carrier's wrongful act does not enlarge the seller's right of stoppage). [*In re* **White**, 205 F. 393 (M.D. Pa. 1913)]

EXAM TIP	gilbert

Remember to closely examine the *role* being played by a carrier in a question about the right to stop delivery. A carrier is not always just a carrier, but may become a *bailee or an agent*. If this occurs, there is no longer a right to stop delivery.

d. **Manner of exercising right of stoppage [§578]**

The seller may exercise the right of stoppage by giving *notice to the carrier* who has possession of the goods to stop delivery. [U.C.C. §2-705(3)(a)]

(1) **Notice—sufficient to prevent delivery [§579]**

The seller's notice must be given under such circumstances that the carrier may, by reasonable diligence, prevent delivery of the goods. Thus, if the goods are in transit across country, the notice must be given in sufficient time to enable the carrier to locate the goods and notify those at the other end to hold up the delivery.

(2) **Expense borne by seller [§580]**

All expenses of redelivering the goods to the seller must be borne by the seller. [U.C.C. §2-705(3)(b)] It is immaterial that they were shipped freight collect. [**Poole v. Houston & T.C. Railway,** 58 Tex. 134 (1882)]

e. **Effect of exercise of right**

(1) **Duties of carrier generally [§581]**

Where the right of stoppage has been properly exercised by the seller, the carrier must hold and deliver the goods according to the seller's directions. [U.C.C. §2-705(3)(b)]

(a) **Limitation [§582]**

If the carrier has issued a *negotiable bill of lading* or other negotiable document of title representing the goods, the carrier is not obliged to redeliver the goods to the seller unless the negotiable bill is first surrendered for cancellation. [U.C.C. §§2-705(3)(c), 7-303]

(b) **Remedies [§583]**

If the carrier fails to comply with a proper notice of stoppage, the carrier is liable to the seller for conversion. On the other hand, if the carrier accedes to a *wrongful* stop notice, the carrier may be liable to the buyer for refusal to deliver the goods. [**Missouri Pacific Railway v. Heidenheimer,** 17 S.W. 608 (Tex. 1891)] Accordingly, where the buyer disputes the seller's notice of stoppage, the carrier will usually protect itself by filing an *interpleader* action. (*See* Civil Procedure Summary.) In any event, the seller must indemnify the carrier for any damages recovered by the buyer. [U.C.C. §2-705, Official Comment 1]

(2) **Exception—sale to buyer in the ordinary course of business [§584]**

If the buyer sells the goods to a buyer in the ordinary course of business *while the goods are in transit*, the second buyer cuts off the seller's right of stoppage. [U.C.C. §2-403(2)]

(a) **Negotiable bill of lading [§585]**

Similarly, where a negotiable bill of lading covering the goods has been issued by the carrier, and the buyer has obtained the bill and negotiated it to a bona fide purchaser, this also will cut off the seller's right of stoppage. [U.C.C. §7-502(2)]

1) And note

This is true whether the bill was negotiated to the bona fide purchaser *before or after* the seller had notified the carrier to stop in transit (*see* above).

(b) Distinguish—creditors [§586]

However, the buyer's creditors are *not* bona fide purchasers and therefore can reach only whatever interest the buyer has in the goods. Thus, where the seller has properly exercised a right of stoppage, the buyer's creditors *cannot* levy on the goods.

5. Identifying Conforming Goods and Salvaging Unfinished Goods [§587]

The seller's primary prelitigation remedy is to resell the goods. However, before the seller can do so, the goods must be "identified" to the contract. Recall that identification consists either of contracting with reference to specific goods (*e.g.*, "this horse") or of designating (by the seller's action) certain goods as being those to be delivered in performance of the contract. [U.C.C. §2-501(1), *see supra*, §§361-362] If the buyer breaches and the seller still has possession of conforming goods not yet identified to the contract or goods in the process of manufacture, what should the seller do?

a. Designating conforming finished goods [§588]

If the seller is in possession or control of conforming goods on learning of the buyer's breach, the seller may *identify the goods* to the contract regardless of their resalability. [U.C.C. §2-704(1)(a)]

Example: Buyer orders 100 cases of dog food from Seller. Seller has 10,000 cases of dog food in a warehouse suitable for delivery in fulfillment of the contract. Buyer then advises Seller that Buyer will not perform. Seller may segregate 100 cases of dog food and mark them as being held for performance of the contract with Buyer. This puts Seller in a position to resell the 100 cases of dog food and recover any difference between the contract price and the resale price.

---

b. Unfinished goods

(1) Identification for resale purposes [§589]

If the goods are in the process of manufacture but are not complete at the time the seller learns of the buyer's breach, the seller may, if the seller so chooses, stop the manufacturing process and identify the goods *in their incomplete state* as those intended under the contract and therefore subject to the right of resale. [U.C.C. §2-704(1)(b)]

(a) Limitation [§590]

The seller may identify incomplete goods as the subject of resale only where the goods are "*demonstrably intended for the particular contract*" (*e.g.,* imprinted calendars).

(2) Completion of manufacture [§591]

Alternatively, the seller may, in the exercise of "*reasonable commercial judgment*" and for the purposes of avoiding loss and of realization of top value, complete the manufacturing process and then identify the completed goods to the contract. [U.C.C. §2-704(2)]

(a) But note

If the seller completes manufacture and in doing so *increases* the damages that the buyer must pay (*i.e.,* adds manufacturing costs that could have been avoided if the goods had been left unfinished), the seller can recover the enhanced damages only if the completion of manufacture was done in the exercise of reasonable commercial judgment.

(3) Salvage [§592]

If the goods are unfinished when the seller learns of the buyer's breach, the seller is also privileged to cease manufacture and resell the unfinished goods for *scrap or salvage value.* [U.C.C. §2-704(2)] Again, the seller can do so only on the exercise of *reasonable commercial judgment* for the purpose of avoiding loss. However, it is unlikely that a court will attempt to "second guess" the seller unless the seller blatantly was acting in bad faith, as to which the buyer would have the burden of proof. [U.C.C. §2-704, Official Comment 2]

6. Resale [§593]

The most logical thing for a seller to do when in possession of goods that the buyer has refused to accept is to resell them and then sue the buyer for any loss sustained by the seller on the resale. The U.C.C. recognizes this course of action and expressly provides that where the seller resells the goods, the seller may recover as damages the difference between the *resale price and the contract price* (less any expenses saved in consequence of the buyer's breach). Of course, the resale must be made in *good faith* and in a *commercially reasonable manner.* [U.C.C. §2-706(1)] (The important point is that the seller is *not* limited by the "market value.") [*See* further discussion of damages, *infra,* §§625 *et seq.*]

a. Public vs. private sale [§594]

The seller has the option to resell at either a public sale (*i.e.,* an auction) or a private sale. [U.C.C. §2-706(2)]

(1) Notice of sale [§595]

In either case, the buyer must be given reasonable notification of the intention to resell. [U.C.C. §2-706(3)] If a *public* sale is contemplated, the seller must also advise the buyer of the time and place of sale, unless the goods are *perishable* or threaten to decline speedily in value, in which case the notice requirement is waived. [U.C.C. §2-706(4)(b)]

(a) Note

Failure to give proper notice results in a denial of any further damages (the "deficiency").

EXAM TIP	**gilbert**

If you see a question where the seller sells goods after buyer breaches, be sure to check the facts about the sale carefully to see if *notice* was given for a *public sale*. If not, the sale is improper, *unless* the goods are *perishable* (*e.g.,* fresh fish or vegetables) or otherwise will quickly *decline in value* (*e.g.,* "championship" T-shirts just before the Superbowl), because in those cases, notice will be excused.

---

(2) Conduct of sale [§596]

Resale of goods, public or private, may be as one unit, or the goods may be sold in parcels. The method, manner, time, and terms of sale may be chosen by the seller, again subject only to the control that all conduct be *commercially reasonable*. [U.C.C. §2-706(2)]

(a) Goods available for inspection [§597]

At a *public* sale, the goods must be in view of those attending the sale or, if not, the advance notice of sale must state the place where the goods are located and provide for their reasonable inspection by prospective bidders. [U.C.C. §2-706(4)(c)]

(b) Resale tied to breach [§598]

The resale, public *or* private, must be reasonably identified as referring to the broken contract. [U.C.C. §2-706(2)]

REQUIREMENTS FOR RESALE OF GOODS—A COMPARISON		**gilbert**
	PUBLIC SALE	**PRIVATE SALE**
IS REASONABLE NOTICE TO THE BUYER REQUIRED?	YES, and notice must include *time* and *place* of sale	YES
MUST THE GOODS BE AVAILABLE FOR INSPECTION?	YES	NO
MUST THE SALE BE IDENTIFIED AS THE RESULT OF THE BROKEN CONTRACT?	YES	YES
IS THE SELLER PERMITTED TO BUY THE GOODS?	YES	NO

---

(3) Right of seller to purchase at sale [§599]

The seller is permitted to buy at a *public* sale, but not a private sale. The idea is that a public sale (*i.e.*, an auction) by its very nature allows public scrutiny of what goes on, an attribute missing in private sales. [U.C.C. §2-706(4)(d)]

b. Title of third party purchaser [§600]

The person to whom the seller resells the goods gets valid title as against the original buyer. [U.C.C. §2-706(5)]

(1) Effect of seller's noncompliance with resale requirements [§601]

The seller's failure to comply with the requirements of section 2-706 does *not* affect a third person's title as against the original buyer. However, it may render the seller liable for *damages* sustained by the original buyer.

c. Profit on resale [§602]

If the seller obtains more on the resale than the original contract price, the seller *may keep the excess* and need *not* account to the buyer therefor. [U.C.C. §2-706(6)]

7. Cancellation [§603]

The final prelitigation remedy afforded the seller by the U.C.C. is to "cancel" the contract [U.C.C. §2-703(f)], cancellation being defined as putting "an end to the contract for reason of breach" [U.C.C. §2-106(4)].

a. Distinguish—rescission [§604]

The U.C.C. avoids the word "rescission" because of the common law election of remedies doctrine, which holds that a seller who rescinds a contract has elected to pursue a remedy inconsistent with any claim for damages. Forswearing the election of remedies doctrine, the Code provides that the seller who cancels a contract is *not* deemed to have elected any remedy, but "retains any remedy for breach of the whole contract or any unperformed balance." [U.C.C. §2-106(4)]

8. Remedies of Third Parties [§605]

Various of the seller's remedies described above may also be exercised by third parties who are financing the particular sales transaction or who otherwise have a financial interest in the sale.

a. Financing agencies [§606]

Where a bank, finance company, or other lender has advanced funds by purchasing or paying a draft drawn by the seller against the buyer (*see supra*, §399), the financing agent acquires not only rights in the draft, but also the rights of the seller-shipper *in the goods* that are the subject of the sale. This includes the right to stop delivery on learning of buyer's insolvency and the right to reclaim the goods. [U.C.C. §2-506(1)]

b. "Person in position of a seller" [§607]

The U.C.C. uses the term "person in position of a seller" to cover an *agent* who has paid or become liable for the price of goods on behalf of the principal or anyone who otherwise holds a *security interest* or right in the goods similar to that of a seller. [U.C.C. §2-707(1)] Such a person has the right to withhold or stop delivery of the goods and to recover incidental damages, but has no other remedies or rights in the goods. [U.C.C. §2-702(2)]

REMEDY	WHEN AVAILABLE	WHO HAS POSSESSION OF GOODS
DEMAND CASH PAYMENT	When Seller learns of Buyer's *insolvency*	Buyer or Seller
WITHHOLD DELIVERY	When Buyer *wrongfully rejects, revokes acceptance, fails to pay,* or *anticipatorily breaches*	Seller
RECLAIM GOODS	In *credit sales*, when Seller learns of Buyer's *insolvency* and demands return within 10 days in writing	Buyer
STOP TRANSIT OF GOODS	When Seller learns of Buyer's *insolvency*, or when Buyer repudiates large shipments, *while goods are in transit*	Carrier
IDENTIFY CONFORMING OR UNFINISHED GOODS	When Seller learns of Buyer's *breach*—unfinished goods may be identified in uncompleted state, finished if commercially reasonable to do so, or sold for scrap	Seller
RESELL GOODS	When Seller learns of Buyer's *breach*—sale must be in good faith and commercially reasonable	Seller
CANCEL CONTRACT	When Seller learns of Buyer's *material breach*, including a repudiation	Seller

B. Buyer's Prelitigation Remedies

1. Sale of Goods to Recover Prepayments [§608]

A buyer who has prepaid all or part of the purchase price and has received goods that do not conform to the contract is in a position substantially similar to that of an unpaid seller still in possession of goods. Therefore, the U.C.C. gives the buyer a *security interest* in the goods for the amount of the prepayment, and provides that if the buyer appropriately *offers to restore* the seller's goods and *demands repayment* of the price paid, and the seller then refuses, the buyer may sell the goods. [U.C.C. §2-711(3)]

a. Note—acceptance irrelevant [§609]

This right exists regardless of whether the buyer ever accepted the goods (*i.e.*, buyer may have rejected them upon receipt, but still be in possession).

b. Excess proceeds returned to seller [§610]

Unlike an unpaid seller, however, the buyer has only a security interest in the goods and therefore must remit to the seller the proceeds from the resale in excess of the buyer's prepayments plus any *costs* incurred in handling, storing, and reselling the goods. [U.C.C. §2-711(3)]

2. Cover [§611]

The most important remedy afforded to a buyer by the U.C.C. is the right to "cover"—to go out into the market and *purchase substitute goods*. As long as the buyer acts reasonably, the buyer can then sue the seller for any excess of the cover price over the contract price (even if the cover price is more than the market price; *see infra*, §656). [U.C.C. §2-712(1)]

a. "Substitute goods" [§612]

Cover involves the procurement of substitute goods. There is no requirement that the buyer purchase precisely the same thing ordered from the seller. However, as a practical matter, it is better for the buyer to do so, since then damages can be more easily determined. However, if precisely the same commodity is unavailable, the purchase of *any commercially reasonable substitute* will be regarded as a cover for U.C.C. purposes. Thus, if the buyer acts reasonably and in good faith, the recovery will be the difference between the cost of the substitute and the contract price—even if this was not the cheapest or most effective substitute that could have been used. [**Farmer's Union Co-op Co. v. Flamme Bros.**, 245 N.W.2d 464 (Neb. 1976)]

b. Cover must be timely [§613]

The cover must be made "*without unreasonable delay*." [U.C.C. §2-712(1)] Again, the purpose of this requirement is to facilitate computation of the buyer's damages. However, this does not mean that the buyer must cover on the same date that the seller was to deliver the goods; the buyer has whatever time is *commercially reasonable* to locate and purchase the precise commodity or the best available substitute.

c. No duty to cover [§614]

The buyer is not required to cover, particularly if the goods are no longer wanted or needed. If the buyer fails to cover, the buyer cannot sue the seller for any cover price/contract price differential, but is still entitled to any other remedy that the circumstances and the U.C.C. may afford. [U.C.C. §2-712(3)]

d. Consequential damages and failure to cover [§615]

Although the buyer is not required to cover, there is a *penalty* for the failure to do so when reasonable: The buyer may not recover *consequential damages* that were *preventable* by reasonable cover attempts. [U.C.C. §§2-712, Official Comment 3; 2-715]

EXAM TIP   **gilbert**

Cover is a very important remedy, so it is very likely to come up on your exam. Whenever you see a question in which the seller has breached the contract, be sure to consider cover. Ask: Did Buyer cover, and if so, *was it reasonable* (*i.e.,* did Buyer purchase the same goods or a commercially reasonable substitute)? If Buyer did not cover and it was reasonable to do so, remember that Buyer will not be able to recover *preventable consequential damages* (although she may be able to recover other damages).

---

e. Analogous to seller's "right of resale" [§616]

Cover is directly analogous to the seller's right of resale, which permits the seller to dispose of the goods the buyer will not take and to hold the buyer for any difference between the resale and contract price (*see supra,* §593). The similarity is best illustrated in the following example.

Example: Seller agrees to sell 100 widgets to Buyer for $20 each. If Buyer breaches and Seller resells the widgets for $18 each, Seller may recover $2 per widget from Buyer. Conversely, if Seller is the one who breaches, and Buyer goes into the market and buys widgets for $22 each, Buyer may recover $2 per widget from Seller.

---

(1) Note

If the market had been stable, so that upon the buyer's breach the seller could have resold for $20, or if on the seller's breach the buyer could have recovered for $20, neither party would be liable to the other in damages.

3. Recoupment [§617]

The U.C.C. accords the buyer the right to deduct from payments to the seller any damages incurred through a nonconformity in the seller's performance under the particular contract. [U.C.C. §2-717] Thus, if the seller's deliveries are short quantity or too late, are freight-collect when they should have been freight-prepaid, or the buyer is damaged in any other way by the seller's breach, the buyer may *deduct damages* from the contract price.

a. Notice [§618]

The U.C.C. requires the buyer to give the seller notice of any nonconformity. [U.C.C. §2-607(3)(a)] In addition, the buyer must also notify the seller of an intention to subtract damages against the price *before* doing so. [U.C.C. §2-717]

b. "Same contract" limitation [§619]

A subtraction of damages against the price can be employed by the buyer only with respect to the "same contract." [U.C.C. §2-717]

4. Prepaying Buyer—"Right" to Goods [§620]

If the buyer has prepaid for the goods (*i.e.*, put them on layaway) and the seller becomes insolvent, the U.C.C. allows the buyer to reclaim the goods only in very narrow circumstances (so narrow as to be almost illusory). Before the buyer may reclaim goods paid for in part or even in full (assuming the goods are still in the seller's possession), *all* of the following must occur:

(i) *The goods must be identified* (*i.e.*, ascertained as belonging) to this one contract between the parties.

(ii) *The buyer must make and keep full tender* of any unpaid purchase price.

(iii) *The seller must have become insolvent within 10 days of the receipt of the buyer's first installment.*

[U.C.C. §2-502]

EXAM TIP   **gilbert**

Be particularly wary of this situation on an exam, especially if you are being tested on the prior version of Article 2. This factual test is so rarely met as to make this section of the U.C.C. a mere joke, *pretending* to give the buyer relief, but so restricting the circumstances of recovery as to fade into *no practical help* to the buyer.

---

a. 2003 revision—no ten-day limitation for consumers [§621]

The revision drops the 10-day limitation in *consumer* layaways (but retains it in commercial ones), and gives consumer buyers the right to recover the goods in all cases where the seller wrongfully refuses to deliver them. [U.C.C. §2R-502(1)(a)]

BUYER'S PRELITIGATION REMEDIES **gilbert**

REMEDY	WHEN AVAILABLE
SELL GOODS TO RECOVER PREPAYMENT	When Buyer has *prepaid* (all or part) and Seller sends non-conforming goods—Buyer gets a *security interest* in goods
COVER (PURCHASE SUBSTITUTE GOODS)	When Seller breaches contract by *not sending* goods or by sending *nonconforming* goods—Buyer may buy same or commercially reasonable goods, if in good faith and without unreasonable delay
RECOUP DAMAGES	When there are any damages due to *nonconformity in Seller's performance* under the contract—Buyer must give Seller notice

C. Preserving Evidence Where Condition of Goods Is in Dispute

1. In General [§622]

Frequently, by the time the case comes to trial, the goods that are the subject of the dispute have long since been resold or consumed, and the trier of fact must deal with conflicting testimony as to whether the goods were in fact in accordance with the contract. U.C.C. section 2-515 attempts to provide a solution to this problem by creating a prelitigation procedure whereby the actual quality and quantity of the goods can be established.

2. Right of Inspection, Testing, and Sampling [§623]

Either party on *reasonable notice* to the other may, for the purpose of ascertaining the facts and preserving evidence, inspect, test, and sample goods in the control of the other party. [U.C.C. §2-515(a)]

a. Rationale

If one party has exclusive control over the goods, the other may not have access to them to establish the basis for later legal contentions. For example, Seller delivers what Buyer contends are nonconforming goods, and Buyer rejects them. Seller retakes possession of the goods, leaving Buyer without any precise objective evidence of how the goods were nonconforming. The U.C.C. seeks to correct this by providing for the above procedure for preserving evidence. [U.C.C. §2-515(a)]

3. Submission to Impartial Arbiter [§624]

The parties, if they so agree, may submit the goods to a third party for inspection and survey so that the third party will be available to testify as to the conformity or condition of the goods. Furthermore, the parties may also *agree* to make the findings by the third party binding upon themselves in any subsequent litigation or adjustment. [U.C.C. §2-515(b)]

D. Seller's Litigation Remedies

1. Action for Full Purchase Price [§625]

At common law, the seller of goods was not allowed to sue for specific performance. Why not? Because, from the seller's point of view, specific performance is actually a *forced sale*, and since the buyer is paying *money*, the courts deemed this sort of thing an action at law for damages. Unlike the common law, the U.C.C. gives the seller a specific performance remedy, calling it an "*action for the price*," but limits the availability to three circumstances:

a. Technical "acceptance" by buyer [§626]

If the buyer has made an "*acceptance*" of the goods (*see supra*, §§439 *et seq.*), the buyer must pay for the goods. [U.C.C. §2-709(1)(a)] (Remember however, that the buyer can avoid this by properly *revoking acceptance*.)

b. Passage to buyer of risk of loss [§627]

If the goods are *harmed or destroyed* after the risk of loss has passed to the buyer (*see supra*, §§521-541), the buyer must pay the full purchase price. [U.C.C. §2-709(1)(a)]

c. "White elephant" goods [§628]

Where the goods still in the seller's possession are such that they *cannot be resold* (so-called white elephant goods), an action for the full price is allowed. This covers goods *manufactured specially to order* (*e.g.*, imprinted calendars), and goods for which there is *no market* other than the buyer. Under such circumstances, if the goods have been identified (designated) to the contract, and the seller after reasonable efforts has been unable to resell them or it is clear such efforts would be unavailing, the seller can sue the buyer for the full price. [U.C.C. §2-709(1)(b)]

(1) Note

A seller who relies on this exception must of course *continue to hold* the goods for the buyer. [U.C.C. §2-709(2)]

(2) And note

If the seller recovers the price of such goods from the buyer, and the buyer still will not take the goods, should the seller later resell them, any proceeds of the sale belong to *the buyer*. [U.C.C. §2-709(2)]

2. Action for Damages for Nonacceptance [§629]

Under the U.C.C., there are three measures of damages available to the seller when the buyer has refused to accept the goods: (i) the difference between the contract and resale prices, (ii) the difference between the contract and market prices, and (iii) lost profits.

a. Contract-resale differential [§630]

As noted, the U.C.C. presumes that the most logical and commercially reasonable action for the seller to take when the buyer refuses to accept goods is to resell them. If the seller does so in accordance with the U.C.C. provision on resale (discussed *supra,* §593), the seller may recover the difference between the resale price and the contract price. [U.C.C. §2-706(1)]

(1) Note

This is true even if the resale was for *less than the* "*market value,*" thus increasing the damage spread. (*But note:* Failure to obtain the market value of the goods may be relevant to whether the seller conducted the resale in a "commercially reasonable" manner.) [**Columbia Nitrogen Corp. v. Royster Co.,** 451 F.2d 3 (4th Cir. 1971)]

(2) Comment

The contract-resale differential measure of damages is of little help where the seller's goods are standard-priced items in unlimited supply. In that case, the resale price will be the same as the original contract price, ending up with the seller recovering no damages (*see infra,* §638).

b. Contract-market differential [§631]

Alternatively, the seller may recover the difference between the contract price and the market price *at the time and place* that the goods were tendered. [U.C.C. §2-708(1)]

(1) Seller's option [§632]

It is not clear from the U.C.C. whether the seller has the choice between a contract-resale and a contract-market recovery. The only light on the subject within the Code itself is the cryptic comment that "[w]hether the pursuit of one remedy bars another depends entirely on the facts of the individual case." [U.C.C. §2-703, Official Comment 1] However, most commentators assume that the seller is permitted to sue for whichever measure of damages is *most favorable.* [48 N.Y.U. L. Rev. 833]

(a) Note—same limitations

In any event, the contract-market differential is subject to the same limitations as the contract-resale differential: It does not help at all where the goods are *unfinished*; and where standard-priced goods in unlimited supply are involved, the seller will end up with no damages.

(2) Proof of market price [§633]

In proving market price at time of tender, the seller may (i) use the price of the goods in any established *commodity market*; (ii) employ *reports in official publications*, trade journals, newspapers or periodicals of general circulation; or (iii) use the *testimony* of witnesses. [U.C.C. §2-724]

(a) Other markets [§634]

If there is no available evidence of market price at time and place of tender, recovery may be based on a market price *within reasonable proximity thereto*, both spatially and chronologically. [U.C.C. §2-723(2); **Sackett v. Spindler,** 248 Cal. App. 2d 220 (1967)]

1) Transportation costs included [§635]

In measuring damages in such cases, appropriate allowance must be made for the cost of transportation to such other place as is used in measuring damages. [U.C.C. §2-723(2)]

2) Notice required [§636]

If the seller proposes to use the market price at a time or place different than the place of tender to prove the market price, the seller must give the buyer *advance notice* of the intention to do so sufficient, in the opinion of the trial court, to prevent unfair surprise. [U.C.C. §2-723(3)]

c. Lost profits [§637]

The U.C.C. also sanctions a lost profits recovery where damages measured by either a contract-resale or contract-market differential formula are "inadequate to put the seller in as good a position as performance would have done." [U.C.C. §2-708(2)] Indeed, in many cases, this measure of damages turns out to be the most realistic one for the seller.

EXAM TIP   **gilbert**

On an exam, if your analysis of the facts shows that the contract-market and con-tract-resale differentials will leave a seller with *no damages*, be sure to look at the possibility of a *lost profits* recovery. You should especially think about the lost profits measure in situations when you see goods that are either *unfinished* or of *unlimited supply*.

---

(1) Standard-priced items in unlimited supply [§638]

The lost profits measure is the appropriate measure of damages to use when the buyer has repudiated the purchase of a standard-priced item in unlimited supply, which the seller is able to resell, at the same price, to another.

Example: Buyer repudiates a contract to purchase a new car from a dealer for $5,000, which is its fair market value. Seller is able to sell the same car to another purchaser for the *same amount* on the very next day. If the U.C.C. required that Seller look to what happened on resale, no recovery would be possible under either the contract-resale or contract-market measure of damage, above. However, Seller has been damaged: But for Buyer's breach, Seller would have made *two* sales instead of only one. Hence, Seller is entitled to recover against Buyer the *profit* that would have been realized had the sale to the first buyer gone through. [**Neri v. Retail Marine Corp.,** 30 N.Y.2d 393 (1972)]

(a) "Lost volume seller" [§639]

A seller in this predicament (one able to recover "lost profit" regardless of what happened on actual resale) is a "lost volume seller." The term refers to a seller who has a virtually *unlimited inventory* and only a *limited number of customers* (like an automobile dealership). If the law made such sellers look to the effect of resale, they would lose *volume* of business. This is unfair, so lost volume sellers may ignore resale recoveries in computing their damages, and instead may sue for lost profit on the first aborted sale.

EXAM TIP   **gilbert**

Although the Code provides that the lost profits measure is used only if the other two measures do not adequately compensate the seller, this is quite often the case in commercial sales contracts. To determine whether the lost profits measure is appropriate, look at the seller's *supply*. If the seller's supply of goods is *unlimited* (*i.e.,* he can obtain all the goods he can sell), then he is a *lost volume seller*, and the lost profits measure can be used. If the seller's supply is limited (*i.e.,* he cannot obtain all the goods he can sell, as when the sale is for a unique item), the lost profits measure cannot be used, and one of the other two measures must be used instead.

(b) Overhead [§640]

Lost "profit" is defined to include the recovery of reasonable "overhead." This term is defined to mean *fixed costs* of the seller's operation that in no way vary with the number of items sold. [U.C.C. §2-708(2); **Vitex Manufacturing Corp. v. Caribtex Corp.,** 377 F.2d 795 (3d Cir. 1967)]

Example: Dealer had $3,000 in general overhead expenses and has made three sales. Thus, the general overhead cost per unit is $1,000. If Dealer made a fourth sale, the general overhead cost per sale would decline to $750. This is an important aspect of the fourth sale. Should that fourth buyer breach, Dealer could successfully claim that the lost profits include this decline in overhead expenses per sale. If it were not for the fourth buyer's breach, Dealer would have received this extra recovery of expenses.

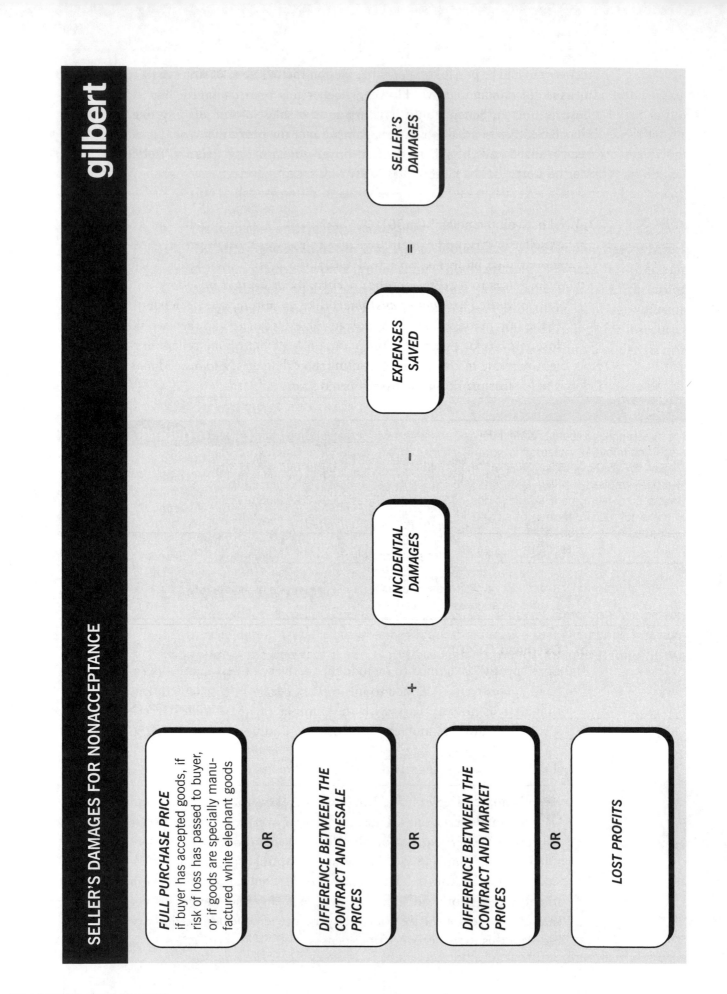

SELLER'S DAMAGES FOR NONACCEPTANCE

FULL PURCHASE PRICE if buyer has accepted goods, if risk of loss has passed to buyer, or if goods are specially manu-factured white elephant goods

OR

DIFFERENCE BETWEEN THE CONTRACT AND RESALE PRICES

OR

DIFFERENCE BETWEEN THE CONTRACT AND MARKET PRICES

OR

LOST PROFITS

+

INCIDENTAL DAMAGES

−

EXPENSES SAVED

=

SELLER'S DAMAGES

d. Incidental damages [§641]

No matter which of the above three damage measures is used—contract-market, contract-resale, or lost profits—the seller is *also* entitled to recover any *incidental damages* occasioned by the buyer's breach. [U.C.C. §§2-706(1), 2-708(1), (2)] "Incidental damages" include expenses or commissions incurred in stopping delivery; in the transportation, care, and custody of goods after the buyer's breach; and in connection with return or resale. Incidental damages also include *all other commercially reasonable* charges. [U.C.C. §2-710]

e. Deduct expenses saved [§642]

From any recovery had by the seller, there must be deducted any expenses *saved* in consequence of the buyer's breach. [U.C.C. §§2-706(1), 2-708(1)] For instance, if the seller was required to deliver the goods to the buyer in special packaging costing $1 per package, but by virtue of the buyer's breach is able to package the goods in the normal manner for 50¢ per package, the 50¢ per unit saved is deducted from the seller's damages.

(1) 2003 revision expands seller's potential recovery [§643]

The common law (and the original version of Article 2) did not allow the disappointed seller to recover any consequential damages other than lost interest, but the revision of Article 2, for the first time, would give the seller *all foreseeable consequential damages*. [U.C.C. §2R-710(2)]

E. Buyer's Litigation Remedies

1. Possessory Actions

a. Replevin [§644]

The U.C.C. authorizes the buyer to seek replevin (*i.e., an action to recover the goods*) in two instances:

(1) Inability to cover [§645]

The buyer may seek replevin if (i) the goods are *identified* to the contract, and (ii) after a reasonable effort, the buyer is *unable to procure substitute goods* (cover) in the market, or the circumstances reasonably indicate that such effort will be unavailing. [U.C.C. §2-716(3)]

(2) Satisfaction of security interest [§646]

An action in replevin may also be maintained if the seller has shipped the goods under reservation and the buyer has made or tendered payment of the price but the seller, some carrier, or bailee has *failed to release the goods* to the buyer. [U.C.C. §2-716(3)]

b. Specific performance

(1) Equity rule [§647]

The traditional rule in equity is that a contract for the sale of chattels may be specifically enforced only where the goods in question are *unique and irreplaceable* (*e.g.*, works of art), so that money damages for the seller's breach are not an "adequate" remedy.

(2) U.C.C. rule [§648]

The U.C.C. permits specific performance in any case where goods are unique *or in other proper circumstances* (*see* below). [U.C.C. §2-716(1)]

(a) Goods in short supply [§649]

The Code codifies case law that has allowed specific performance wherever goods are in scarce or short supply. *Inability to cover* (which justifies replevin, above) is strong evidence of "other proper circumstances." [U.C.C. §2-716, Official Comment 2]

(b) Damages inadequate or indeterminable [§650]

Moreover, specific performance is proper where damages would simply be *inadequate* or *too difficult to determine* (*e.g.*, output and requirements contracts).

1) Limitation on damages [§651]

The fact that the buyer obtained a closeout price from the seller that could not be duplicated is not enough to entitle the buyer to specific performance. Rather the buyer is limited to an action for damages between the price quoted and replacement cost. This is true even where buying at the replacement price imposes a heavy financial burden on the buyer.

2) Scope of order of specific performance [§652]

The U.C.C. also empowers a court decreeing specific performance to *include terms and conditions* as to payment of the price, damages, or other relief, as the court deems just. [U.C.C. §2-716(2)]

EXAM TIP   **gilbert**

While many exam questions will focus on the computation of the buyer's damages, remember that *replevin and specific performance* are options, too. Keep these two options in mind, especially where the goods are *unique or irreplaceable*.

---

2. Action for Damages for Nondelivery [§653]

Under the U.C.C., there are several measures of damages available to the buyer when the seller fails to deliver the goods contracted for.

a. Contract-cover differential [§654]

As noted, the U.C.C. presumes that the most logical and commercially reasonable thing for the buyer to do when the seller fails to deliver goods is to go into the market and *purchase substitute goods*, *i.e.*, "cover." If the buyer does so, the buyer may recover the difference between the cover price and the contract price—as long as the cover was chosen in *good faith*. [U.C.C. §2-712(2)]

b. Contract-market differential [§655]

Alternatively, the buyer may recover against the seller the difference between the contract price and the market price at the time the buyer learned of the breach. [U.C.C. §2-713(1)]

(1) Buyer's option [§656]

The choice of whether to cover rests entirely with the buyer (*see supra*, §§611-616). A buyer choosing to cover is entitled to whatever added cost is incurred in obtaining replacement goods (as long as everything was done in good faith), even if the buyer has to pay *above* market value to get the substitute goods. On the other hand, a buyer electing *not* to cover is limited to the contract-market differential.

(2) "Market" [§657]

The place for establishing the "market" is the *place where the seller should have tendered* the goods if the seller refuses to deliver. If the seller has made a nonconforming tender, which the buyer rightfully rejects (or later revokes acceptance on), then the place for determining market price is the *place of arrival*. [U.C.C. §2-713(2)]

(3) Proof of market price [§658]

The discussion with reference to proof of market price as to the seller's damages, *supra*, §633, is applicable here as well.

c. Consequential damages [§659]

In addition to the "contract-cover" or "contract-market" differential, the U.C.C. permits the buyer to recover for "any loss resulting from general or particular requirements and needs of which the seller at the time of contracting *had reason to know* and which *could not reasonably be prevented* by cover or otherwise." [U.C.C. §2-715(2)(a)—emphasis added; *see supra*, §338]

(1) Lost profits [§660]

In brief, this sanctions a lost profits recovery where the buyer cannot go out into the market to cover and is thus deprived of profits on resale, etc. Note that lost profits can include loss of *future* profits (goodwill) as well.

(2) Cover requirement [§661]

Normally the buyer cannot recover consequential damages unless the buyer made an attempt to "cover" (*see supra*, §615). However, this rule does not apply where cover would be *unreasonable*. For example, where the buyer had contracted to purchase the seller's bar equipment at a very low price and simply could not afford to buy similar equipment from another supplier at a much higher price, the failure to "cover" would *not* bar a claim for consequential damages. [**Gerwin v. Southeastern California Association of Seventh Day Adventists**, 14 Cal. App. 3d 209 (1971)]

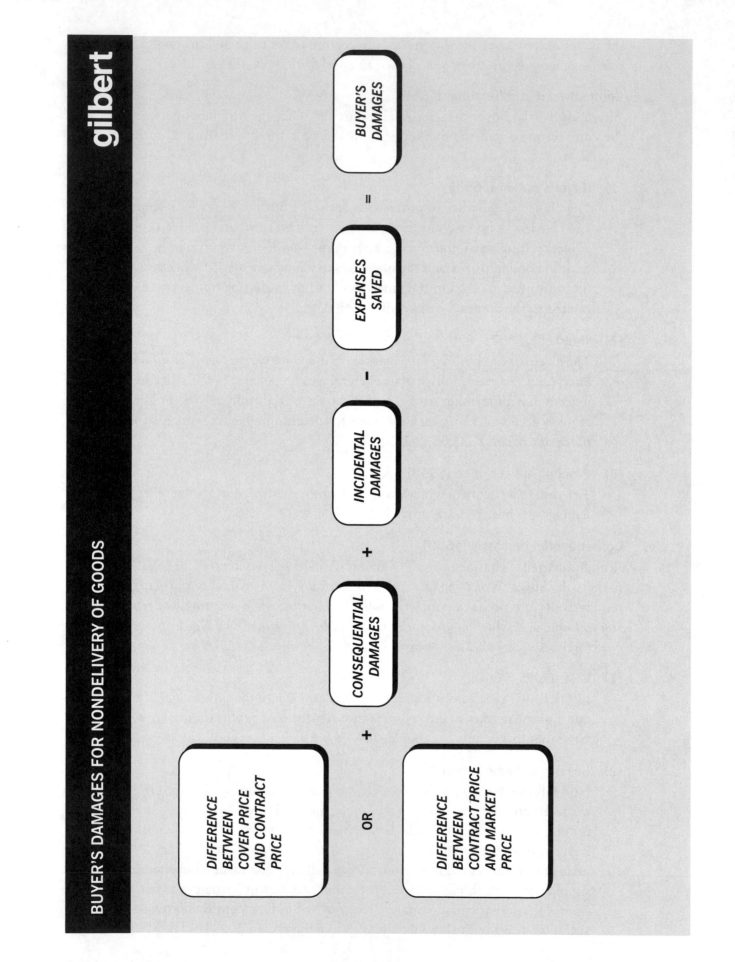

BUYER'S DAMAGES FOR NONDELIVERY OF GOODS

gilbert

DIFFERENCE BETWEEN COVER PRICE AND CONTRACT PRICE

OR

DIFFERENCE BETWEEN CONTRACT PRICE AND MARKET PRICE

+

CONSEQUENTIAL DAMAGES

+

INCIDENTAL DAMAGES

−

EXPENSES SAVED

=

BUYER'S DAMAGES

d. **Incidental damages [§662]**

In addition, the buyer is entitled to recover any incidental damages resulting from the seller's failure to deliver conforming goods. These damages include expenses reasonably incurred in inspection, receipt, transportation, care, and custody of goods rightfully rejected; any commercially reasonable charges in connection with effecting cover; and any other reasonable expense incident to the delay or other breach. [U.C.C. §2-715(1)]

(1) But note

The U.C.C. does *not allow punitive damages*, no matter how aggravated the seller's breach. [U.C.C. §1-106]

e. **Deduction for expenses saved [§663]**

From any recovery had by the buyer, there must be deducted any expenses saved in consequence of the seller's breach (*e.g.,* savings on cover must be deducted from any claimed incidental damages). [U.C.C. §§2-712(2), 2-713(1)]

3. Remedies for Breach of Warranty

See discussion of breach of warranty, *supra,* §§335-343.

4. Restitution of Payments Where Buyer in Default [§664]

A problem that has plagued buyers since common law times is the right to recover advance payment on the purchase price where the *buyer* has defaulted, but the default has not caused much damage to the seller.

Example: Buyer agrees to purchase a machine from Seller for $1,000, against which price there is a down payment of $500. Later, Buyer repudiates the contract and Seller resells the machine to someone else for $1,200. Seller has not been damaged by Buyer's breach; indeed, Seller is better off because of it. Can Seller nevertheless retain the $500 advance deposit made by the buyer?

a. **U.C.C.—"rule of thumb offset" [§665]**

The U.C.C. attempts to deal with the problem, although its solution might be described as a halfway house. The Code provides that the buyer is entitled to restitution of the amount by which the advance payments *exceed 20% of the purchase price or $500*, whichever is smaller. This is the so-called rule of thumb offset. [U.C.C. §2-718(2)(b)]

Example: Thus, in the above example, the U.C.C. solution would require Seller to return $300 as the amount exceeding 20% of the purchase price.

b. **Effect of valid liquidated damages provision [§666]**

The result may differ if the contract contains a valid liquidated damages clause. In such a case, if the buyer breaches, the seller may be required to refund only any excess of the buyer's prepayments over the amount of valid liquidation damages. [U.C.C. §2-718(2)(a)] (Liquidated damages are discussed *supra,* §§653-659.)

c. 2003 revision—eliminates rule of thumb offset [§667]

The revision drops this formula entirely, and allows the breaching buyer to recover any amount paid that *exceeds the liquidated damages* specified in the contract, or, if there is no liquidated damages clause, the amount seller proves it suffered as harm from the buyer's repudiation. [U.C.C. §2R-718(2)]

d. Seller's right to other damages

(1) Greater damages [§668]

The "rule of thumb offset" applies *only* where the seller cannot prove greater damages. If the seller proves damages *greater* than $500 or 20% of the purchase price, the seller may recover accordingly. [U.C.C. §2-718(3)]

> **Example:** In the example above, if Seller had been unable to resell the machine and its market value was only $400, the loss of profit would be $600, and Seller would be entitled to retain the $500 down payment and recover another $100 from Buyer.

(2) No provable damages [§669]

Even where the seller cannot prove *any* damages, *in addition* to the "rule of thumb offset," the seller can recover:

(i) Any *incidental damages* sustained as a result of the buyer's breach (*e.g.,* expenses of resale, costs of storing goods, etc.); and

(ii) The value of any *benefits received* by the buyer (as where the buyer had possession of the goods).

[U.C.C. §2-718(3)]

> **EXAM TIP** gilbert
>
> Be sure to recall the provisions regarding *incidental damages* and *benefit received* by buyer when you run across a fact pattern that seems to provide no recovery for the seller. Even when the seller is unable to prove damages, the U.C.C. will provide this minimal recovery.

F. Limitation of Remedies

1. In General [§670]

Many times a sales contract of a small object costing a few pennies or a few dollars can involve huge consequential damages in the event of breach (*e.g.,* airplane factory shut down by seller's refusal to deliver critical parts). Similarly, a buyer's failure to perform may cause substantial lost profits or other large consequential damages to the seller. For these reasons, parties to sales contracts may seek to stipulate as to their ultimate liability by special provisions in their contract.

2. Liquidated Damages Provision

a. Common law [§671]

The common law rule (as to all types of common law) is that the parties can liquidate (*i.e.,* establish in advance) the damages in the event of breach only in those situations where from the nature of the case it would be *impracticable or extremely difficult* to fix the actual damages. [**Better Food Markets, Inc. v. American District Telephone Co.**, 40 Cal. 2d 179 (1953)]

b. U.C.C. rule [§672]

The U.C.C. sets forth a new set of standards for determining the validity of liquidated damages clauses in sales contracts:

(1) Reasonable amount [§673]

First, the amount of damages pre-established to be paid in the event of default or breach by one or both parties must be reasonable. "Reasonableness" is measured in light of (i) the *anticipated or actual harm* caused by the breach, (ii) the *difficulties of proof of loss*, and (iii) the *inconvenience or nonfeasibility* of otherwise obtaining an *adequate remedy*. [U.C.C. §2-718(1)]

(a) No actual damages [§674]

If the liquidated damages provision was "reasonable" at the time the contract was made, some (but not all) courts will enforce the stipulated amount, and the defendant will have to pay that amount *even where there are no actual damages* at the time of breach. [**Bethlehem Steel Co. v. City of Chicago**, 234 F. Supp. 726 (N.D. Ill. 1964)—goods resold for more than contract price]

(b) Greater damages [§675]

Conversely, the damages will be *limited* to the liquidated damages set forth in the contract, even though the plaintiff can prove a greater loss.

(c) Invalid measure void as penalty [§676]

If the sales contract fixes *unreasonably large or small* liquidated damages, the clause is *void* as a penalty. [U.C.C. §2-718(1), Official Comment 1]

Example: Provisions forfeiting a buyer's down payment in event of default may be held unenforceable if the amount of the down payment greatly exceeds any actual damages suffered by the seller.

1) But note

In such a case, the seller may still enforce the contract so as to recover whatever actual damages are provable. [**Security Safety Corp. v. Kuznicki**, 213 N.E.2d 866 (Mass. 1966)]

> **cf.** **Compare:** A provision requiring a defaulting party to pay 30% of any monies due as a "reasonable attorney's fee" to the seller has been held *valid* where there was no showing that this amount was greatly disproportionate to the normal fee an attorney would charge for collection of the claim. [**Equitable Lumber Corp. v. IPA Land Development Corp.**, 38 N.Y.2d 516 (1976)]

(2) "Unconscionability" limitation [§677]

A liquidated damages provision may also be subject to attack as "unconscionable" under U.C.C. section 2-302 if it is shown that there was *great disparity in bargaining power* between the parties, or that it otherwise resulted from *oppressive practices*. [*See* **Equitable Lumber Corp. v. IPA Land Development Corp.**, *supra*]

LIQUIDATED DAMAGES—A CHECKLIST   gilbert

FOR A LIQUIDATED DAMAGES CLAUSE TO BE VALID UNDER THE U.C.C.:

☑ The *amount* of damages pre-established *must be reasonable* in light of:

- *Anticipated or actual harm* caused by the breach;
- *Difficulties of proof of loss*; and
- *Inconvenience or nonfeasibility of otherwise obtaining an adequate remedy*

or it will be *void* as a penalty.

☑ There must *not be great disparity in bargaining power* between the parties or *oppressive practices*.

---

(3) Variation—2003 revision [§678]

The revision allows for the recovery of liquidated damages for reasonable amounts caused by the breach. In *consumer contracts* only, the revision also measures the validity of the clause by the difficulty of proving loss and the inconvenience of otherwise obtaining an adequate remedy. This means that it will be easier to get liquidated damages in commercial contexts than it will be where the buyer is a consumer. [U.C.C. §2R-718(1)]

3. Limitations on Damages [§679]

Clauses limiting the buyer's remedies are frequently found in provisions *disclaiming express or implied warranties* (*see supra*, §§267-298). Probably the most well-known of these clauses is found in the standard automobile dealer's "warranty," which permits the purchaser to recover for breach of warranty only the cost of any part or parts shown to the satisfaction of the manufacturer to be defective. These clauses have generated intense litigation because they severely limit the buyer's recovery in situations where defective goods have caused personal injuries.

a. **General rule [§680]**

The U.C.C. specifically permits the parties to *limit* or *alter* the measure of damages otherwise recoverable under the Code. Specific examples of permissible limitations include clauses restricting the buyer to a return of the goods and repayment of the price, or to repair and replacement of nonconforming goods and parts. [U.C.C. §2-719(1)(a)]

b. **Consequential damages exception [§681]**

It is also permissible for the parties to limit or exclude consequential damage recoveries *unless* the limitation or exclusion is "unconscionable" within the meaning of U.C.C. section 2-302. [U.C.C. §2-719(3)]

(1) **Presumption of "unconscionability" in consumer goods cases [§682]**

However—and this is extremely important—where *consumer goods* are involved (*i.e.,* goods used or bought for use primarily for personal, family, or household purposes), and the goods cause *personal injuries*, there is a *presumption* in the buyer's favor that the limitation of remedy clause is unconscionable and therefore inoperative. [U.C.C. §2-719(3)]

 Example: A tire manufacturer's express "warranty" against blowouts, which purported to limit liability to repair or replacement of the defective tire, has been held ineffective to bar claims for personal injuries and property damage resulting from a blowout. It would be "patently unconscionable for the manufacturer to be permitted to limit its damages for a breach of warranty resulting in the purchaser's injury or death to a price refund or replacement of the tire." [**Collins v. Uniroyal, Inc.**, 315 A.2d 16 (N.J. 1974)—New Jersey has extended this presumption of unconscionability to situations where breach of warranty in the sale of consumer goods causes only *property* damage; *see* **Gladden v. Cadillac Motor Car Division**, 416 A.2d 394 (N.J. 1980)]

(a) **But note**

In states where a manufacturer or retailer can be held *strictly liable in tort* in products liability cases, the presumption of unconscionability is not necessary since any disclaimer would apply only to a warranty (contract) action. [**Vandermark v. Ford Motor Co.**, 61 Cal. 2d 256 (1964); *see supra,* §§317-323]

(2) **Other cases [§683]**

Where the loss is only "commercial," there is *no* presumption that a disclaimer or limitation on damages clause is unconscionable. [U.C.C. §2-719(3)] It is up to the buyer to *prove* that the clause is in fact "unconscionable" (*i.e.,* grossly unfair).

 Example: A contract for the sale of a home furnace limits the buyer's remedies to return and replacement of defective parts. A defective part causes a fire that destroys a $50,000 home, but no personal injuries are involved. The owner's right to recover against the furnace seller depends on whether the clause limiting remedies is, under the circumstances, "unconscionable." [**Shroeder v. Fageol Motors, Inc.**, 544 P.2d 20 (Wash. 1975)]

REQUIREMENTS FOR PRESUMPTION OF UNCONSCIONABILITY — gilbert

THE PRESUMPTION OF UNCONSCIONABILITY ARISES ONLY WHEN THERE ARE:

☑ *Consumer goods* involved (those used primarily for personal, family, or household purposes), **and**

☑ *Personal injuries* suffered by party seeking damages.

---

4. "Exclusive Remedy" Provision [§684]

The parties are given broad latitude under the U.C.C. in choosing their own remedies, as long as *minimum* adequate remedies are available. If the contract provides for its own remedies in the event of default, resort to those remedies is *optional* at the discretion of the aggrieved party *unless* the contract declares the remedy to be "exclusive," in which case it is the sole remedy. [U.C.C. §2-719(1)(b); **Dow Corning Corp. v. Capital Aviation, Inc.**, 411 F.2d 622 (7th Cir. 1969)]

a. Limitation [§685]

Any claimed "exclusive remedy" provision must be clear. Otherwise, courts will interpret around it.

---

e.g. **Example:** A contract provided: "We will repair goods at any time within one year; otherwise, no other warranty, express or implied, is given." This was held to be only a disclaimer as to warranty liability; it did *not* operate to limit remedies to repair of the goods. Hence, the buyer was entitled to rescind and demand a refund when the goods did not work. [**Herbstman v. Eastman Kodak Co.**, 330 A.2d 384 (N.J. 1974)]

---

5. Failure of Essential Purpose of Remedy Limitation [§686]

If circumstances cause an exclusive or limited remedy to *fail of its essential purpose*, then the aggrieved party may resort to the usual U.C.C. remedies. Thus, for example, where the seller narrows the remedies to one (*e.g.*, repair or replacement of defective merchandise) and that fails to function as contemplated (*e.g.*, seller cannot repair the goods), the buyer can *ignore the exclusive remedy* and have recourse to the full set of remedies available to buyers under the U.C.C. [U.C.C. §2-719(2); *see* **Wilson Trading Corp. v. David Ferguson, Ltd.**, 23 N.Y.2d 398 (1968)]

a. Minimum adequate remedies required [§687]

Sellers giving warranties must play fair in allowing the buyer to realize on those warranties should the goods prove defective, and any limitation on the remedy will "fail of its essential purpose" unless "at least *minimum adequate remedies* are provided." [U.C.C. §2-719, Official Comment 1]

> **Example:** The purchaser of a new car, which turns out to be a "lemon" and which defies the manufacturer's continuous attempts to repair it, may claim that the manufacturer's limited warranty ("to repair or replace defective parts") has failed of its essential purpose, and the purchaser is entitled to sue for full warranty damages (*i.e.*, the difference between the price paid and the value of the "lemon" received). [**Goddard v. General Motors,** 396 N.E.2d 761 (Ohio 1979)]

6. Relationship Between Consequential Damages and Failure of Limitation of Remedies [§688]

If a limitation of remedy fails of its essential purpose under section 2-719(2), may the buyer now recover consequential damages even though the seller had disclaimed such damages in the contract, or to recover the consequential damages must the buyer still convince the courts that the disclaimer is unconscionable under section 2-718(3)? Phrased another way, are these subsections *dependent* or *independent*? If dependent, then on a finding of failure of essential purpose, the buyer would always get appropriate consequential damages, but if independent, then the buyer would also have to jump through the next hoop of convincing the court that the disclaimer of consequential damages was unconscionable.

> **Example:** An automobile sales contract provided that Buyer's remedy for breach was limited to repair of the vehicle, and that Seller would not be liable for consequential damages. When Seller failed to fix the defects, Buyer sued and asked for damages that included consequential losses (such as medical expenses caused by the car crash). Having proved that Seller cannot repair the vehicle (and thus that the limitation to repair "failed of its essential purpose"), does Buyer now get consequential damages automatically, or must Buyer also prove that the disclaimer of these damages was "unconscionable" under the tests of section 2-719(3)?

a. Results vary in consumer cases vs. commercial cases [§689]

Courts have reached both results in this independent/dependent quandary, but are more likely to find the clauses *dependent in consumer cases* (so the consumer more easily gets consequential damages), and *independent in commercial cases* (so the commercial buyer must also prove unconscionability). [**Pierce v. Catalina Yachts,** 2 P.3d 618 (Alaska 1999)]

G. Statute of Limitations

1. Statute of Limitations Under the U.C.C. [§690]

The U.C.C. creates a *four-year statute of limitations* on actions to enforce rights or obligations under any contract sale, *oral or written*. [U.C.C. §2-725(1)]

2. Parties' Agreement [§691]

The parties are permitted to *shorten* the statute of limitations by agreement to *no less than one year*, but they are *not* permitted to *lengthen* it. The U.C.C. drafters chose four years as a reasonable period for the keeping of records. [U.C.C. §2-725, Official Comment]

EXAM TIP   **gilbert**

It is easier to recall the U.C.C. provisions regarding the statute of limitations once you realize they are common sense (*e.g.*, parties may shorten, but not lengthen, the statutory period), especially when you consider the reason that such statutes exist—to curtail a party's ability to bring an action to a reasonable time following the transgression.

---

3. Accrual of Actions [§692]

The statutory period starts to run *when the cause of action accrues*. When is that? The cause of action accrues when the aggrieved party could bring suit—*i.e.*, *when the breach occurs*. Normally, this is the date on which the other party's *performance was due* under the contract. The statutory period starts to run regardless of the aggrieved party's knowledge or lack of knowledge of the breach. [U.C.C. §2-725(2)]

4. Breach of Warranty Actions [§693]

In a breach of warranty action, the U.C.C. presumes that the breach occurs (and hence the four-year period starts running) *at delivery* of the goods. This is true even if the buyer does not discover the breach until much later.

a. Express warranty of future performance [§694]

This rule is harsh, and thus it is softened in effect by the rule that "where a warranty explicitly extends to future performance of the goods and discovery of the breach must await the time of such performance," then the four-year period does not start to run until the time when the buyer *should have discovered* the breach.

 Example: A new car had a "five-year warranty" and it first broke down in the third year. The four-year statute of limitations will run from that moment, and not the moment of delivery.

---

(1) Distinguish—implied warranties breached on delivery [§695]

Since there is no way that an implied warranty can "explicitly extend" to future performance, all implied warranties are breached (if at all) on delivery and die, as causes of action, unless the lawsuit is brought within the four years thereafter. [**Holdridge v. Heyer-Schulte Corp.**, 440 F. Supp. 1088 (N.D.N.Y. 1977)]

5. Statute of Limitations Under the 2003 Revision [§696]

The revision makes a large number of changes to the statute of limitations rules.

a. New time periods [§697]

Under section 2R-725(1), the statute of limitations is four years from the accrual of the cause of action *or one year after the breach was or should have been discovered* (in no event longer than five years after the cause of action accrued). As before, the parties may by agreement reduce the period to no less than one year (except in consumer cases, where it cannot be reduced at all).

b. Remedial promise of repair [§698]

Under the original section it was not clear where a breach of a promise of repair fit—was it a breach of warranty (so the statute of limitations would start running at delivery of the goods) or was it not breached until the repair was not made as agreed? The revision now calls promises of repair "*remedial promises*" and provides that they are breached only when the repair is not accomplished as agreed. [U.C.C. §2R-725(2)(c)—"remedial promise" is defined in §2R-103(1)(n)]

c. Indemnity actions [§699]

If the buyer has resold goods and then been sued for breach of warranty, and the original buyer wants to pass the loss on to its seller for *indemnification*, this cause of action accrues when the claim was *first asserted* against the original buyer by its buyer. [U.C.C. §2R-725(2)(d)]

Chapter Nine:
Documents of Title

CONTENTS

Chapter Approach

Sales questions involve transfers of goods or transfers of documents representing the goods. In the latter case, it is important to remember that for the most part possession of the document means ownership of the goods.

This chapter covers the two major types of documents of title: *bills of lading* and *warehouse receipts*. Although the documents may be different in form and/or uses, the issues related to them are basically the same. You should especially consider two issues:

1. **Is the Document Negotiable?**

    If not, it is merely a receipt for the goods and a contract for their carriage. If it is negotiable, it is tantamount to *ownership* of the goods. Remember too that with negotiation certain warranties arise, but these warranties are in addition to the warranties that pertain to the goods themselves.

2. **Who Is Entitled to Possession of the Goods?**

    Questions often ask you to consider whether the bailee made delivery to the proper person. Make sure that the bailee followed the terms of the document and delivered to the holder of a negotiable document or according to the bailor's instructions if the document is nonnegotiable.

A. Introduction

1. **Possession of Documents Equals Ownership of Goods [§700]**

    The ownership of goods is frequently evidenced by documents of title that arise from the shipment and/or storage of goods. Such documents are more than mere conveyances of title, such as bills of sale or assignments. Rather, *if negotiable*, they are deemed to *represent the goods themselves*. Therefore, possession of the documents is, to varying degrees, the equivalent of ownership of the goods. Since it is easier to hold, transfer, and keep track of papers rather than the goods themselves, such documents of title are popular in the commercial world.

2. **Applicable Law [§701]**

    Article 7 of the U.C.C. is devoted entirely to documents of title. It replaces comparable provisions of the Uniform Sales Act, the Uniform Bill of Lading Act, and the Uniform Warehouse Receipts Act. Federal law (most importantly, the Federal Bill of Lading Act, 49 U.S.C. §§81 *et seq.*) governs the interstate shipment of goods, and thus Article 7 of the U.C.C. is limited in effect to intrastate shipments. However, federal law does not differ dramatically from the rules of Article 7. (*Note:* A revision of Article 7 is in the works, but it makes few changes other than providing for *electronic* documents of title.)

B. Bills of Lading

1. **Definition [§702]**

   A bill of lading is a document issued by a carrier to the shipper of goods. It *lists the goods* received by the carrier, states the *agreed destination* for the goods, and the *terms* under which the carrier undertakes to deliver them. Bills of lading may be either negotiable or nonnegotiable (*see* below).

2. **Meaning of "Negotiable" [§703]**

   The word "negotiable" means that the parties have put the piece of paper in such a form that they intend transferees of the paper to take it *free from the normal defenses* that would otherwise transfer with it (*e.g.*, mistaken delivery, fraud, breach of the underlying contract, etc.).

3. **Other Terminology in Article 7**

   a. **"Shipper" [§704]**

   The shipper is the person who *delivers the goods to the carrier* for shipment.

EXAM TIP	gilbert
Although in the ordinary use of the words the two terms "shipper" and "carrier" seem interchangeable, *in the context of the U.C.C.,* they are *not*. Be sure not to confuse the shipper with the carrier, who is the one who transports the goods. The shipper will appear first in the timeline of delivery.	

   b. **"Consign" [§705]**

   To consign is to "send" something to another. Hence, the shipper is the *consignor*, and the person to whom the goods are to be delivered is the *consignee*.

   c. **"Issuer" [§706]**

   The issuer of the document of title is the person who *creates* it and hands it to another. Typically, the issuer will be the carrier (or if the document is a "warehouse receipt," the warehouser, *see* below).

4. **Nonnegotiable Bills ("Straight Bills") [§707]**

   Under federal law, a nonnegotiable bill of lading (*i.e.*, one that travels *with* its defenses) is called a "straight bill." A straight bill of lading is one stating that the goods are consigned to a *specified person* (*e.g.*, "consigned to the XYZ Co."), but not to that person's "order" (*e.g.*, "consign to the order of XYZ Co."). [U.C.C. §7-104] Under such a bill, the carrier is contractually obligated to deliver the goods to the named consignee only. A straight bill is nothing more than a *receipt for the goods* and a *contract for their carriage*.

a. **Carrier's obligation under straight bill [§708]**

Under a straight bill, a carrier may be held liable for conversion of the goods if the carrier delivers them to someone other than the named consignee—even though such person was in possession of the straight bill covering their shipment.

(1) **Delivery orders [§709]**

Of course, delivery to someone other than the named consignee is proper if the carrier has received *written instructions* from the *shipper* to make such a delivery. [U.C.C. §7-303(1)(b)—on "diversion"] Such instructions in writing are called "delivery orders." [U.C.C. §7-102(1)(d)]

b. **Consignee's rights [§710]**

Again, due to the nature of the document, it is not necessary that the consignee present or surrender the bill of lading in order to pick up the goods. The consignee has the right to receive the goods, and the carrier is obligated to deliver them, *without the surrender of the straight bill.*

5. **Negotiable Bills [§711]**

A negotiable bill is a bill of lading that is more than a mere receipt for the goods and a contract for their carriage. Rather, the carrier undertakes to deliver the goods *to whomever is legally in possession of the bill.* The person who is in legal possession of a negotiable bill is entitled to possession of the goods described in the bill, and for this reason, legal possession of the bill is *tantamount to ownership* of the goods. Accordingly, negotiable bills are effective "documents of title." [U.C.C. §7-403(3)]

a. **Types of negotiable bills [§712]**

A negotiable bill may be either an *order bill* (*e.g.,* "consign to the order of XYZ Co.") or a *bearer bill* (*e.g.,* "consign to bearer"). [U.C.C. §7-104(1)(a)]

b. **Manner of "negotiation"**

(1) **Bearer bill [§713]**

A bearer bill can be negotiated by mere *delivery* of the bill. [U.C.C. §7-501(1)(2)(a)]

(2) **Order bill [§714]**

An order bill is negotiated by *indorsement* by the named consignee *plus* delivery to the party to whom the bill is being negotiated. [U.C.C. §7-501(1), (2)(b)]

c. **Types of indorsements [§715]**

An order bill may be indorsed in blank (*i.e.,* the consignee merely signs the bill), which continues the *full negotiability* of the instrument. Or the indorsement may be *special* (*i.e.,* naming a specific transferee—"deliver to Jones Co."), which *limits* the further negotiability of the instrument to the named transferee. *But note:* The named transferee may indorse it in blank (the transferee's name only) and restore full negotiability. [U.C.C. §7-501(3)]

d. Effect of failure to indorse [§716]

If an order bill has been transferred for value, but the transferor has failed to indorse it properly, no rights pass. However, the transferee can compel the transferor (by an equitable action for specific performance) to make an indorsement. The indorsement is effective, however, only as of the time it is made. [U.C.C. §7-506]

e. Warranties on negotiation [§717]

One who negotiates a negotiable bill (by indorsement and delivery of an order bill or by delivery of a bearer bill) thereby warrants that (i) the document is *genuine*, (ii) the transferor has a *legal right to transfer* it and the goods it represents, and (iii) the transferor has *no knowledge* of any fact that would *impair the validity* or worth of the document. [U.C.C. §7-507]

(1) Warranties that run with goods unaffected [§718]

The fact that a seller chooses to transfer ownership by a document of title rather than by physical delivery of the goods has no effect on the warranties that run with the goods. The party negotiating a negotiable bill makes the warranties mentioned above *in addition to* any warranty made in selling the goods. [U.C.C. §7-507] Thus, unless disclaimed, the usual express and implied warranties that are made in connection with the goods are also made on the sale of the document of title representing the goods. (*See supra,* §§210 *et seq.*)

WARRANTIES AND NEGOTIABLE BILLS　　　　**gilbert**

THE FOLLOWING WARRANTIES ARE IMPLICIT IN A NEGOTIABLE BILL:

- ☑ *Genuineness* of document;
- ☑ Legal *right to transfer* the bill and the goods represented therein;
- ☑ *No knowledge* of facts that could *devalue* the bill; and
- ☑ Any additional warranty made in the *sale of the goods* (*i.e.,* express and implied warranties of merchantability, fitness for a particular purpose, etc.) unless disclaimed.

---

(2) No guarantee of delivery [§719]

The above warranties on negotiation do *not* include a guarantee that the goods will be delivered by the carrier. [U.C.C. §7-505]

(3) Warranties arise on negotiation [§720]

The above warranties arise only where there is a negotiation—an *outright transfer* of the bill. If the document is merely assigned for collection, the warranties do not apply [**Johnson v. Mayo,** 256 F.2d 761 (5th Cir. 1958)]—instead, the collecting intermediary warrants by the transfer only its good faith and authority to act. [U.C.C. §7-508]

---

e.g. **Example:** The typical case is that of a *bank* that acquires a negotiable bill as *security* for monies advanced by the bank on the goods shipped. When the bank forwards the bill to the buyer's bank for collection, there are no warranties made except good faith and authority to act in the transfer between the two banks.

---

6. Carrier's Obligations

a. To deliver goods [§721]

Having issued a negotiable bill, the carrier is obligated to deliver the goods to the *bearer* of the bill if it is a bearer bill, or if it is an order bill, to the lawful current *holder* of the bill (*i.e.*, the consignee or some person to whom the consignee has negotiated the bill). If the carrier improperly delivers the goods, the carrier is liable for *conversion*. [*See* U.C.C. §7-404]

(1) Note

The carrier is always protected by complying with the *terms of the document*. This is true even if the shipper was not authorized to ship the goods or the party to whom the carrier delivered the goods had no authority to receive them. As long as the carrier delivers the goods in accordance with the bill (to the bearer or indorsee of a negotiable bill, or to the consignee on a nonnegotiable bill), the duty of delivery is satisfied, and the carrier is not liable for misdelivery. [U.C.C. §7-404; **Rohr v. Logan,** 213 A.2d 166 (Pa. 1965)]

b. Taking up the bill [§722]

It is also the carrier's duty to take up and *cancel* the negotiable bill upon delivery, or, if the delivery is partial, to note conspicuously on the face of the bill the amount of the partial delivery. [U.C.C. §7-403(3)] If the carrier fails to do so, and the holder thereafter sells the bill (a "spent bill") to a bona fide purchaser, the carrier is liable for the loss. Similarly, if the document of title is a warehouse receipt (*see* below), the warehouser who has issued a negotiable warehouse receipt must be careful to get it back before releasing the goods from the warehouse. [U.C.C. §7-403(3)]

C. Warehouse Receipts

1. Definitions [§723]

A warehouse receipt is a document issued by a warehouser, *acknowledging receipt and storage of the goods* identified in the document. The receipt usually also specifies the date of receipt, the rate being charged for storage, and the like. Such receipts may be negotiable or nonnegotiable.

2. Purpose of Warehouse Receipts [§724]

Warehouse receipts are used to finance the sale of merchandise held in storage. Sometimes the storage is at the warehouser's premises, and at other times it is on the owner's premises in what is called a *"field warehouse."* Field warehousing is widely practiced as a security device. (*See* Secured Transactions Summary.)

3. Procedure [§725]

Warehouse receipt financing is accomplished by the owner's storing goods with the warehouser and receiving in return the warehouse receipt. The owner (bailor) then takes the receipt and sells it or pledges it as *security for a loan.* Or, where a buyer has not paid for goods ordered from a seller, the seller may ship the goods to a warehouse and have a warehouse receipt issued in the buyer's name, to be delivered to the buyer upon receipt of payment. Transfer of a *negotiable* warehouse receipt is tantamount to *transfer of ownership* of the goods covered thereby. And as mentioned above (*see supra*, §717), transfer leads to the *making of warranties* for the sale of goods under U.C.C. Article 2.

4. Bills of Lading—Same Rules Apply [§726]

The problems encountered and rules applicable to warehouse receipts are *substantially the same* as with those pertaining to bills of lading. [U.C.C. §§7-201 - 7-210] The discussion and rules in the section on bills of lading above are therefore applicable to warehouse receipts as well, and reference should be made to them when handling any similar problems dealing with warehouse receipts.

D. Rights of Third Parties

1. Rights of Third Parties Under Document Not Regularly Issued [§727]

All of the above discussion of the negotiable character of the documents presumes that the documents were regularly issued. If the document is a forgery, or if its issuance was obtained by fraud or deception upon the issuer or without the authority of the owner (*e.g.,* a thief steals goods and obtains issuance of document), *no rights* can be created thereunder as against the true owner of the goods. [U.C.C. §7-503(1); **Dunagan v. Griffin,** 151 S.W.2d 250 (Tex. 1941)]

a. Exception—document wrongfully procured by bailee to whom owner had entrusted goods [§728]

The result is different when the person who procured the issuance of the negotiable document was a bailee to whom the owner had given possession of the goods (or another document covering the goods) and who had *actual or apparent authority* to obtain the issuance of the document. [U.C.C. §7-503(1)(a)]

e.g. **Example:** Owner employed Bailee to deliver goods, but instead Bailee sold the goods to a bona fide purchaser, T, and shipped them to T under a negotiable document that Bailee negotiated to T. T will prevail over Owner when the carrier is faced with the claims of both for the goods. [U.C.C. §7-403(1), (3)] *Rationale:* As between two innocent parties, the one who caused the loss must suffer. Here, Owner caused the loss by entrusting goods to a dishonest bailee.

cf. **Compare:** A thief broke into Owner's warehouse and stole a valuable piece of machinery. The thief took the machinery to a warehouse and procured a negotiable warehouse receipt for the machinery. The thief then pledged the warehouse receipt to a bank for a loan. Since Owner in no way entrusted the goods to the thief, Owner can recover the machinery from the warehouser without having to surrender the document. The bank's only recourse is against the thief for breach of the warranty of title (or breach of the pledge contract). [U.C.C. §7-403(1), (3); *and see supra,* §717—breach of the warranties accompanying the transfer of the document of title to the bank]

(1) Meaning of "entrustment" [§729]

If the true owner of goods or documents "entrusts" (delivers) them to someone else, that person has at least *apparent authority* to transfer good title to innocent parties. Entrustment means "any delivery and any acquiescence in retention of possession regardless of any condition expressed between the parties to the delivery" and regardless of whether the subsequent conduct of the entrustee is punishable under the criminal law. [U.C.C. §2-403(3)]

(a) Entrustment to merchant [§730]

Under Article 2 of the U.C.C., if the true owner of goods entrusts them to someone who *deals regularly in goods of that kind* (*i.e.,* a merchant), and the merchant sells the goods to a buyer in the ordinary course of business (who has no knowledge of the true situation), the buyer gets *good title* to the items purchased. [U.C.C. §2-403(2)]

e.g. **Example:** The owner of a valuable watch took it to a jeweler to be cleaned. The jeweler sold the watch to a customer who came into the store. Assuming that the jeweler regularly sold watches of this kind and that there was nothing suspicious about the sale, the customer would get clear title to the watch.

1) Bailee still liable [§731]

Even though the true owner of goods (or documents covering the goods) has lost them to an innocent purchaser, the owner may still sue the bailee (*i.e.,* the merchant) for breach of the bailment contract, conversion, quasi-contract, negligence, etc.

Note that the requirements for entrustment are **very specific**. The merchant must be one who **ordinarily deals in goods of the kind** (e.g., a television repair shop that only repairs televisions does not qualify). The sale must be **in the ordinary course of business** (e.g., seizure by a creditor to satisfy a lien does not qualify).

2. Rights of Third Parties Under Document Regularly Issued But Negotiated Without Authority [§732]

To be distinguished from the above is the situation where a negotiable document has been *validly issued* but subsequently has been *negotiated without authority* to an innocent purchaser.

Example: Seller ships goods to Buyer and obtains a negotiable bearer bill of lading therefor (valid issuance). Later, Seller delivers the document to X with instructions to forward it to Buyer as soon as Buyer's payment for the goods is received. Instead, X wrongfully negotiates the document to T, an innocent purchaser. What rights, if any, does T obtain?

a. Effect of "due negotiation" [§733]

If an innocent purchaser (T in the last example) takes by "due negotiation" and thereby becomes a "holder to whom a negotiable document of title has been duly negotiated" (Article 7's protected party), the innocent purchaser gets *full title* to the document and the goods it represents. [U.C.C. §7-502] This is true notwithstanding that the person negotiating the document had obtained possession thereof by defrauding the owner of the document, or had breached some duty to the owner in negotiating the document. [U.C.C. §7-502]

(1) Meaning of "due negotiation" [§734]

"Due negotiation" is the transfer of the document to the holder who buys in *good faith* and *without notice* of problems, in the regular course of business or financing or the payment of a debt. [U.C.C. §7-501(4)]

(2) Effect [§735]

The Code thus accords documents of title the same full negotiability that is accorded to checks and notes, and the holders in due course thereof. (*See* Commercial Paper & Payment Law Summary.)

3. Rights of Third Parties Under Document Issued to Cover Nonexistent Goods [§736]

Another problem arises when a careless or dishonest issuer issues a document showing that it has received certain goods, when in fact it has not. When the goods turn up missing, who bears the loss—the issuer or the holder of the document? This problem most often arises with carriers who issue bills of lading. A common practice is for a carrier to permit the shipper (the bailor) to load the truck or railroad car and fill out the bill of lading for the carrier to sign. Since the carrier did not really see what went into the shipment, the carrier may be deceived into signing a bill showing shipment of nonexistent goods.

a. Common law [§737]

At common law, issuers could absolve themselves of liability by noting on the document itself the words *"shipper's weight, load, and count"* or language of similar import, in which case (provided that in fact it had been "shipper's weight, load, and count"), the courts held the carriers *free from liability* for missing goods. [**D.H. Overmeyer Co. v. Nelson-Brantley Glass Co.**, 168 S.E.2d 176 (Ga. 1969)]

b. U.C.C. rule [§738]

The U.C.C. follows case law in permitting a carrier to limit its liability by using the "shipper's weight, load, and count" phrase, and, if the phrase is true, absolving the carrier of liability. Failure to insert such a phrase passes the *burden of proof* to the carrier to explain what went on, and the omission of the phrase makes the carrier liable to a consignee of a nonnegotiable bill or a holder of a negotiable bill to whom there has been a due negotiation of the document. [U.C.C. §7-301]

4. Bills Drawn to Seller or Seller's Order—Divided Property Interests [§739]

A seller who does not wish to ship goods to a buyer on open credit may *consign the goods to the seller* (straight bill) or to *the order of seller* (an order bill), although the destination may be the buyer's place of business. In such a case, the seller retains the right to possession of the goods until payment is received from the buyer, and the buyer cannot obtain the goods from the carrier until the seller has negotiated to the buyer the bill of lading covering the shipment. If the carrier delivers the goods to the buyer without obtaining the bill, the carrier is liable to the seller for conversion. [**Roundtree v. Lydick-Barmann Co.**, 150 S.W.2d 173 (Tex. 1941)]

a. "Shipping under reservation" [§740]

This practice is called "shipping under reservation," meaning that seller has reserved title and thus maintained control over the goods. It gives the seller a *security interest* in the goods shipped. [U.C.C. §2-505]

b. Practical advantage [§741]

Another advantage of the seller's consignment to the seller is that if the buyer fails to pay, the seller can indorse the document to a third party in the buyer's vicinity and save the expense of having the goods shipped back.

Chapter Ten:
Lease of Goods

CONTENTS

Chapter Approach

In the late 1980s, the drafters of the Uniform Commercial Code proposed for adoption a new Article 2A, governing the lease of goods. The application of the original Article 2 (Sale of Goods) to leases was unclear, and the courts were reaching conflicting results. In a climate where leasing is big business ($200 billion a year and rising), such chaos compelled the creation of Article 2A. Because of a negative reaction to the original proposed version of Article 2A, the drafters made major changes in its wording in 1990, and it is that version which is described below.

The first task of someone approaching Article 2A is to make sure that the Article applies at all—*i.e.,* is it really a lease? The terminology used by the parties is *not conclusive.* For various reasons, parties to a *sale on credit* may wish to disguise it as a lease. In such a case, Articles 2 (Sale of Goods) and 9 (Secured Transactions) apply and Article 2A does not.

The rules of Article 2A are copied slavishly from those of Article 2, making an explanation of the law easier. However, there are some major differences between the two Articles, and they are given detailed treatment in this chapter.

A. Scope of Article 2A

1. **Lease Defined [§742]**
   The definition of "lease" in Article 2A restricts its coverage to a lease of *goods.* [U.C.C. §2A-103(1)(j)] In turn, "goods" are defined in the same way as in Article 2: "all things that are moveable at the time of identification to the lease contract." [U.C.C. §2A-103(1)(h)]

   a. **Sublease included**
      The definition of a "lease" includes a sublease. [U.C.C. §2A-103(1)(h)]

2. **Lease vs. Disguised Sale on Credit [§743]**
   Article 2A applies only to true leases. If the so-called lease is really a sale of goods on credit, Article 2A does not apply. Instead the "lessor" is really a seller of goods (so that Article 2 governs the transaction) and is also an Article 9 *secured party* and had better take the steps Article 9 requires for perfection of the seller's security interest in the goods. If the "lessor" fails to do this, the lessor risks losing the goods to other claimants. (*See* Secured Transactions Summary.)

   Example: For tax reasons, the buyer of goods wanted the transaction disguised as a lease of the goods. The seller agreed, and the contract between them was

Does the lessee have the *right to terminate* the lease and return the goods at any time?

YES

NO

This is a *true lease*. Article 9 does not apply, and Article 2A will apply.

Are *either* of the following true?

- At the end of the lease, the leased goods will have *no remaining economic value* (or the lessee can *renew* the lease for nominal or no additional consideration until the goods have no remaining economic value)

- The lessee will become the *owner* of the goods or has an *option to purchase* them for *nominal or no additional consideration*

NO

YES

This is a *secured transaction* (*i.e.,* sale on credit) disguised as a lease. The "lessor" must comply with Article 9 to protect his interest in the "leased" goods.

called a "lease," with the seller being the "lessor" and the buyer being the "lessee." The so-called lease ran for five years, the entire useful life of the goods. The lease payments slightly exceeded the original market value of the goods. The lease provided that at the end of the lease period the goods became the property of the lessee on the payment of $1. Obviously this is not a true lease, but a disguised sale on credit. The "lessor" is an Article 2 seller of goods and, because the seller reserves the right to repossess in the event of nonpayment, the lessor also is an Article 9 secured party. Consequently the transaction creates a security interest in the goods, so Articles 2 and 9 and not Article 2A will govern the transaction.

---

a.   Tests for telling a lease from a disguised sale [§744]

Jurisdictions adopting Article 2A have also adopted an expanded definition of "security interest" in U.C.C. section 1-201(37) containing a detailed test for telling a true lease from a secured transaction. While the definition is imposing, it is not as complicated as it looks. Its rules can be boiled down to the following:

(1)   Termination clause [§745]

If the contract contains a clause that permits the lessee to *terminate* the lease at any time and *return* the leased goods, a true lease results. Such a right of termination is not an attribute of a sale of goods.

(2)   No remaining economic life [§746]

If the lease is for the *entire economic life* of the leased goods, with or without renewal, a disguised sale has occurred. Thus, if as in the above example, the goods are worthless at the end of the lease period (the "scrap heap" test), Article 2A does not apply.

(3)   Option to purchase [§747]

If the lease contains an option to purchase for *nominal* or *no additional consideration*, a disguised sale has occurred.

(4)   Other provisions [§748]

Section 1-201(37) goes on to provide that in other situations the nature of the transaction must be determined by the facts of the case and that a transaction is not necessarily a disguised sale merely because (i) the lessee pays consideration equal to or even greater than the *fair market value* of the leased goods (as long as the lease does not cover the total economic life of the goods) or (ii) the lessee assumes *major duties* (paying taxes, assuming the risk of loss, etc.) as to the goods.

b.   Protective Article 9 filing [§749]

In situations that are doubtful one way or another, the careful attorney advises the lessor-client to make a protective filing under Article 9. Section 9-505 permits the filing of a financing statement using the terms "lessor" and "lessee" instead of the usual Article 9 terms "secured party" and "debtor." If the alleged lease is subsequently judged to be a secured transaction, this filing will protect the seller from other creditors without in any way being a legal admission that anything other than a true lease has occurred.

B. Article 2 Rules Copied

1. Article 2A Rarely Differs from Article 2 [§750]

With minor exceptions throughout, Article 2A slavishly copies the rules of Article 2 that make up the bulk of this Summary. Consequently, they will not be repeated here. However, there are some differences of note.

2. Statute of Frauds [§751]

The lease must be in writing if the total of payments thereunder will be *$1,000 or more,* and the writing must be signed, describe the leased goods and the lease term, and indicate that a lease contract has been made between the parties. As in Article 2, the writing must specify the *quantity* of the leased goods. [U.C.C. §2A-201]

STATUTE OF FRAUDS—A COMPARISON CHART	**gilbert**
ARTICLE 2 REQUIREMENTS	**ARTICLE 2A REQUIREMENTS**
• Sale of goods for *$500* or more.	• Lease of goods for *$1,000* or more.
• Writing must be *signed* by party to be charged.	• Writing must be *signed* by party to be charged.
• Writing must specify *quantity*.	• Writing must specify *quantity, lease term,* and *describe the leased goods*.

3. Battle of the Forms [§752]

Recognizing the wisdom of avoiding all the trouble caused by the original, Article 2A has no "battle of the forms" section at all. (For a discussion of the battle of the forms in Article 2, *see supra*, §§76-89.)

4. Consumer Protection [§753]

If the lessee is a consumer, a consumer lease arises. [U.C.C. §2A-103(1)(e)] Article 2A contains various rules protecting the consumer. Among these are the following:

a. Option to accelerate at will [§754]

If the lease contains a term allowing acceleration of the entire lease obligation at the will of the lessor, the term is enforceable only if the lessor exercises it *in good faith*, which the lessor has the burden of proving. [U.C.C. §2A-109(2)]

b. Unconscionability [§755]

Article 2A contains an unconscionability section modeled on U.C.C. section 2-302, but going a bit further. Like its predecessor, section 2A-108 does not define unconscionability, but does have the following rules:

(1) Substantive unconscionability not required [§756]

Unlike the original, Article 2A's rules on unconscionability do not require both procedural *and* substantive unconscionability (*see supra,* §22). If a consumer lease has been *induced* by unconscionable conduct, the court may award appropriate relief even though the lease is otherwise fair. The same rule applies if the lessee engages in unconscionable conduct in the *collection* of a claim arising from the lease (such as using force or violence). [U.C.C. §2A-108(2)]

(2) Attorney's fees [§757]

In consumer lease litigation, the successful consumer is permitted to recover attorney's fees. The amount of the fees is not limited by the amount of the recovery. If the consumer loses the lawsuit and the court finds that the consumer brought an action that the consumer knew to be groundless, the consumer must pay attorney's fees to the lessor. [U.C.C. §2A-108(4)]

c. Limitation of consequential damages [§758]

Just as in section 2-719(3), Article 2A provides in section 2A-503(3) that a disclaimer of liability for consequential damages for personal injury in a consumer lease is *prima facie unconscionable.*

C. Warranties

1. Few Distinctions from Article 2 [§759]

In an Article 2A lease, the lessor makes all the usual warranties that are made by a seller in Article 2. There is one major exception: the finance lease.

2. Finance Lease Defined [§760]

In a "finance lease," the lessee, instead of buying goods and financing the sale somehow, has the lessor buy the goods from a seller (called a *supplier* in Article 2A) and then lease them to the lessee. [U.C.C. §2A-103(1)(g)]

Example: Waldo picked out the car of his dreams from Façade Motors, but for tax reasons did not want to buy the car and instead wished to lease it. Waldo went to Last National Bank ("LNB") and asked LNB if it would buy the car from Façade Motors and then lease it to Waldo for three years. LNB did this. This transaction is called a finance lease. LNB is the lessor, Waldo is the lessee, and Façade Motors is the supplier.

---

a. Lessee must select the goods [§761]

If the lessor is in the business of selecting or manufacturing or selling these kinds of goods, no finance lease occurs. The lessor must be a *true financer*, and the lessee must be the entity that selects the goods or approves their purchase.

EXAM TIP   **gilbert**

On your exam, be wary if the facts provide for an entity other than a bank or finance company as the lessor. This may be a sign that the party is a seller or a manufacturer, *not a true financer*.

---

b.   Lessee's understanding of warranty rights [§762]

If the lessee did not receive or approve a copy of the contract between the supplier and the lessor, the lessee must be given enough information to enable the lessee to understand all the warranty rights involved (either these will be described or the lessee will be told to communicate with the supplier on the topic).

3.   Warranties in a Finance Lease [§763]

In a finance lease, the *lessor makes no implied warranties*, but instead any warranties, express or implied, made by the *supplier* to the lessor are *passed on* to the lessee, who has a direct cause of action on them against the supplier, regardless of the lack of privity between the lessee and the supplier. [U.C.C. §2A-209]

4.   The "Hell or High Water" Clause [§764]

A finance lease imposes an *absolute obligation* on the lessee to make payments to the lessor no matter how badly the leased goods perform or break down. The lessor is supposed to deal with the supplier to work out problems, and must keep making the lease payments in the meanwhile. This is called a "hell or high water" clause, and, whether or not specifically provided for in the lease, it is the law. [U.C.C. §2A-407] The rule kicks into effect as soon as the lessee "accepts" the goods. [U.C.C. §§2A-407(1), 2A-515] Note, however, that the rule *does not apply to consumer leases*.

D. Remedies

1.   Default Under Article 2A [§765]

Part 5 of Article 2A contains the rules on default by the parties involved. These rules are derived in part from Article 2 and in part from the repossession rules of Article 9.

2.   Default by Lessor [§766]

Default by the lessor gives the lessee the same rights and remedies the lessee would have had if the transaction had been a sale and Article 2 applied. [U.C.C. §§2A-508 - 2A-522] Thus, the lessee may accept the goods and recover damages for breach of warranty, or may reject the goods and cover, or seek the market price-lease differential. [U.C.C. §2A-508] Revocation of acceptance is permitted under rules similar to Article 2, except that in a finance lease, revocation of acceptance *is not* permitted for *quality* problems first arising after acceptance, but only for substantial breaches of the lease agreement between the lessor and the lessee. [U.C.C. §2A-516, and Official Comment]

3. Default by Lessee [§767]

Default by the lessee invokes remedies similar to those given a seller in Article 2. [U.C.C. §§2A-523 - 2A-532] The lessor may cancel the lease only if the lessee's default is *material*, and for nonmaterial breaches the lessor is relegated to an action for damages. [U.C.C. §2A-523, and Official Comment] The lessor is given the right to repossess the goods without a court proceeding if repossession can be done *without a breach of the peace*. [U.C.C. §2A-525(3)]

4. Repossession by the Lessor [§768]

At common law and as a matter of contract, lessors frequently repossessed and then sued the lessee for the entire amount of rent called for in the lease. Article 2A does not allow the lessor to get a windfall of this magnitude, but relegates the lessor to the *actual damages* suffered, which the lessor must prove. [U.C.C. §2A-528] If the lessor repossesses and then relets the goods to someone else, the new lease is a mitigating factor and must be taken into account in computing damages. [U.C.C. §2A-527]

a. Action for the rent [§769]

The most controversial section in Part 5 of Article 2A is section 2A-529, "Lessor's Action for the Rent." As originally written, this section (copied almost word for word from section 2-709) made little sense (it apparently permitted the lessor to repossess *and* recover the unpaid rent), and this led to non-uniform amendments by the legislatures adopting it. The 1990 amendments to Article 2A resulted in a more coherent rule. The lessor may sue for the entire future rent on a substantial default by the lessee, but only if the goods were *neither repossessed nor tendered* by the lessee (because, for example, they have been destroyed or have ceased to have any value). An action for the rent also lies where the lessor proves that the return of the goods was in no way a mitigating factor, as, for example, where the lessor proves to have an inventory of leased goods that would cover any number of rentals, so that the lessor has *lost volume* by the refusal of the lessee to go through with the deal. [U.C.C. §2A-529, Official Comment 2]

E. Priority Disputes

1. Ability to Sublease [§770]

In spite of an agreement otherwise, section 2A-303 clearly allows subleasing (or any transfer of the lease). This is done in the interest of commerce.

a. Sublease as material violation of prime lease [§771]

However, Article 2A also provides that a transfer of the lease in *material* violation of the terms of the prime lease is a ground for default and gives rise to an action for damages, or allows a court "to grant other appropriate relief, including cancellation of the lease contract or an injunction against the transfer." [U.C.C. §2A-303(5)(b)]

b. Meaning of "material" [§772]

The statute does not define "material," but the parties may set standards to determine its meaning. [U.C.C. §2A-303, Official Comment 2]

c. Assignment of right of payment allowed [§773]

When the lessor has no remaining significant affirmative duties (called in the trade a "*nonoperating lease*"), a transfer of a right to payment arising out of a lease is *not* a material transfer and is allowed despite an agreement otherwise. On the other hand, where the lessor has significant remaining duties, such as maintenance of the leased property (a so-called *operating lease*), a transfer of a right to payment without the agreement of the lessee would be a ground for default. [U.C.C. §2A-303(4), Official Comment 7]

d. Security interest in lessor's rights allowed [§774]

Section 2A-303(3) permits the lessor to grant a security interest in the lessor's interests under the lease despite agreement otherwise, and does not allow the lessee to claim that doing so is a breach of the lease agreement.

2. Rights of Sublessee [§775]

Generally, a sublessee is subject to the terms of the prime lease and gets no better rights in the leased goods than the sublessor had. [U.C.C. §2A-305] Thus a sublessee faces the prospect that a default by the sublessor on the prime lease could result in repossession of the leased goods from the sublessee.

a. Exception—entrustment [§776]

One major exception is based on the entrusting rule of section 2-403(2) in Article 2 (*see supra*, §730), adapted to leases in sections 2A-304 and 2A-305. If anyone entrusts goods to a merchant who deals in goods of that kind, a buyer or lessee in the ordinary course takes free of the claims of the entruster. This means that if the sublessor is someone who regularly leases goods to others, the sublessee in the ordinary course of business will *prevail* over the prime lessor's rights in the leased goods.

3. Creditors' Rights [§777]

Generally, creditors of either party to the lease get no better rights than their debtors have in the leased property. Thus, creditors of the lessor cannot levy on the leased property in the hands of the lessee, and creditors of the lessee cannot seize the leased property and appropriate it to pay the debt owed by the lessee to the creditors. [U.C.C. §2A-307] There are, however, exceptions.

a. Not a true lease [§778]

Repeating what was said above (*see supra*, §§743-749), if the so-called lease is not a true lease but is instead a sale on credit, the "lessor" is really an unpaid seller. If the "lessor" has not taken the steps required by Article 9 to *perfect* a security interest in the leased goods, the creditors of the lessee will prevail. [U.C.C. §9-301]

b. Statutory lienholders [§779]

In a rule similar to the one found in section 9-310, section 2A-306 gives a valid lien to artisans who perform work on the leased property, and this lien prevails over all other claimants as long as the artisan maintains possession. Thus if the lessee takes the leased goods to a repair shop for servicing, the repair shop would obtain an artisan's lien on the goods for the value of the repairs, and as long as the repair shop did not surrender possession of the goods, its lien would prevail over the rights of all other parties.

c. Lessor's preexisting creditors [§780]

A creditor of the lessor whose lien or security interest attaches to the leased goods *after* the lease was in effect cannot realize on the leased property to the prejudice of the lessee. However, a creditor of the lessor whose lien or security interest attached *prior* to the lease may repossess unless the lessor leased the goods in the ordinary course of the lessor's business to a lessee who gave value and was unaware that the lease was in violation of the rights of the creditor. [U.C.C. §2A-307]

Chapter Eleven:
The International Sale
of Goods

CONTENTS

Chapter Approach

Chapter Approach

Effective January 1, 1988, the United States became bound by a treaty, the United Nations Convention on Contracts for the International Sale of Goods, that governs international contracts for sale between parties in signatory nations. To the extent this treaty is covered in your law school course, keep in mind that its rules typically are similar to the rules in Article 2.

A. United Nations Convention on Contracts for the International Sale of Goods

1. Application of the Treaty [§781]

As the world grows smaller and trade broadens, even attorneys in the heartland of the United States are going to be faced with international trade. Ideally the attorney may be able to make the foreign party in a sales contract agree to be bound by United States law (*i.e.*, the Uniform Commercial Code), and now that may be possible. The United Nations Convention on Contracts for the International Sale of Goods ("CISG") clearly authorizes contractual agreements choosing a source of law other than the treaty itself. If the foreign party is not willing to agree to be bound by United States law, and the domestic attorney is unwilling to agree to the law of the foreign jurisdiction, selection of the treaty as the source of law is indicated (and if nothing is said about choice of law, the treaty would automatically apply if both parties are located in contracting states). However, there is good news, even if CISG applies: CISG is modeled on the Uniform Commercial Code in large part, with a few foreign ideas thrown in, and should look reassuringly familiar to anyone who has mastered the rules of Article 2.

B. Scope of the Treaty

1. Basic Application [§782]

Generally, the treaty applies when the parties are in different countries, *both* countries are signatories to the treaty ("contracting states" in the language of the treaty), and the parties do not agree to be bound by some other body of law. [CISG Article 1]

a. **Signatory countries [§783]**

At the printing of this book, the following countries had joined in the treaty: Argentina, Australia, Austria, Belarus, Bosnia and Herzegovina, Bulgaria, Canada, Chile, China, Cuba, Czech Republic, Denmark, Ecuador, Egypt, Estonia, Finland, France, Georgia, Germany, Ghana, Guinea, Hungary, Iraq, Italy, Lesotho, Mexico, Netherlands, New Zealand, Norway, Poland, Republic of Moldova, Romania, Russian Federation, Singapore, Slovakia, Slovenia, Spain, Sweden, Switzerland, Syrian Arab Republic, Uganda, Ukraine, United States of America, Venezuela, Yugoslavia, and Zambia.

EXAM TIP	gilbert

Remember that, although the United States has joined in the CISG, the treaty will only apply in situations where **both** countries have adopted its provisions. Therefore, be cautious and do not automatically apply the CISG to every international transaction.

2. **Exclusions [§784]**

The treaty does *not* apply to or regulate the following:

a. *Personal injury* [CISG Article 5];

b. *The sale of consumer goods* [CISG Article 2(a)];

c. *Goods sold by auction or pursuant to execution* [CISG Article 2(b), (c)];

d. *The sale of ships, vessels, hovercraft, or aircraft* [CISG Article 2(e)]; or

e. *The sale of electricity* [CISG Article 2(f)].

3. **Validity of the Contract [§785]**

The treaty does *not* regulate matters of validity of the sales contract. [CISG Article 4] This means that issues of capacity, fraud, mistake, etc., are not addressed anywhere in the treaty and will have to be litigated according to other law.

C. Some Substantive Issues

1. **Rules Based on Article 2 [§786]**

As mentioned above, the treaty's substantive provisions are unremarkable, being based on Article 2 of the Uniform Commercial Code. Thus, the treaty has the usual rules on *usage of trade*, contract *formation*, *warranties*, *risk of loss*, and *remedies*. Some of the variations from the norm follow.

2. **Statute of Frauds [§787]**

There is *no* Statute of Frauds, and thus the treaty recognizes oral contracts for the sale of goods. [CISG Article 11]

3. Mailbox Rule [§788]

The mailbox rule of contracts law (acceptance effective on dispatch) is altered. Under CISG, an acceptance is not effective until *received*. [CISG Article 18(2)] However, the offeror is not permitted to revoke the offer once the acceptance has been dispatched. [CISG Article 16(1)]

4. Battle of the Forms [§789]

The battle of the forms (*see supra,* §§76-89) has been simplified. A reply to an offer that purports to be an acceptance but contains additions, limitations, or other modifications is a rejection of the offer and constitutes a counteroffer. However, a reply to an offer that purports to be an acceptance but contains additional or different terms that do not materially alter the terms of the offer constitutes an acceptance, unless the offeror, without undue delay, *objects orally* to the discrepancy or dispatches a notice to that effect. If there is no such objection, the terms of the contract are the terms of the offer with the modifications contained in the acceptance. Additional or different terms relating, among other things, to the price, payment, quality and quantity of the goods, place and time of delivery, extent of one party's liability to the other, or the settlement of disputes are considered to alter the terms of the offer materially. [CISG Article 19]

5. Fundamental Breach [§790]

The treaty borrows from civil law the concept of "fundamental breach." [CISG Article 25] Fundamental breach is similar to "material breach" in the Restatement (Second) of Contracts section 241 (which is the opposite of "substantial performance"). Under Article 25:

> A breach of contract committed by one of the parties is fundamental if it results in such detriment to the other party as substantially to deprive him of what he is entitled to expect under the contract, unless the party in breach did not foresee, and a reasonable person of the same kind in the same circumstances would not have foreseen, such a result.

On a finding of fundamental breach, the aggrieved party is given a broader range of remedies (including contract termination) than for non-fundamental breaches. [*See, e.g.,* CISG Articles 49, 51(2), 64, 72, 73]

6. Notice of Breach [§791]

The buyer must give the seller notice of any claimed breach of warranty/contract within a reasonable time, but in no event longer than *two years* after the goods were actually handed over to the buyer. [CISG Article 39]

7. Remedies

a. Specific performance [§792]

CISG has a *presumption* in favor of the ability of the parties to get *specific performance.* [*See* CISG Articles 46, 62] Note, however, that Article 28 does not permit specific performance if the court asked to do so would not do so were its own law applied. For example, in the United States specific performance is never granted where it would require undue court supervision, and so a United States court might use this ground to duck an order of specific performance.

b. **Rejection by buyer [§793]**

The buyer may not reject goods and require delivery of conforming goods unless the seller's original tender is so deficient as to constitute a fundamental breach. [CISG Article 46(2)]

c. **Grace periods to resolve disputes [§794]**

The buyer may notify the seller of a grace period in which the seller must remedy the claimed defects, and if the buyer has done so, the buyer must not resort to other remedies during the period (unless the seller refuses to do the repairs/replacements). [CISG Article 47] Similarly, where the buyer claims breach, the seller may propose a grace period for remedial actions, and, unless the buyer objects to this proposal, the buyer cannot resort to any remedy during this period, but retains a claim for damages caused by the delay. [CISG Article 48] Where the buyer is in breach, the parties may also propose to one another similar grace periods. [CISG Article 63] These grace period proposals are commonly called *"Nachfrist" notices* ("Nachfrist" is German for "extension").

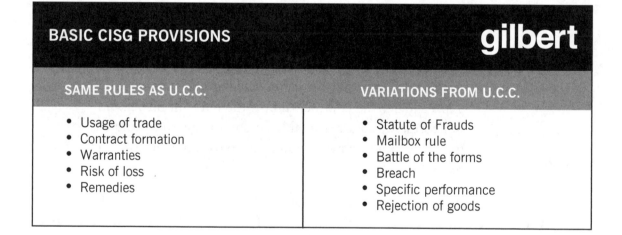

BASIC CISG PROVISIONS	gilbert
SAME RULES AS U.C.C.	**VARIATIONS FROM U.C.C.**
• Usage of trade • Contract formation • Warranties • Risk of loss • Remedies	• Statute of Frauds • Mailbox rule • Battle of the forms • Breach • Specific performance • Rejection of goods

Review Questions
and Answers

Review Questions

SALES CONTRACTS—IN GENERAL

1. Which of the following transactions is not subject to Article 2 of the U.C.C.?   _____

    (A) Owner of land sells subsurface coal and iron ore to Buyer, who is to mine and remove the coal and iron ore.

    (B) Owner of land agrees to allow Buyer to cut down and take all trees growing on Owner's land.

    (C) Owner of land sells to Buyer all oranges growing and to be grown on Owner's trees for next five years, Buyer to pick the fruit from the trees.

    (D) Owner of land sells to Buyer wheat crop now growing on Owner's land, Buyer to harvest the crop and remove it.

2. Which of the following transactions is a "sale" of goods under Article 2?   _____

    (A) Blood injected into a patient as part of an operation.

    (B) A product put on a person's hair as part of a haircut.

    (C) The sale of the unborn young of animals.

    (D) A lease of a rental car by an agency.

3. Farmer sends the following signed letter to Food Processor: "I am offering you my current crop of potatoes at $85 per ton; delivery August 1. This offer is firm for next 10 days only." Can Farmer revoke the offer prior to the expiration of 10 days?   _____

4. Wholesaler sends out a printed notice to various retail accounts, offering them special price reductions on orders received during the next 30 days. The notice states that it is a "firm offer" and will not be revoked. Can Wholesaler revoke the offer notwithstanding the promise to hold it open?   _____

5. Wholesaler telegraphs Flower Grower as follows: "Send 100 dozen yellow roses by air freight at usual price." Flower Grower has only 50 dozen yellow roses on hand, and therefore sends them together with 50 dozen red roses. The following morning, and before receipt of the roses, Wholesaler telegraphs: "Cancel yesterday's order; market conditions have changed." By the time the flowers arrive, they are a glut on the market and cannot be sold.

a. Grower sues for the price. Wholesaler defends on the ground that Grower had not acknowledged the order prior to shipment and therefore Wholesaler had no way of knowing that the goods were en route when Wholesaler canceled, so that the revocation should be held effective. Who wins? _____

b. Assume there was an enforceable contract. Can Grower recover the full price? _____

6. On March 1, Wholesaler writes Flower Grower: "I hereby offer to purchase 600 dozen No. 1 red roses for delivery on December 15." Grower immediately goes out and plants extra rosebushes to fill this order. On March 15, Wholesaler telegraphs Grower: "Not having heard from you, I am revoking my offer and placing my order with another grower."

a. If Grower sues Wholesaler for breach of contract, who wins? _____

b. Assume that on March 5, Grower mailed Wholesaler a memo: "Your roses are being planted this week." However, this memo was delayed in the mail and was not received by Wholesaler until after March 15. Under these facts, who wins the Grower v. Wholesaler lawsuit? _____

7. Printer sends a purchase order to Pressco for a new printing press. The order is on Printer's form and expressly states that the press is to be delivered "no later than June 1." Instead of signing Printer's form, Pressco mails Printer its own "acknowledgment of order" form which contains numerous provisions, one of which states: "Any delivery date shown on your purchase order is approximate only; our failure to deliver on said date shall not constitute a breach of this sales contract." Printer fails to object thereto. Pressco fails to deliver on June 1. On June 2, Printer cancels the contract and sues for damages. Pressco defends on the ground that (i) the delivery date was only approximate; and (ii) there is no contract. Who wins? _____

8. Farmer telephones Wholesaler for a price quote on Farmer's corn crop. Wholesaler says "$275 a ton." Farmer says "It's a deal." Wholesaler immediately sends a written confirmation stating "$275 per ton, upon delivery to my storage facility in Middleton." Farmer refuses to deliver and is sued for damages. Farmer claims no contract. Who wins? _____

9. Farmer buys a used tractor from Dealer for $3,000 and later sues for breach of warranty. There was a written contract signed by both Dealer and Farmer which made no mention of any warranties. Farmer claims Dealer orally warranted the condition of the tractor. Dealer defends on the ground that the sale was for more than $500 and was required to be in writing under the Statute of Frauds. Who wins? _____

10. Farmer orally agrees to purchase a used tractor from Dealer for $3,000. The only thing in writing signed by Farmer is an application for transfer of the vehicle license.

If Farmer later backs out of the sale, can Dealer enforce it notwithstanding the lack of a signed contract? _____

11. Farmer orally agrees to sell 5,000 bushels of corn to Wholesaler at $3.75 per bushel. Wholesaler sends a check to Farmer marked "deposit on corn contract," which Farmer indorses and cashes. Later, Farmer refuses to deliver and tenders back the money received from Wholesaler. Can Wholesaler enforce the sale notwithstanding the lack of a signed contract? _____

12. Farmer orally agrees to sell 5,000 bushels of corn to Wholesaler at $3.75 per bushel. Farmer sends Wholesaler a written confirmation of the sale, but Wholesaler makes no response thereto. Later, Wholesaler refuses to purchase at the agreed price. Can Farmer enforce the sale notwithstanding the lack of a signed contract? _____

13. Farmer orally agrees to sell 5,000 bushels of corn to Wholesaler at $3.75 per bushel, to be delivered in two shipments of 2,500 bushels each. Farmer delivers and Wholesaler pays for the first shipment. When Farmer tenders the second shipment, Wholesaler rejects it without cause. Can Farmer enforce the sale notwithstanding the lack of a signed contract? _____

14. Farmer orally agrees to purchase a tractor from Dealer for $5,000 and pays $100 cash as a down payment. Later, Farmer has a change of heart and refuses to proceed with the purchase. Can Dealer enforce the sale notwithstanding the lack of a signed contract? _____

15. Aerospace Co. telephones an order to Toolco to design and manufacture a special machine tool for Aerospace. Toolco engineers create a design and submit it to Aerospace for approval, at which point Aerospace cancels the order without cause. Can Toolco enforce the sale notwithstanding the lack of a signed contract? _____

16. Which of the following sales agreements is enforceable? _____

(A) Buyer promises to pay for goods "at whatever price we mutually agree upon at time of delivery."

(B) Buyer promises to pay for goods "at whatever price you (seller) fix at time of delivery."

(C) Buyer promises to pay for goods "at price to be fixed by me at time of delivery."

17. Steelco agrees to sell its entire output of slag (a byproduct from steel mill operation) to Processor for a period of one year at $10 per ton. Due to adverse business conditions, Steelco decides to close its own steel mill. Processor has to pay $15 a ton to obtain slag elsewhere. Is Steelco liable for damages? _____

18. Steelco agrees to sell its entire output of No. 30 pig iron ingots to Fabricator for a period of one year at $600 per ton. Due to increased labor costs, Steelco finds that

it costs in excess of $600 a ton to manufacture these particular ingots, and hence discontinues manufacture. Processor has to pay $800 a ton to obtain similar ingots elsewhere. Is Steelco liable for damages?

19. Boatco displays one of its new models at Boat Show. The day the show closes it sells its display model to Salty, but the contract does not mention anything about delivery. Is Boatco under an obligation to deliver the boat to Salty's dock?

20. To obtain a price discount, Trucker agrees to purchase exclusively from Gas Station all gas and oil which Trucker needs to operate Trucker's fleet of trucks. Nothing is said about how long this arrangement is to continue. Two weeks later, Trucker finds another gas dealer who is willing to give Trucker a bigger discount. Can Trucker terminate the agreement with Gas Station at will?

21. On August 1, Seller ships goods to Buyer and sends an invoice dated the same date marked "net 30 days; 2% discount 10 days." The invoice is received August 5. If Buyer tenders payment on August 12, is Buyer entitled to the discount?

22. Auto Manufacturer has a written contract with Battery Co. to deliver 5,000 batteries on November 1, at a price of $20 each. On October 15, Battery Co. indicates that it may be unable to deliver on time. To insure timely delivery, Auto Manufacturer orally agrees to pay a bonus of $5,000 for full and prompt performance. If Battery Co. meets the deadline, can it collect the bonus?

   a. Could Battery Co. collect the bonus if Auto Manufacturer had put its promise in writing?

23. Auto Manufacturer has a written contract with Battery Co. to deliver 5,000 batteries on November 1. The contract stipulates that "no modification of any term shall be effective unless in writing." On October 1, the parties orally agree that delivery may be postponed for 30 days. On October 5, Manufacturer changes its mind and demands delivery on November 1. Is Battery Co. obligated to perform on November 1?

TYPES OF SALES

24. Aerospace orders a special machine tool from Toolco for $100,000. Nothing is stated in the contract as to when payment is to be made. Is Toolco entitled to insist upon cash payment at time of delivery?

   a. If Aerospace gave Toolco a check for the purchase price at the time of delivery, and the check was returned for nonsufficient funds, can Toolco reclaim the goods?

   b. Assume that Aerospace had in the interim sold the tool to BFP, an innocent purchaser for value. Could Toolco reclaim the tool from BFP?

25. Manufacturer delivers to Dealer five heavy-duty sewing machines for resale to others. A signed contract indicates this is an outright sale, although Manufacturer has verbally assured Dealer that the machines are "on approval."

    a.   Assume Dealer decides to return the goods to Manufacturer, but Manufacturer refuses to accept the goods back because the right to return was not in writing. Is Manufacturer obliged to take the goods back? _____

    b.   Assume the machines were stolen while on Dealer's premises, despite reasonable care by Dealer. Who bears the loss? _____

    c.   Assume that before Dealer notified Manufacturer of Dealer's desire to return the goods, Dealer's creditors levied on the goods in Dealer's store. In litigation between the creditors and the unpaid Manufacturer, who is entitled to the goods? _____

26. Dealer delivers a heavy-duty sewing machine to User. A signed contract indicates this is an outright sale, although Dealer has verbally assured User that the sale is "subject to your approval."

    a.   Assume User tries the machine but is dissatisfied and notifies Dealer that User wants to return the machine. Is Dealer obliged to take the goods back? _____

    b.   If the machine is stolen while on User's premises, despite reasonable care by User, who bears the loss? _____

    c.   Assume User's creditors levied on the machine while it was on User's premises. In litigation between the creditors and the unpaid Dealer who would prevail? _____

WARRANTIES

27. Battery Co. publishes national advertisements asserting that its batteries will provide "years of quick starts, even in subfreezing weather!" Later, tests show that Battery Co. batteries do not last more than six months in subfreezing climates.

    a.   Can a Florida purchaser rescind for breach of warranty even though the purchaser has never used the battery in subfreezing climates? _____

    b.   Would your answer be the same if the advertisement had claimed merely that Battery Co. batteries "perform dependably, even in subfreezing weather"? _____

    c.   Is it relevant that Battery Co. had reason to believe its advertising was true at the time it was published? _____

    d.   Assume that Battery Co.'s advertising campaign started *after* the time of purchase. Would this affect the Florida purchaser's right to rescind? _____

28. Neighbor sells her used car to Friend. Does Neighbor impliedly warrant that the car is fit for driving?

29. Auto Dealer sells both new and used cars. Will warranties be implied on the sales of *used* cars?

30. Ivana buys a boatload of wheat from Grainco. Upon delivery, a small portion of the wheat is contaminated. Is Ivana entitled to sue for breach of implied warranty of merchantability?

31. Trucker orders a "Battery Co. Model 12" truck battery from Dealer. This battery proves inadequate to power the refrigerated system on Trucker's truck. Is there a breach of warranty of merchantability or fitness?

32. Self-Service Cafeteria offers for breakfast boxes of cereal containing individual servings. Hungry selects a box of "Wheatos" packaged by National Mills. Hungry breaks a tooth on a small pebble which has somehow found its way into the cereal box. Has Cafeteria made or breached any warranty as to the contents of the "Wheatos" cereal?

33. Buyer ordered 300 bushels of potatoes from Seller. Upon delivery, Buyer made only a casual inspection of the potatoes and found nothing wrong. A thorough inspection would have disclosed that a substantial portion of the shipment was rotten. Has Buyer waived any claim as to breach of warranty?

    a. Would your answer be the same if Seller had written Buyer prior to delivery, "I will not honor any claim as to the condition of the potatoes being shipped to you unless you inspect and return any potatoes that you find defective"?

34. Dealer sells a used tractor to Farmer, representing that it has a "load hauling capacity of at least three tons." However, the written sales contract does not include this representation and specifically disclaims "all warranties, express or implied."

    a. Does this disclaimer in the sales contract bar an action by Farmer against Dealer for breach of representation regarding hauling capacity?

    b. Assume the tractor has the hauling capacity represented, but otherwise proves inoperative. Would the disclaimer in the sales contract bar an action by Farmer for breach of the implied warranty of merchantability?

    c. Assume Farmer made known special needs to Dealer, and Dealer picked out this particular tractor for Farmer. Would the disclaimer in the sales contract bar an action by Farmer for breach of the implied warranty of fitness for particular purpose?

    d. Assume an action for breach of implied warranty of merchantability would otherwise lie. Could Farmer establish that the tractor was not "merchantable" because normally tractors have a load hauling capacity of at least *five* tons (whereas Dealer had represented only three-ton capacity)? _____

35. Homeowner is operating a new Lawnco gasoline engine lawnmower, which Homeowner purchased from Dealer, when a blade breaks loose and goes flying into Neighbor's house, where it destroys a valuable painting. Could Neighbor maintain a *warranty* action against either Homeowner, Dealer, or Lawnco? _____

36. Hungry became seriously ill after consuming food at Leftomaine Restaurant. Hungry files an action for breach of implied warranty against Leftomaine. Leftomaine moves to dismiss Hungry's complaint because it fails to allege that Hungry gave Leftomaine any notice of having become ill before suit was filed. How should the court rule on Leftomaine's motion? _____

37. Hungry filed a lawsuit against Leftomaine Restaurant for breach of implied warranty, alleging that Hungry became seriously ill after consuming food served there. Leftomaine moves to dismiss on the ground that Hungry has failed to allege any actual damage or that the illness was caused by the food Hungry consumed. How should the court rule on Leftomaine's motion? _____

38. Trucker purchases a new truck that is designed so poorly that it turns over in normal operation, causing extensive damage both to the truck and to the load being carried.

    a. Are the damages to both the truck and the load recoverable in an action for breach of warranty? _____

    b. Suppose that while the truck was being repaired, Trucker was unable to haul other loads, and thereby lost profits Trucker otherwise would have earned. Would such profits be recoverable in a warranty action? _____

    c. Assume a local statute of limitations requires that "any action based on injury to person or property be filed within one year following date of such injury." Would Trucker be barred if Trucker failed to file the action for breach of warranty within one year? _____

PERFORMANCE OF THE CONTRACT

39. Spudco sells 3,000 bushels of potatoes to Chipco. Nothing is said about delivery except that Spudco is to pay all freight charges to Chipco's plant.

    a. Is Spudco required to deliver the goods to Chipco's plant? _____

    b. Is Spudco required to make shipping arrangements to get the potatoes to Chipco's plant? _____

    c. Who bears the risk of loss if the potatoes are accidentally damaged or destroyed en route to Chipco's plant? _____

40. Mines sells 1,000 tons of iron ore to Steelco at an agreed price, "F.O.B. Steelco mill."

   a. Who is obliged to pay for the freight charges in getting the iron ore to the Steelco mill?

   _____

   b. Who bears the risk of loss if the iron ore is accidentally damaged or destroyed en route to the steel mill?

   _____

41. Manufacturer has stored its excess inventory of widgets at Warehouse, obtaining a negotiable warehouse receipt therefor. On June 1, it sells this excess inventory to Dealer, and indorses the warehouse receipt to Dealer. On June 2, before Dealer has a chance to obtain the inventory, the Warehouse is destroyed by fire. As between Manufacturer and Dealer, who bears the loss?

   _____

42. On August 1, Stable sells a riding horse to Rider, who agrees to pick up the horse on August 5. On August 2, the horse is killed by lightning. Who bears the loss?

   _____

43. On September 1, Neighbor sells Neighbor's used car to Friend, and gives Friend the keys to the car, which is still in Neighbor's garage. If the car is accidentally destroyed that night, before Friend has taken possession, who bears the loss?

   _____

44. Spudco sells 3,000 bushels of potatoes to Chipco. It tenders delivery of 2,950 bushels and offers a discount on the purchase price for the missing 50 bushels. Chipco rejects delivery. Spudco sues for breach. Who wins?

   _____

45. Spudco sells 3,000 bushels of potatoes to Chipco, delivery to be made in five separate shipments of 600 bushels each. Spudco's first shipment contains only 550 bushels. Chipco rejects delivery and cancels the contract. Spudco sues for breach. Who wins?

   _____

46. Spudco sells 3,000 bushels of potatoes to Chipco, delivery to be made "via commercial truck carrier to arrive at Chipco plant on or about June 5." To save freight expense, Spudco sends the potatoes via rail carrier, which is slower and arrives on June 8. If Chipco rejects delivery and suit ensues, who wins?

   _____

47. Spudco sells 3,000 bushels of potatoes to Chipco, delivery to be made "no later than June 10." On June 5, Spudco tenders delivery of 2,500 bushels and Chipco rejects. Spudco immediately notifies Chipco that it will cure the shortage by shipping the balance of potatoes immediately, so that they will arrive on or about June 15. Chipco rejects the second shipment as well. Who wins?

   _____

   a. Would your answer be the same if Chipco had previously accepted and paid for shipments which were short in quantity and Spudco reasonably believed that Chipco would do so on this occasion as well?

   _____

   b. Assume the sale required delivery "on or about June 10." Who wins under these facts?

   _____

48. Spudco sells 3,000 bushels of potatoes to Chipco, payment to be made "C.O.D." Upon arrival of the shipment, Chipco demands the right to inspect the potatoes before paying. Spudco refuses to permit inspection. Chipco thereupon "cancels" the sale. Suit ensues. Who wins? _____

49. Same facts, except assume that Chipco acceded to Spudco's demand, and paid for the potatoes before inspection. If, after payment, Chipco inspected the shipment and found the potatoes were rotten, can it reject the shipment and recover its money? _____

   a. Assume only 500 bushels were rotten, and the balance fine, could Chipco reject the shipment in part and retain the good potatoes? _____

   b. Assume that Chipco did not discover that 500 bushels were rotten at the time of delivery. Rather, the condition became apparent only after Chipco had notified Spudco that the potatoes were accepted and the shipment had been processed by Chipco. Would Chipco be barred from any recovery for the rotten potatoes? _____

50. Spudco sells 3,000 bushels of potatoes to Chipco, payment to be made "C.O.D." Upon arrival of the shipment, Chipco tenders a personal check for the purchase price. Spudco refuses to take a personal check and thereupon sells the potatoes to another buyer. Chipco sues for damages. Who wins? _____

51. Spudco sells 3,000 bushels of potatoes to Chipco, delivery to be made no later than June 10. The shipment arrives on that date, but Chipco finds that 50 bushels are rotten. Chipco thereupon writes Spudco, "I am rejecting your shipment because it is defective." Is this an effective rejection even though Chipco failed to specify what was wrong? _____

   a. Would your answer be the same if the shipment had arrived on June 1, instead of June 10 (the date when delivery was due)? _____

   b. Assume that on June 15, Spudco wrote a letter to Chipco demanding that Chipco state in detail what was wrong with the shipment. Chipco ignored Spudco's letter. Spudco thereupon sued for damages. Who wins? _____

52. Spudco sells 3,000 bushels of potatoes to Chipco. Upon arrival at Chipco's plant, half the shipment is rotten, and Chipco promptly and properly rejects the shipment.

   a. In the absence of any instruction or request from Spudco, is Chipco under any duty with respect to the potatoes? _____

   b. Assume that Chipco took it upon itself to *sell* the potatoes on the open market, without any request or instruction from Spudco. The sale realized only $2,500. Of this sum, Chipco kept $1,000 for its time and effort in disposing of the potatoes, and sent the balance to Spudco. Spudco now sues for conversion. Who wins? _____

c. Assume that the potatoes were accidentally destroyed (through no fault of Chipco) before they could be sold. Who bears the loss?

_____

53. Printer orders a new printing press from Pressco, built to Printer's special order, paying $10,000 down on a purchase price of $50,000. Upon delivery, Printer tests and inspects the press and accepts it. However, within a few weeks, operating problems develop and it becomes apparent that the press will never function as per the specifications in the contract. Printer notifies Pressco in writing of the problems and states that Printer is revoking acceptance. Pressco sues for the purchase price. Who wins?

_____

a. Assume that after notifying Pressco that Printer was revoking his acceptance, Printer continued to use the press because Printer had no other printing equipment available. Would this waive the right to assert the defects as a defense to Pressco's action?

_____

b. Assume that Printer had properly revoked acceptance. Can Printer thereafter sue Pressco for damages for breach of warranty?

_____

c. Assume that Printer had properly revoked his acceptance and demanded that Pressco take back the press, but Pressco refused. Would Printer have any right to *sell* the press?

_____

BREAKDOWN OF THE BARGAIN

54. Salty agrees to purchase a cabin cruiser that is to be specially built to order by Shipco. The purchase price is $150,000. Shipco commences construction. When the hull is about one-third complete, Salty notifies Shipco that Salty is canceling the sale, although Salty has no cause to do so.

a. Assume Shipco thereupon suspends further work on the boat and sells the uncompleted hull for its scrap value, $1,000. Shipco then sues Salty for $149,000. Salty defends on the ground that if Shipco had completed the boat, it could have been sold for more than $150,000 and hence Shipco would have no claim for damages. Who wins?

_____

b. Assume that *before* Shipco disposed of the hull, Salty wrote another letter saying he had "reconsidered" and wanted to go ahead with the purchase. Shipco thereupon sent a letter demanding that Salty give some assurance that Salty would pay for the boat when completed. Salty refused to do so, and Shipco refused to do any further work on the boat. If Shipco now sues for the balance of the purchase price, and Salty cross-complains for damages, who wins?

_____

55. Oilco agrees to supply Trucker with all of Trucker's requirements of gasoline for a period of one year at 60¢ per gallon. At the time the contract was made, Oilco was obtaining its gasoline from the refinery at 50¢ per gallon. Six months later, however,

all refineries raised their prices to $1 per gallon, so that Oilco would lose 40¢ on each gallon sold to Trucker. Is Oilco excused from supplying Trucker's reasonable requirements during the remainder of the year? _____

56. Mines agrees to deliver 1,000 tons of iron ore to Steelco on June 1. If its miners go out on strike and there is no stockpile of ore to ship from, is Mines excused from delivery on the date specified? _____

   a. Assume Mines had a stockpile of 500 tons on hand. Could Steelco compel Mines to deliver at least this amount? _____

   b. Assume Mines had a stockpile on hand sufficient to enable it to tender delivery of 500 tons of iron ore to Steelco. Would Steelco be obligated to accept such tender? _____

REMEDIES

57. Spudco sells 3,000 bushels of potatoes to Chipco, to be delivered in five monthly shipments of 600 bushels each; Chipco agrees to pay for each within 10 days after receipt.

   a. Assume that the first shipment was delivered, but Chipco fails to pay for it within the agreed 10 days. If Spudco fails to tender delivery of the next installment, is it in breach of the sales contract? _____

   b. Assume that the first shipment was made on June 1 and that on June 15 Spudco learned that Chipco was insolvent at all times. Spudco immediately makes a written demand for return of the potatoes. Chipco refuses. Spudco sues to reclaim the potatoes. Who wins? _____

   c. Assume that the first shipment was made on June 1 and was paid for by June 10, even though Chipco was at all times insolvent. On July 1, Spudco tendered the second shipment but demanded cash on delivery. Chipco insisted it was entitled to 10 days' credit as per the sales agreement. Who wins? _____

   d. Assume that Spudco was entitled to demand cash on delivery for the second shipment on July 1 and did so, and that Chipco gave its check, which was returned for insufficient funds. On July 15, Spudco files suit to reclaim the July 1 shipment. Who wins? _____

58. If a seller has successfully reclaimed goods from the buyer, does this prevent the seller from later suing the buyer for the profits that the seller would have made on the sale? _____

59. If a seller has the right to reclaim goods, but the buyer has gone into bankruptcy, can the seller reclaim the goods as against the trustee in bankruptcy? _____

60. Pressco ships a new printing press on credit to Printer via rail carrier. Before the press is received, Pressco discovers that Printer is insolvent. Meanwhile, Printer has sold the press to an innocent purchaser for value, BFP. To whom should the carrier deliver the press?

    _____

61. Pressco builds a new printing press to printer's order for an agreed price of $60,000. Printer repudiates the contract before the press is complete. Nonetheless, Pressco completes manufacture and later sells it to another purchaser for $50,000. Pressco now sues Printer for $10,000. Which, if any, of the following is a valid defense to Pressco's suit?

    _____

    (A)   Seller has no right to complete manufacture after buyer's breach.

    (B)   Seller has no right to sell goods at a private sale without notice to buyer.

    (C)   Market value of the press was at all times in excess of $50,000.

62. Following Printer's repudiation of its contract to purchase a new press, Pressco sells the press at a public auction sale.

    a.   Is Pressco entitled to bid on and purchase the press at the sale?

    _____

    b.   Assume the press is sold to BFP, an innocent purchaser for value. Can Printer later move to set aside the sale because Printer was not given adequate notice thereof?

    _____

63. Chipco orders 3,000 bushels of "No. 2 Rose-medium" potatoes from Spudco at $1 per bushel, but Spudco fails to deliver on the agreed date. Chipco thereupon purchases from another supplier 5,000 bushels of "No. 1 Rose-large" potatoes at $1.10 per bushel. Is Chipco entitled to recover 10¢ per bushel damages from Spudco?

    _____

    a.   Would your answer be the same if it was proved that at all times the market value of potatoes (both grades) was $1 per bushel?

    _____

64. Chipco orders 3,000 bushels of potatoes from Spudco, in shipments of 500 bushels each, the shipments to be paid for upon receipt. The first shipment is received and paid for, but Chipco later discovers a shortage of 50 bushels. Is Chipco authorized to subtract the amount paid for the missing potatoes against the purchase price for the next shipment?

    _____

65. Printer orders a new printing press from Pressco, paying $1,000 down on a purchase price of $5,000. Pressco completes manufacture of the press, but before it is shipped, Pressco goes into bankruptcy. The trustee in bankruptcy wants to sell the press for more money to someone else. Can Printer force the trustee to turn the press over to Printer (by tendering the balance of the purchase price)?

    _____

66. Salty repudiates a contract to purchase a new cabin cruiser from Shipco. Shipco sues Salty for the full purchase price. Salty defends on the ground that Shipco has

made no effort to sell the cruiser, but is instead using it as a show model. Is this a valid defense? _____

67. Salty repudiates a contract to purchase a new cabin cruiser from Shipco. Salty had agreed to pay $30,000 for the boat, and Shipco is able to resell the boat to another purchaser for the same amount. Is Shipco entitled to any damages against Salty? _____

68. Salty repudiates a contract to purchase a new cabin cruiser from Shipco. Salty had agreed to pay $30,000 for the boat, and had paid $1,000 down. After Salty's repudiation, Shipco is able to resell the boat to another purchaser for $37,500 but in the interim had incurred storage and other expenses of resale totaling $2,500. Salty sues Shipco for return of its $1,000 down payment. How much, if anything, should the court award? _____

69. Salty repudiates a contract to purchase a new cabin cruiser from Shipco after the boat is only partially built. Shipco *reasonably* decides to scrap the partially built hull rather than finish the boat. The cost of work completed was $5,000. The price Salty agreed to pay for the boat was $30,000, which would have included a $10,000 profit to Shipco. What is the proper measure of damages to Shipco? _____

70. Steelco has accumulated a mountain of slag (a byproduct of steel mill operation). It sells the slag to Processor at $10 per ton, payable as Processor takes delivery. Before Processor can remove much of the slag, another purchaser offers Steelco $15 per ton, and Steelco therefore repudiates its contract with Processor. Processor sues to compel Steelco to allow it to remove the balance of the slag. Who wins? _____

71. Same facts, except assume that slag is available from another source at $15 per ton, which is its market value. Processor *reasonably* concludes that it cannot stay in the business which it is in if it has to pay $15 per ton for slag. Therefore, it closes down its business, and sues Steelco for damages. Steelco defends on the ground that Processor is not entitled to any damages because it has failed to cover. Who wins? _____

72. Same facts, except assume that Processor "covered" by purchasing slag from another source at $20 a ton. Processor now sues Steelco for $10 per ton damages. Steelco defends on the ground that the fair market value of slag at all times was no more than $15 a ton. Who wins? _____

73. Same facts, except assume that the contract between Steelco and Processor contained a provision drafted by Steelco's attorney as follows: "No claim for damages exceeding $500 shall be valid in the event of breach by either party." Would this provision limit the damages to which Processor would otherwise be entitled? _____

a. Would this provision bar Processor's right to specific performance of the contract (assuming specific performance was otherwise available)? _____

DOCUMENTS OF TITLE

74. Distiller ships a boatload of scotch whiskey to Wholesaler. The carrier issues a bill of lading covering the shipment consigned to the order of "bearer." Distiller entrusts this bill of lading to Agent with instructions to deliver it to Wholesaler upon receipt of payment for the whiskey. However, Agent wrongfully sells the bill of lading to innocent purchaser, BFP. Upon arrival of the boat, BFP and Wholesaler both demand delivery of the whiskey. Who wins? _____

    a. Assume that carrier delivered the whiskey to Wholesaler. Would BFP have any cause of action against the *carrier*? _____

    b. If the whiskey had been shipped pursuant to a straight bill of lading and Distiller had ordered the carrier to deliver the goods to Wholesaler, but the bill had been sold to BFP, to whom should the carrier deliver the goods? _____

75. Distiller ships whiskey via carrier and obtains an order bill of lading therefor, which it proceeds to negotiate to the bank in return for a loan. Distiller then sells the shipment to a dealer, giving the dealer written authority to obtain the shipment from the carrier. Is the carrier authorized to deliver the whiskey to the dealer? _____

76. Same facts, except assume the bill covered "500 cases as per consignor's count," but actually there were only 300 cases in the shipment. Distiller defaults on the loan, and Bank demands 500 cases from the carrier. Is the carrier liable for the missing cases? _____

    a. Does Bank have any cause of action against Distiller for the missing cases? _____

LEASE OF GOODS

77. Lessee leases a computer for a five-year period during which the lease payments amount to 1.5 times the original market price of the computer had it been sold rather than leased. At the end of the lease period, the computer has a remaining economic life of four years. Is this a true lease or a disguised sale? _____

78. Big Bank agreed to finance the following transaction: Retailer picked out a computer system that it wanted. Big Bank then bought the system from its manufacturer, Computers of the World, and leased the system to Retailer. If the computer system does not comply with the warranties that Computers of the World gave to its buyer, Big Bank, may Retailer withhold the lease payments owed to Big Bank? _____

    a. Is Retailer in sufficient privity to bring a breach of warranty action against Computers of the World? _____

INTERNATIONAL SALES

79. If two contracting parties are located in different countries (both of which are signatories of the United Nations Convention on the International Sale of Goods), they are bound by the treaty's rules and may not agree otherwise. True or false? _____

80. Under the United Nations Convention on the International Sale of Goods, an acceptance of an offer creates a contract only when received by the offeror. True or false? _____

Answers to Review Questions

1. **(A)**   Sales of growing crops or timber are subject to the U.C.C. whether the crop is annual (D) or perennial (C), and regardless of whether the seller or buyer is to harvest the crop or cut the timber. Sales of minerals and the like are subject to the U.C.C. only if the *seller* (owner of the land) is to sever; where Buyer is to sever (A), there is an implicit conveyance to him of an interest in the land (to enable him to remove the minerals), and hence it is outside the Code. [§§37-44]

2. **ONLY (C) FOR CERTAIN**   The sale of blood as part of an operation may or may not be primarily the rendition of a service or the sale of goods, but such a transaction is typically covered by a statute stating that the sale of blood is *not* a sale. A product put on hair during a haircut would be a sale of goods only if the sale of services aspect of the transaction did not *predominate*, which it probably would. [§53] The *lease* of a vehicle is not a sale, and the U.C.C. provisions requiring a "sale" (in which title passes from the seller to the buyer), such as the warranty sections or the Code's Statute of Frauds, would not apply to a lease. [§55] However, rules similar to those might be applied to the lease if the jurisdiction has adopted Article 2A. [§§742-779] The sale of the unborn young of animals is covered by Article 2 of the Code. [§44]

3. **DEPENDS**   On whether Farmer is a "merchant." (Courts are presently split on this.) If Farmer is, the offer is irrevocable as a "firm offer." [§§30, 60]

4. **DEPENDS**   There must be a "signed" writing; a printed notice will qualify only if it is "signed," a word defined very broadly under the Code to include any mark made with intent to authenticate (including the letterhead; *see* Official Comment 39 to U.C.C. §1-201). [§§60, 106-107]

5.a. **GROWER**   An offer requesting "prompt or immediate shipment" impliedly invites acceptance *by shipment* (or by a promise to ship). Hence, Grower's failure to acknowledge the order prior to shipment is immaterial. [§67]

b. **NO**   The shipment of nonconforming goods (red roses instead of yellow) is a *breach* of the contract formed by shipment. [§70] Such a breach violates the "perfect tender rule" [§416], and permits the buyer to reject the entire shipment [§465].

6.a. **WHOLESALER**   Beginning performance is an effective acceptance of an offer, but if the offeror will not know of the acceptance in the ordinary course of things, the offeree's contract lapses unless the performance is coupled with *notice* within a reasonable time that performance has begun. [§74]

b. **GROWER**   The memo would probably be construed as an acceptance of an offer, and hence effective upon mailing (whether or not received). [§74]

<table>
<tr><td>7.</td><td>**PRINTER**</td><td>Since it appears that the parties intended an enforceable bargain, there is a contract despite the clash of forms. Printer's offer clearly made time an important condition ("no later than . . ."). Pressco's response *materially altered* the time provision, and hence did not become part of the contract (both parties are merchants, and Printer's alteration in the terms of the contract did not preserve its ability to be a counteroffer by requiring *express* agreement thereto). [§§78-87] (*Note*: Under the 2003 revision the answer is less clear. Per section 2R-206(3), differing terms do not prevent a response from acting as an acceptance, but if the parties behave as if they have a contract, the contract consists of the terms on which they agree, plus the supplementary provision of the Code to fill in the gaps. Query: whether here the parties have behaved as if they have a contract (no goods have been shipped). If not, there is no liability on either party. If so, the Code presumes that delivery must be made within "a reasonable time." [U.C.C. §2R-309(1)])</td></tr>
</table>

8. **WHOLESALER**

Wholesaler's additional term is construed as a mere proposal for addition to the contract, and, if both parties are deemed merchants, would become part of the contract unless it was a *material alteration* of the oral deal. If viewed as a material alteration, it would be stricken from the deal, but the rest of the deal would still be a valid contract (containing the usual U.C.C. presumption of delivery at seller's place of business; *see* §145). [§83] The writing sent by Wholesaler would also be sufficient to deprive Farmer of a Statute of Frauds defense if Farmer is deemed to be a merchant who failed to object to its terms within 10 days of its receipt. [§109] (*Note*: Under the 2003 revision, a contract would also exist, and the supplementary provisions of the Code would be used to fill in the blanks on the place of delivery, which presumes that the *seller's* place of business is the appropriate location for delivery. [U.C.C. §2R-308(a)])

9. **FARMER**

Proof of the oral warranty is permitted by the parol evidence rule, as long as the terms thereof are not inconsistent with the written contract, and are admissible unless it is shown that the parties intended the writing to be the exclusive and complete statement of their agreement. [§92] The Statute of Frauds is not relevant here since it does not require all of the terms of the contract to be in the writing (as the common law did). [§§101-102]

10. **YES**

All that is required is a "writing sufficient" to indicate that a contract for sale has been made; an application for transfer of license would so indicate. It need not specify price; only the quantity term is essential. [§102]

11. **NO**

Because the only writing (the check indorsed by Farmer) does not mention the quantity term, which is essential. (If it had, the check itself would have been a sufficient writing.) [§105]

12. **YES**

Where the party to be charged is a *merchant* (Wholesaler), the party is bound if the party fails to object within 10 days to a written confirmation of an oral sale agreement sent by another merchant. If Farmer were held not to be a "merchant," the result would be to the contrary. [§109]

13.	**NO**	Partial acceptance of an oral sale takes the contract out of the Statute only to the extent of the goods accepted (the first shipment). [§115]
14.	**YES**	U.C.C. §2-201(3)(c) provides that an oral sale is enforceable as to goods "for which *payment* has been made." The courts have uniformly held that a down payment on an indivisible item removes the whole item (the tractor) from the writing requirement of the Statute of Frauds. [§117]
15.	**DEPENDS**	On whether the design work would be considered a "substantial beginning" on the manufacture. If so, it would fall within the specially manufactured goods exception to the Statute. [§119]
16.	**ALL**	(A) Agreements to agree are enforceable at a reasonable price. [§128] (B) and (C): Agreements reserving to one party the power to fix a price are enforceable at whatever price is set in good faith; otherwise, the other party may cancel or fix the price in good faith. [§§132-134]
17.	**NO**	Output contracts are not enforceable where a seller's output terminates for good faith business reasons. [§141]
18.	**YES**	Increased cost of manufacture is *not* a "good faith" reason to terminate output. [§143]
19.	**NO**	In absence of agreement, the place of delivery is the seller's place of business or if (as here) the goods are elsewhere, the place where they are located. [§145]
20.	**NO**	The right to terminate a contract of indefinite duration is conditioned on giving *reasonable advance notice*. [§149]
21.	**NO**	Where an invoice is sent concurrently with a shipment, the credit period runs from the date of the shipment. [§§154-156]
22.	**NO**	The Statute of Frauds requires that all modifications of contracts within the coverage of U.C.C. §2-201 be in writing. A court might find that promissory estoppel or some similar doctrine permitted Battery Co. to recover. [§163]
a.	**PROBABLY**	Because a modification of a sales contract needs no consideration to be enforceable, as long as made in *good faith*. [§161]
23.	**DEPENDS**	On whether it changed its position in any way between October 1 and October 5 in reliance on the oral extension. If it did, Manufacturer would be estopped to insist on Battery Co.'s performance. If no estoppel, Auto Manufacturer can retract the oral waiver. [§165]
24.	**YES**	In the absence of other agreement, a cash sale is presumed. [§174]
a.	**YES**	Accepting buyer's check is not a waiver of seller's right to withhold possession until payment. [§177]

b. **NO** The U.C.C. protects BFP even though the party from whom BFP purchased had voidable title (having given a nonsufficient funds check for goods in a cash sale). [§183]

25.a. **NO** Even though the parties have denominated the transaction as a sale "on approval," the goods were ordered for *resale* to others and hence a "sale or return" was contemplated. Such an arrangement must appear in the writing or it is not enforceable. [§§186-187]

b. **DEALER** Buyer bears risk of loss until the goods are actually returned to Dealer. [§191]

c. **CREDITORS** As a matter of law, goods purchased for resale are treated as the property of the buyer until actually returned to the seller; and hence are subject to the claims of buyer's creditors, unless the dealer files an Article 9 financing statement or demonstrates that the buyer was generally known by buyer's creditors to be substantially engaged in selling the goods of others. [§199]

26.a. **YES** The goods were ordered primarily for use, and hence this is a "sale on approval." A "sale on approval" need not be evidenced in writing (as must a "sale or return"). [§186]

b. **DEALER** Seller retains all incidents of ownership until buyer evidences his approval. [§197]

c. **DEALER** As indicated, the seller retains all incidents of ownership. Thus only the *dealer's* creditors are entitled to the goods. [§195]

27.a. **YES** A manufacturer's advertisements are deemed warranties to the ultimate consumer, establishing the necessary privity. Such warranties are deemed "part of the basis of the bargain (purchase)." It will be up to the manufacturer to *prove* that the Florida purchaser *did not rely* on its warranty at time of purchase. (*Note:* The burden is on the seller, not the buyer.) [§§219-222, 225-226]

b. **YES** The issue is whether "dependably" is an affirmation of fact or opinion. The strong trend is to limit "puffing" by manufacturers regarding their products, by finding their representations to constitute warranties. [§224]

c. **NO** Seller's intent or negligence is immaterial. [§223]

d. **YES** Statements made after sale are probably *not* "part of the basis of the bargain." [§§227, 229]

28. **NO** A warranty of merchantability is implied only in sales by "merchants." [§234]

29. **YES** Implied warranties of merchantability arise in every sale by a merchant. [§234]

30. **NO** It is sufficient that the *bulk* of the goods is of "fair average quality." Small variations do not affect merchantability in the sale of fungible goods. [§237]

31. **PROBABLY NOT**   Trucker's designating the brand and model number indicates Trucker was *not* relying on seller's judgment in selecting goods, and hence no implied warranty of fitness for a particular purpose; and there is no showing here that the battery was not merchantable (fit for ordinary use). [§§242-244, 249-251, 238]

32. **YES**   A restaurant impliedly warrants the wholesomeness of the food it offers for sale—even where, as here, the food was in a sealed container prepackaged by another. The warranty of merchantability was breached by presence of a non-indigenous object (pebble). [§§257, 260]

33. **NO**   There is no waiver of implied warranties unless there has been an *actual* inspection of the goods. Express warranties are unaffected by inspection. [§§290-291]

   a. **PROBABLY NOT**   Implied warranties *may* be excluded by seller's demand that buyer inspect *before entering the contract*, but here the demand appears to have come after the contract was entered into. [§290]

34.a. **PROBABLY NOT**   The oral representation would probably be construed as an *express warranty*. Express warranties generally *cannot* be disclaimed, as long as proved to be an essential part of the bargain, though the buyer will have to find a way around the parol evidence rule to get in the evidence of the oral express warranty. [§§270-274]

   b. **NO**   Because there can be no effective disclaimer of the merchantability warranty unless "merchantability" is specifically mentioned, or goods are sold "as is," etc. [§§275-293]

   c. **YES**   As long as it was in writing and conspicuous, the disclaimer is effective ("fitness" need not be specifically mentioned). [§283]

   d. **NO**   Because in the event of conflict, express warranties ("three tons") displace any inconsistent implied warranty of merchantability. [§306]

35. **NO**   Under traditional concepts, there is no "privity" because Neighbor was only a bystander (not a purchaser or member of household, etc.). Moreover, even in some states which have relaxed the "privity" requirement, liability usually extends only to *personal injury* claims (not property damage, as here). [§§308-328]

36. **GRANTED**   Notice of breach is an essential element of the cause of action for breach of warranty (notice may be written or oral), and most courts have held that filing suit is not sufficient notice. [§§330, 333]

37. **GRANTED**   In an action for breach of warranty, allegations of damage and proximate causation are essential. [§329]

38.a.	**YES**	Consequential damages (damages which the seller had reason to know or foresee at time of the sale) are recoverable. [§338]
b.	**YES**	Again, as consequential damages. [§338]
c.	**NO**	A warranty action is governed by the U.C.C. four-year period notwithstanding other statutes of limitations. [§690]
39.a.	**NO**	In the absence of an *express* undertaking to deliver, sales contracts are presumed to be "shipment" rather than "destination" contracts; mere agreement to pay freight is not enough to make it a "destination" contract. [§376]
b.	**YES**	If the parties understood that the goods would be shipped to the buyer, the seller must make reasonable arrangements on behalf of the buyer, and must notify the buyer of the shipment. [§§376-377]
c.	**CHIPCO**	Under a "shipment" contract, the risk of loss passes to the buyer when the goods are delivered to the carrier. [§375]
40.a.	**MINES**	This is an "F.O.B." destination contract and hence all freight and loading charges are borne by Seller. [§385]
b.	**MINES**	Under a "destination" contract, the risk of loss does not pass until the goods reach their destination. [§375]
41.	**DEALER**	Indorsement of a negotiable document of title constitutes delivery where goods are in possession of bailee, and risk of loss passes at that time. [§§411-412, 532]
42.	**STABLE**	Where the seller is a *merchant*, the risk of loss passes only when the buyer *actually receives* the goods. [§535]
43.	**FRIEND**	Where the seller is *not* a "merchant," risk of loss passes on tender of delivery alone. [§535]
44.	**CHIPCO**	The Code retains the rule of "perfect tender" as to most sales contracts (subject to seller's right to cure if time for performance has not yet expired). [§416]
45.	**SPUDCO**	The "rule of perfect tender" does *not* apply to *installment* sales contracts. Substantial performance is sufficient. Buyer can reject only if the 50-bushel defect "substantially impairs the value of the installment"; and can cancel only if the defect "substantially impairs the value of the whole contract." [§§418-420]
46.	**DEPENDS**	On whether the delay is *material* (probably not, since order called for "on or about" June 5). The perfect tender rule does *not* apply to shipping arrangements. [§422]

47.	**CHIPCO**	A "cure" can be made only by a conforming tender *within the time* provided in the original contract. [§424]
a.	**NO**	A "surprise rejection" gives the seller a "reasonable period" even after time for performance has expired. [§426]
b.	**SPUDCO**	Time for performance here would be a "reasonable period" before or after June 10; June 15 would probably be within bounds. [§424]
48.	**SPUDCO**	The buyer's right to inspect the goods prior to payment is waived in a "C.O.D." sale. [§436]
49.	**YES**	Payment in a "C.O.D." sale is *not* an acceptance so as to waive the right of inspection. [§438]
a.	**YES**	The buyer may accept any commercial unit or units and reject the rest if nonconforming. [§446]
b.	**NO**	Chipco might be entitled to *revoke* its acceptance if the defect was "latent" (not reasonably apparent at time of inspection) and "substantially impaired the value of the goods to the buyer," and "processed" does not mean that the goods have been substantially changed. Otherwise, an acceptance waives the right to reject for later-discovered defects. Even if it is too late to reject/revoke, the buyer may pursue an action for damages for breach of warranty. [§483]
50.	**CHIPCO**	Unless the seller has given prior notice that cash will be required, payment may be tendered in any manner reasonable in the ordinary course of business. If seller then demands cash, seller must give buyer an *extension of time* to obtain it. [§452]
51.	**YES**	A general rejection of nonconforming goods on the date delivery is due is normally sufficient. [§469]
a.	**NO**	Where the time for performance has not yet expired, buyer *must* specify the defect to enable seller to cure within the requisite time. [§470]
b.	**SPUDCO**	Where both parties are *merchants*, seller is entitled to demand in writing that buyer specify defects on which buyer proposes to rely. If buyer fails to comply, buyer is *barred* from raising the defects as a defense. [§470]
52.a.	**YES**	A buyer who has rejected goods and still has possession must exercise reasonable care until seller has opportunity to remove them. Where goods are *perishable*, merchant buyers *must* make reasonable efforts to *sell* the goods (with or without request from seller). [§§472-482]
b.	**CHIPCO**	As long as Chipco acted in *good faith*, it was authorized to sell perishable goods rejected for nonconformity. It was also authorized to deduct its costs and expenses (including reasonable compensation to itself). [§§472-482]

c. **SPUDCO** — Where buyer has rightfully rejected nonconforming goods, risk of loss remains with seller. [§538]

53. **DEPENDS** — On whether the operating problems "substantially impair the value of the goods"; a buyer cannot revoke acceptance for anything less. [§485]

a. **DEPENDS** — Most courts will excuse post-rejection use of the goods *if* the use is unavoidable. [§474]

b. **NO** — Revocation of acceptance is an alternative to a suit for breach of warranty, but following the revocation, buyer is entitled to a return of the price paid and any consequential and incidental damages the breach caused. [§493]

c. **YES** — Having made a $10,000 down payment on the purchase price, Printer is deemed to have a security interest in the press and can sell it to enforce this interest. Printer must remit to Pressco any excess above the down payment and expenses. [§§479, 481]

54.a. **SHIPCO (BUT NOT FOR $149,000)** — Where buyer repudiates while seller is in the process of manufacture, seller may *either* complete manufacture or suspend further performance and sell what seller has for scrap, as long as seller acts in **good faith**. [§§589-592] However, seller's recovery will generally not be the difference between the contract price and the salvage price because seller must deduct expenses saved. [§642]

b. **SHIPCO** — A repudiating party is free to retract the repudiation where (as here) the other party has not materially altered position (*e.g.*, by disposing of the hull). However, the retraction entitles the other party to demand adequate assurances of performance and to refuse further performance until it is received. [§§500-504]

55. **PROBABLY NOT** — Increased costs of performance are normally held foreseeable (particularly in a fuel-short economy). [§§513-516]

56. **YES** — Provided the nonoccurrence of labor strike was a basic assumption on which the sale was made. [§§507, 513-514]

a. **NOT NECESSARILY** — Mines would be required to *allocate* this stockpile in any reasonable fashion, and could even include regular customers not then under contract. [§516]

b. **DEPENDS** — On whether the deficiency is such that it "substantially" impairs the value of the contract. If it does, buyer can terminate the entire contract. [§518]

57.a. **NO** — Seller has the right to withhold delivery where buyer fails to pay for a previous shipment when due. [§550]

b. **CHIPCO** — Unless buyer has made a written misrepresentation of solvency in the three months prior to the delivery, seller's right to reclaim goods upon discovery of buyer's insolvency exists only where the demand for return is made ***within 10 days*** after buyer's receipt of the goods. [§553] (*Note*: Under the revision there are no set time periods, but seller must demand return of the goods within a reasonable time after delivery to the buyer.)

c. **SPUDCO**   If buyer has become insolvent, seller is entitled to demand cash on ***future*** shipments, regardless of the credit terms of the contract and regardless of whether seller had any right of reclamation as to earlier shipments. [§553]

d. **SPUDCO**   The check was a written misrepresentation of solvency in the three months prior to delivery, so that the 10-day limitation of U.C.C. §2-702(2) does not apply. [§555] (*Note*: There is no such time period in the revision, which gives a seller a "reasonable time" after delivery to demand return of the goods.)

58. **YES**   Successful reclamation excludes all other remedies. [§562]

59. **YES**   The Bankruptcy Code so provides. [§566]

60. **BFP**   The sale to a bona fide purchaser while the goods are still in transit cuts off seller's right of stoppage. [§584]

61. **ONLY (B)**   (A) is wrong as long as completion was in the exercise of reasonable commercial judgment to mitigate loss [§591], and (C) is wrong because if resale was proper, resale price—not market value—is the measure of damages [§593]. However, (B) is correct; buyer is entitled to notice whether resale is public or private. [§595]

62.a. **YES**   Seller can purchase at a ***public*** sale. [§599]

b. **NO**   Seller's failure to comply with resale requirements may bar seller from damages but does ***not*** affect the title of an innocent purchaser. [§601]

63. **DEPENDS**   On whether Chipco's purchase from the other supplier was a commercially reasonable "cover." It need not be the same amount or grade. [§§611-612]

a. **NO**   If "cover" was proper, Chipco is entitled to recover the difference between the contract and cover price regardless of the market price, although the fact that the market price was lower than the cover price may demonstrate that the cover attempt was not reasonable. [§611]

64. **PROBABLY**   Installment deliveries under a single contract would be viewed as part of the "same contract" to assure the right of subtraction. [§619]

65. **UNCLEAR**   The U.C.C. provides that if seller became ***insolvent within 10 days after*** buyer made the prepayment, buyer who has prepaid any part of the purchase price has a right of "capture" once the goods are identified to the contract. However, it is unclear whether the U.C.C. right can be asserted against an unwilling trustee in bankruptcy. [§620]

66.	**YES**	Where seller has retained possession of the goods, seller is generally limited to an action for incidental damages (cannot recover full purchase price and retain goods at same time). [§641]
67.	**YES**	Even though there is no difference between the contract price and resale price, Shipco is entitled to recover the *profit* it lost on the original sale, assuming that Shipco qualifies as a "lost volume seller" (one who has an unlimited inventory, and who would therefore have made the second sale anyway). [§639]
68.	**$500**	Where buyer is in default, he is entitled to restitution of the amount by which the down payment exceeds 20% of the purchase price or $500, whichever is smaller. Here, 20% of the purchase price would be $6,000, so $500 is the appropriate amount. Because seller made a profit on the resale, seller has no other damages to offset against the $500. [§§664-665] (*Note*: The revision drops this formula and allows the buyer to get back the down payment, minus the damages suffered by the seller.)
69.	**$15,000**	As long as the decision to scrap the boat was *reasonable*, seller is entitled to the cost of the work completed prior to the repudiation and to lost profits. [§592]
70.	**DEPENDS**	On whether slag is available from another source. Suit is in effect to compel specific performance of the contract, and this remedy is available where goods are in *short supply*. [§§648-649]
71.	**PROCESSOR**	Cover is an *option* only. Having failed to cover, Processor may sue Steelco for the difference between the contract price and market price (*i.e.*, $5 per ton) *plus* possibly consequential damages as well (being forced out of business) if this was foreseeable to Steelco at time of contracting. (*Note:* Normally, failure to cover precludes recovery of consequential damages; but here, the failure to cover was a reasonable choice.) [§§654-659]
72.	**PROCESSOR**	As long as Processor covered in *good faith*, damages are measured by the contract-cover differential regardless of market value, although, again, the huge difference between the cover price and the market price may show that the cover was not reasonable or that Processor did not cover in good faith. [§654]
73.	**PROBABLY**	Disclaimers and limitations on damages in sales contracts between *business entities* are usually upheld. It would be up to Processor to prove that it was somehow "unconscionable." (Fact that it was included may be why Steelco agreed to sell at low price.) [§§672-677]
a.	**NO**	Because the limitation refers only to damages and does *not* appear to be an "exclusive" remedy provision. [§684]
74.	**BFP**	Unauthorized negotiation of negotiable bill of lading vests in the innocent purchaser full ownership of the bill and of the goods represented thereby. [§732]

a.	**YES**	For the tort of conversion. [§721]
b.	**WHOLESALER**	Possession of a straight (*i.e.*, nonnegotiable) bill of lading does not give the possessor the right to the goods. Instead the bailee will deliver the goods to the person the bailor designates. [§§707-708]
75.	**NO**	Having issued a negotiable bill of lading, the bailee must insist upon its return before releasing the goods covered thereby. [§711]
76.	**NO**	Assuming that the carrier does not know that the description is wrong and that the consignor and not the carrier counted the goods, the bailee has no liability where the receipt indicates that the shipper counted the goods. [§§736-738]
a.	**YES**	The transfer of a bill warrants that the transferor has no knowledge of any fact that would impair its worth. [§717]
77.	**TRUE LEASE**	The amount paid under the lease is irrelevant. The major question asked by U.C.C. §1-201(37) is whether there is any economic life left in the leased goods at the end of the lease period. If there is, it is a true lease. [§§744-748]
78.	**NO**	In what is called the "hell or high water clause" (now implied) in a finance lease such as this, a business lessee must make lease payments even if the goods do not conform. [§764]
a.	**YES**	In a finance lease, the lessee may pursue warranty theories against the original seller (called a "supplier"). [§763]
79.	**FALSE**	The parties are always free to agree to law other than the treaty. [§780]
80.	**TRUE**	This reverses the mailbox rule of the American common law. However, the offeror is forbidden the right to revoke the offer once the acceptance is mailed. [§788]

Exam Questions
and Answers

QUESTION I

Jack Point was a professional nightclub entertainer. He was tired of living in hotel rooms and went to Yeoman Mobile Homes to buy a trailer. Point told the salesman, Leonard Merill, of his occupation and his desire to be free of hotel living, and Merill showed Point many models. Finally, Merill talked Point into buying a 2006 Guardian Mobile Home (three-ton, 60-foot trailer) for $75,000. The contract stated that the object sold was a "2006 Guardian Mobile Home" and that it would be delivered the following week. As Point signed the contract, Merill remarked, "This trailer will be perfect for you in your business." Point paid cash for the trailer. When it was ready the following week, Point was handed a booklet describing the care and handling of the trailer. In the booklet, on page 2, was this conspicuous statement: "Sold AS IS; this sale is made with no warranties express or implied, especially not the warranties of merchantability or fitness for a particular purpose." The mobile home had been manufactured on July 1, 2005.

Point drove the mobile home 3,000 miles to his first professional engagement and took it to a trailer park. There it was much admired by the residents, but they all told him that it was far too big a trailer to be suitable for much travel. Point consulted experts, who informed him that this type of trailer would fall apart if moved more than two or three times for any distance.

Disgusted, Point wrote Yeoman Mobile Homes a letter saying, "This trailer is no good for traveling, and I don't want it. It's parked at Tower City Trailer Park; go get it and give me my money back." Point then left the trailer at Tower City (3,000 miles from Yeoman Mobile Home's place of business) and flew to London to do a show. Yeoman ignored the letter, and two months later, the mobile home was stolen from the Tower City lot. It has never been recovered. Answer the following questions:

1. Were any express warranties created during the sale?

2. Were any implied warranties created?

3. Were any warranties effectively disclaimed? Consider the Magnuson-Moss Act.

4. What was the legal effect, if any, of Point's letter?

5. If Point sues, what are his possible theories, what defenses will Yeoman raise, and how should the judge rule?

QUESTION II

Fifty "Voice of Japan" television sets were stolen from a pier in San Francisco in 2003. At that time they were owned by Nippon, Inc. The sets were sold and resold several times before coming into the hands of Imports, Ltd., a reputable importing firm, which paid full price for them and which had no idea that the sets had ever been stolen.

In 2006, Ohio Appliances ordered 50 such sets from Imports, Ltd., the contract calling for a $15,000 "C.I.F. Columbus, Ohio," payment to be made by a letter of credit. The letter of credit was sent to Imports, Ltd. at Ohio Appliance's request by Octopus National Bank ("ONB").

Imports, Ltd. made a proper contract of shipment with Righton Railroad, received a negotiable bill of lading consigning the goods to ONB, and sent the bill, along with all of the documents called for by the terms of the letter of credit, on to a collecting bank in Columbus, which presented the documents to ONB for payment.

Before ONB paid, it was contacted by Ohio Appliances, which informed ONB of two things: (i) it had found out that Nippon, Inc. really owned the sets, and (ii) some of the sets had been damaged in transit. ONB paid on the letter of credit anyway.

When the sets arrived in Columbus, both ONB and Nippon, Inc. demanded the goods. Ohio Appliances refused to reimburse ONB for the amount of the letter of credit ($15,000).

ONB sued Ohio Appliance for $15,000, and the railroad filed an interpleader action asking the court to determine who should get the sets. Decide the issues involved.

QUESTION III

On January 3, 2006, Howard Prexy, President of Yellow Pencils, Inc., sent the following letter to Donna Stall, the owner of Errata Erasers:

> Dear Donna:
>
> We wish to buy 60,000 #16 erasers at two cents each for delivery as follows: 5,000 per month beginning February 28, 2006, and ending March 1, 2007, supplemental contract terms as per our usual purchase order.
>
> Howard Prexy

When Stall received the letter on January 5, 2006, she called Prexy and said, "I accept your offer, subject to our usual shipping terms. We'll meet the delivery schedule stated in your letter." Prexy said that he was "delighted to hear this," and the conversation ended. Prexy mailed Stall the usual Yellow Pencil purchase order, on which the above terms were typed, followed by a lot of fine print. On February 28, 2006, the first shipment of 5,000 erasers came in the mail, but the warehouse supervisor refused to accept the shipment because the packages were obviously damaged in transit. Prexy called Stall and told her that damaged erasers were unacceptable; at which point, Stall replied that the erasers had conformed to the contract when mailed. Stall insisted that Prexy take and pay for the goods, but Prexy refused, adding that "as far as I'm concerned, the whole deal is off."

The next day, Errata Erasers filed a suit against Yellow Pencils. Plaintiff's complaint charged breach of contract, submitting as exhibit "A" a copy of Prexy's first letter to Stall, and stating that Errata had orally accepted this offer with the addition of Errata's usual shipping terms. Exhibit "B" was an Errata shipping invoice, which the complaint alleged accompanied the first shipment. The invoice was as follows:

ERRATA ERASERS
Contents: 5,000 #16 erasers
Date mailed: February 28, 2006
Terms as per reverse side

On the reverse side, 30 fine print terms appeared, one of which stated: "Buyer takes complete risk of damage to goods in mailing thereof."

Yellow Pencil's answer, while admitting that all of the above took place, denied liability, arguing in the alternative: (i) there was no contract, and (ii) if there were a contract, Errata breached it by tendering damaged goods and that Yellow Pencil was excused from the entire contract. In support of this answer, Yellow Pencil attached its purchase order, labeled exhibit "C." One of the fine print terms of the purchase order read as follows:

Seller, by accepting the terms of this purchase order and acting thereunder, agrees to accept risk of damage to the goods while in the mail.
Buyer may reject damaged goods without further liability.

Answer these questions:

1. What are the bases for Yellow Pencil's two contentions in its answer?

2. What will be Errata's probable arguments in reply?

3. How should this case be resolved?

QUESTION IV

Carl Ice was the world's greatest snowmobile racer, and one day he went down to Wyoming Snow Vehicles ("WSV") to purchase a competitive machine. Carl's only profession was racing snowmobiles. The salesman, Ralph Teeth, showed Carl the new Japanese Snowglider, which had the largest horsepower of any snowmobile in the world, and told Carl that the machine was obviously the best snowmobile in the state and a "cinch" to win next year's Wyoming Snowmobile Championship. Carl bought the Snowglider for $8,000 and was given a "LIMITED SIX MONTH WARRANTY" covering the defect-free performance of the machine for that period. The warranty also conspicuously disclaimed all other express or implied warranties, specifically mentioning merchantability.

Over the two weeks after the sale, Carl took the vehicle out into the woods for many practice sessions. Except for the fact that the gas gauge never worked (it always showed that the tank was empty), the snowmobile worked perfectly. When Ralph Teeth called to find out how things were going (he and Carl were personal friends), Carl replied that he was very satisfied (although he mentioned the gas gauge problem and Ralph said to bring the machine in for easy repair).

Three weeks after the sale, the Secretary of the Interior issued an order banning the use of snowmobiles for recreational or contest purposes anywhere in the United States. The next day, Carl Ice put the machine in his own locked garage and gave Wyoming Snow Vehicles a notice of rescission, stating that he canceled the sale because of the government's actions and the gas gauge problem and demanding back the $8,000 he had paid. He refused to return the snowmobile until this amount was refunded. WSV ignored the letter. Four days after receipt of the letter by WSV, marauding children broke into the garage and stole the snowmobile. It was never seen again.

Carl, who had no insurance covering this loss, brought suit against WSV for $8,000 plus $5,000 consequential damages (the prize amount for the winner of the Wyoming Snow-mobile Championship), plus costs and attorney's fees.

Explain Carl's best arguments. How will WSV respond? How should the judge rule?

QUESTION V

Helen Humbug was the owner of the Happy Doll Company, a leading toy doll manufac-turing enterprise. On September 25, she phoned Kris Claus, president of the Toy Spe-cialty Shop, and contracted to buy from the shop 4,000 sets of doll eyes (1,000 sets each of blue, brown, grey, and green eyes). Happy Doll agreed to pay $450 per each 1,000 sets on delivery, which was agreed to be as follows: blue, March 1; brown, May 1; grey, September 1; and green, November 1. Before hanging up the phone, Humbug said, "You know, of course, that the success of our entire Christmas season depends on our getting these doll eyes in time to install them in the dolls." Claus said he knew this, and they hung up.

The Toy Specialty Shop began immediate manufacture of the four sets of doll eyes. On March 2, the company shipped 1,000 sets of blue eyes to Happy Doll; the eyes arrived on March 5. Happy Doll accepted the eyes and paid for them.

On May 10, Toy Specialty shipped the brown eyes, but when they arrived three days later at Happy Doll's plant, they were refused and returned. Humbug phoned Claus and said, "The brown eyes were late so the deal is off." Claus was outraged. He knew that Happy Doll was not planning to put the dolls on the market until early in December and that the 1,000 sets of eyes could be placed in the dolls in one week's time. Claus replied, "You have no right to reject these eyes. I'm going to call my lawyer. In the meantime, I hope you're going to accept the other shipments." Humbug said nothing but just slammed down the phone receiver.

The next day, lightning struck the eyes storage shop at Toy Specialty and completely destroyed the 1,000 sets of grey eyes and the rejected 1,000 sets of brown eyes. Claus phoned Humbug and, not getting her directly, left a message about the destruction. On November 1, Toy Specialty shipped the green eyes, which Happy Doll refused to receive when the shipment arrived.

On December 1, Toy Specialty filed suit against Happy Doll and Humbug, alleging breach of contract and asking for damages. What theories will each of the parties argue, and how will the court decide this case?

QUESTION VI

After much urging by his wife, Paul Listless decided to buy a new family car. He went down to Flash Motors and fell into the hands of Sam "Sales" Sullivan, the best car salesperson Flash employed. Sullivan tried to sell Listless a $20,000 Chrome-Special wagon, telling him that the car "would be perfect for your family," but Listless resisted and Sullivan kept reducing the price. Listless, who did not really want to buy a car at all, kept trying to leave. Finally, an exasperated Sullivan offered to sell the car for $16,000. Listless, aware that this was a fantastic buy, said, "I accept," and took $500 out of his wallet. "Is this enough of a down payment until I can get to the bank?" he asked. Sullivan, stunned that he had been so lax as to make such an offer, nodded and took the money.

Listless went to the bank and withdrew $15,500 and promptly returned to Flash Motors, where he tendered this amount to Sullivan. Sullivan, fearing for his job, denied making the deal at the low figure of $16,000. Listless stormed out and went home. The dealership mailed him a check for $500, which he refused to cash. Instead, he filed suit the next day.

What defense will Flash Motors raise, what will Listless argue; how would you decide the case if you were the judge?

QUESTION VII

For his wife's birthday, Andy Milk decided to buy her a new car. He chose to make the purchase from Smiles Motors because it had the best reputation in town for satisfying its customers.

He negotiated a deal with Smiles for a 2007 Chrome-Special. The price was $10,000. Andy wrote out a check for $1,000 (the down payment), payable to Smiles Motors, Inc. He told the salesperson that the car was a birthday gift for his wife. The car was ordered from the factory; the arrival date was to be June 7, 2006. He went home and told his wife what he had done; she kissed him.

The next day (June 1, 2006), Smiles Motors, Inc. sold its entire operation to Teeth Motors, Inc., a new corporate entity run by a group of people who had no prior experience in the automobile business, but which rehired all of Smiles's salespeople and auto mechanics. Teeth Motors also took from Smiles an assignment of "all contracts and accounts receivable with Smiles Motors's existing customers."

When Andy Milk found out about the sale of the business, he became furious. On June 4, he stopped payment on the check. He brought suit against Teeth Motors and Smiles Motors for return of his down payment, and Teeth counterclaimed for the unpaid purchase price.

Give the arguments of the parties and explain the result the judge should reach.

ANSWER TO QUESTION I

1. Point will argue that Merill's statement that the trailer will be "perfect for you in your business" was an express warranty. Yeoman Motor Homes will reply that since the statement was made after Point had made a decision to buy, the statement did not go to the "basis of the bargain" and thus was not a warranty. [§219] However, the U.C.C. provides that a statement made after the sale can be part of the basis of the bargain, and if it is, it is deemed a modification of the contract effective even without consideration. [§229] Thus, here Point will probably prevail in the argument that the statement was a modification of the original deal and part of the basis of the bargain, and thus an express warranty.

2. The implied warranty of merchantability was made. The U.C.C. imposes a warranty in any sale of goods by a seller who is a merchant with respect to goods of that kind that the goods are of "merchantable" quality. [§234] However, this warranty is not relevant to Point's case because it was not breached; the trailer was "merchantable"; it was fit for its ordinary purpose—being a semi-permanent residence.

   The implied warranty of fitness for a particular purpose, on the other hand, is important to Point. An implied warranty of fitness for a particular purpose arises when a seller has reason to know of the buyer's particular contemplated use of goods and that the buyer is relying on the seller's judgment to select goods suitable for that purpose. [§245] In this case, Point told Merill of the particular purpose he had in mind for the trailer (*i.e.,* extensive travel). Point obviously relied on Merill's skill to select a trailer suitable for this purpose, and thus there arose an implied warranty that the trailer would be suitable for Point's purpose.

3. Although the seller in this case attempted to disclaim all express and implied warranties, it was not successful. The booklet attempted to disclaim all warranties and generally met the Code requirements: the disclaimer was conspicuous, in writing (necessary to disclaim fitness for a particular purpose), and mentioned "merchantability" (necessary to disclaim that implied warranty). [§§275 *et seq.*] However, the Magnuson-Moss Act forbids the disclaimer of implied warranties if the warrantor makes a written warranty covering a consumer product. [§§344 *et seq.*] Since the trailer is a consumer product (*i.e.,* purchased primarily for personal, family, or household purposes), it falls under the Act. Since Yeoman Motor Homes had a written warranty section in its booklet, it cannot, under the Act, disclaim the implied warranties. Therefore, the implied warranties of merchantability and fitness for a particular purpose have not been effectively disclaimed.

4. The letter is either a rejection or a revocation of acceptance, depending on the court's interpretation of the facts: If Point's letter was within the trial use period to which a buyer is entitled, then the letter is a rejection; if the court finds that this period has passed, and thus Point is deemed to have accepted the trailer, then the letter is a revocation of acceptance. In either case, the letter works a rescission of the contract. [§§465, 483]

5. Point will argue that Yeoman breached the implied warranty of fitness for a particular purpose that it made to him, and therefore he rejected or revoked acceptance of the trailer (as discussed above). Point will ask for his money back, and he will say that the trailer was destroyed after the risk of loss passed to Yeoman. [*See* U.C.C. §2-510; *supra*, §§537-541]

Yeoman's defense will be that it breached no warranties, an argument it will probably lose. It will also argue that the risk of loss was on Point because he did not take reasonable care of the trailer following rescission of the contract [§470], and thus Point is not entitled to a refund of his money.

The court will find that the implied warranty of fitness for a particular purpose was breached, but it will probably deny Point recovery of his money. Although the risk of loss is on the seller when seller is in breach, the buyer has a duty to use reasonable care to store the goods until seller can retrieve them. [§477] The court will most likely find that Point failed to use reasonable care; rather, he merely sent notice to Yeoman and abandoned the trailer in a park far from Yeoman's place of business. Therefore, the risk of loss remained with Point, and with the trailer went his hope of recovery.

ANSWER TO QUESTION II

The first issue is who should get the television sets. Nippon, the true owner of the sets, is entitled to them since the sets were stolen from it. It does not matter how many innocent hands the sets went through. [§§212-214] A purchaser receives the title the seller had, and a thief has no title. The innocent parties must each sue their sellers for breach of warranty of title until the loss is passed back to the thief.

Another issue is whether Ohio Appliances must reimburse ONB for the $15,000 it paid on the letter of credit. Assuming that Imports, Ltd. presented the required documents to ONB, ONB was quite right to honor the letter of credit. The letter of credit is an obligation of the bank totally independent of the underlying sale and of any breach of contract arising from the sale. [§§458-463] Therefore, ONB acted properly and is entitled to reimbursement for the $15,000 paid. Ohio Appliances will have to seek recovery from Imports, Ltd.

As to who will bear the risk of loss in this situation, the loss rests with Imports, Ltd. because it breached the warranty of good title—*i.e.*, that it had good title to the goods it sold. As mentioned, Imports had no title since the goods were stolen, and thus the sale to Ohio Appliances breached this warranty. Therefore, Imports is liable to Ohio.

Although not actually at issue here, the loss for transit damage also rests with Imports. Normally, the "C.I.F." term would put the risk of loss on the buyer [§528], but here, because of the title problem, the goods were nonconforming and so the risk of transit damages remained with Imports, Ltd. [§537]

ANSWER TO QUESTION III

1. As to its first contention—that there was no contract—Yellow Pencil will argue that the parties never reached an agreement. There was no "meeting of the minds," because the apparent offer and acceptance contained such contradictory risk of loss terms. [§86]

    As to its second contention, Yellow Pencil will argue that even if there is a contract, the risk of transit loss is on Errata. Under U.C.C. section 2-207(3), where the parties have sent each other forms with inconsistent terms, the court looks to the parties' conduct to see if they have acted as if a contract has been formed. If so, a contract exists, consisting of the terms on which the parties agreed; the inconsistent terms are replaced by the usual Code rule or by custom. [§89] Here, the parties acted as if there was a contract, and so the inconsistent terms pertaining to risk of loss should be replaced with the usual U.C.C. rule. The Code puts the risk on the seller because it presumes that the contract is a shipment contract, and the seller must make reasonable contract with a carrier or the risk remains with the seller. [§377] Yellow Pencil will argue that the contract with the carrier was not reasonable.

2. Errata will reply that the parties had reached an oral agreement during the telephone conversation between Prexy and Stall. This oral agreement contained Errata's "usual shipping terms." Since the course of dealing between the parties showed that these shipping terms placed the risk of transit damage on the buyer, Yellow Pencil's purchase order, with its inconsistent shipping terms, was a written confirmation that tried to modify the existing contract terms. Under U.C.C. section 2-207(1) and (2), this attempted modification of the transit damage agreement is a material alteration of the contract and is stricken from the purchase order. The rest of the purchase order remains valid as an acceptance of the oral agreement. [§83] Thus, the risk of transit damage (per the original agreement) was on Yellow Pencil.

3. A court could go either way in this case. Much will depend on the course of dealing between the parties. If past transactions between Errata and Yellow Pencil put the risk on the buyer, then the court will assume that was the intention of the parties in this contract, and Errata will prevail.

    (*Note:* Under the revision, the contract would consist of the terms on which the parties have agreed, and the Code's supplementary provisions would fill in the gaps. The Code presumes that transit damage is the risk of the buyer if the parties have not agreed otherwise (*i.e.,* a shipment contract is presumed). [U.C.C. §§2R-207, 2R-509(1)]

ANSWER TO QUESTION IV

Carl will argue that WSV made both express and implied warranties which were breached. Carl will argue that an express warranty was made by Teeth when he stated that the machine was a "cinch" to win the Wyoming Snowmobile Championship. This warranty was breached because the machine cannot win the Championship since it has been canceled by government decree. Although WSV will contend that this warranty was disclaimed and that the parol evidence rule keeps this warranty out altogether, Carl may be able to get around these contentions. Express warranties cannot be disclaimed [§§267-270], and the oral warranty can probably be introduced in spite of the parol evidence rule because otherwise, Carl will argue, the contract is unconscionable, any other result condones fraud, and he did not intend the writing to be a final expression of the agreement. [§§271-273]

Carl will also argue that the implied warranty of merchantability was made and breached. Carl will say that the snowmobile was not merchantable because it had no working gas gauge. This warranty was not effectively disclaimed, because the Magnuson-Moss Act applies here and prohibits disclaimer of implied warranties. [§348]

Finally, Carl will argue that since these warranties were breached, his rejection of the snowmobile was proper. [§465] Once the vehicle was rejected, the risk of loss on it passed to the seller, as long as Carl took reasonable care of it. [§§471, 477] Carl locked the vehicle in his garage and will argue that this was reasonable care. Therefore, WSV should bear the loss.

WSV will argue that the oral "warranty" was mere puffing and no warranty at all. Even if the statement were a warranty, WSV will argue that it was not breached; WSV cannot be held responsible for unforeseen governmental action.

As for the implied warranty, WSV will argue that the warranty was effectively disclaimed because Magnuson-Moss applies only to consumer goods, and this snowmobile was purchased for professional use. [§§344-345] Furthermore, even if the implied warranty was not effectively disclaimed, the warranty was not breached, because the defect was minor and easily repairable. In any event, WSV will state that Carl clearly made an acceptance of the snowmobile and drove it for three weeks (more than a mere trial use period) and agreed that it was fine. [§§440 *et seq.*] Thus, the risk of loss was on him since he had no basis for revoking his acceptance. [§§448, 535]

The court is likely to agree with Carl that Magnuson-Moss applies. The Act covers consumer goods—goods used for personal, family, or household purposes—and a snowmobile is a consumer good. It does not matter that the snowmobile was purchased for professional use; as long as it is the sort of good that is usually sold to consumers, it is covered by the Act. [§344] Therefore, the warranties were not effectively disclaimed.

However, the court is likely to find that the warranties were not breached. The gauge defect was minor; the snowmobile was still "merchantable." The court will quite possibly find that the "express" warranty was mere puffing, but even if the court considers the statement to be a warranty, the court will hold that the risk of government action was not clearly on the seller. Thus, since Carl clearly made an acceptance of the goods and has no grounds for revoking acceptance, the risk of loss remained with him. The court will rule for WSV.

ANSWER TO QUESTION V

Toy Specialty will argue that Happy Doll wrongfully rejected the shipments and unjustifiably repudiated the contract. Specifically, the rejection of the brown eyes was improper for two reasons: (i) The late shipment of the first set of eyes and its acceptance by Happy Doll established a course of performance that allowed slightly late tender. Therefore, the slightly late shipment of the brown eyes was not justification for rejection. (ii) Also, under the U.C.C., in installment contracts, only substantial performance is required [§418]; the buyer is entitled to reject an installment only if the defect in tender substantially impairs the value of that installment. [§419] Toy Specialty will argue that the slightly late arrival of the eyes did not impair the value of the installment.

Furthermore, Toy Specialty will argue that the repudiation is likewise wrongful. Happy Doll had no right to repudiate the contract because to cancel an installment contract, the defect in an installment must substantially impair the value of the whole contract. [§420] Here, the shipment, although late, was still timely enough to allow Happy Doll to get its product out for Christmas; thus, the late shipment did not impair the value of the whole contract.

Finally, Toy Specialty will argue that since the rejection/repudiation was wrongful, the risk of loss on the brown eyes was with Happy Doll. [§541] Therefore, Happy Doll should pay Toy Specialty for the brown eyes, as well as paying damages for the rejection of the green eyes.

Happy Doll will counter these arguments by claiming that no course of performance was established, but rather that it was absolutely necessary that the shipments be on time. Happy Doll will say that it made that quite clear—that the timing was essential—and thus, when the shipment was late its value was substantially impaired, as well as the value of the whole contract. Rejection/repudiation was therefore proper. Even if the repudiation was improper, the U.C.C. puts the risk of loss on the seller to the extent of its insurance coverage [§540], and so Happy Doll would not be liable for the full amount of the destroyed eyes. Furthermore, Happy Doll will argue that, upon repudiation, the seller must take action within a reasonable period of time to mitigate damages. [§497] Toy Specialty took no action but unreasonably waited for several months, hoping that Happy Doll would retract its repudiation.

The court's decision will depend on its interpretation of the facts. Probably, it will agree with Happy Doll that the delay was a substantial impairment of the contract and rule in Happy Doll's favor.

ANSWER TO QUESTION VI

The only defense Flash Motors appears to have is the Statute of Frauds. Under the U.C.C. Statute of Frauds, a contract for the sale of goods having a price of $500 ($1,000 under the revision) or more must be evidenced by a writing signed by the party being sued and containing a quantity term. [§§96-102] Without such a writing, the contract is unenforceable. [§98] Here, there was no writing. Therefore, Listless cannot enforce the contract; all he can recover is his down payment, which he will have if he cashes the check.

Listless will argue that the check that the dealership mailed him is sufficient evidence of the sales contract. The U.C.C. does not require the writing to be a formal contract, merely that it meet the requirements stated above. [§104] The check meets these requirements: It is a writing, signed by the party being sued, and it at least implies a quantity of one.

In case the court does not accept this argument, Listless will also argue that the down payment satisfies the part payment exception to the Statute of Frauds. [§117] A down payment on a single item such as a car completely removes the whole transaction from the Statute's writing requirement, and therefore, the contract should be enforced.

The court should rule for Listless because the contract is enforceable under the Statute of Frauds.

ANSWER TO QUESTION VII

The issues here are the validity of the assignment of Andy's contract, the delegation of duties under that contract, and the resulting responsibility of Andy.

Andy will argue that the delegation of duties is improper. Under the U.C.C., all duties are delegable unless otherwise agreed or unless the obligee has a substantial interest in the personal performance of the original promisor. [§167] Andy will argue that he had such a substantial interest. He chose Smiles Motors because of its reputation for customer service. Now he finds that the duties have been delegated to people who know nothing about the business. Thus the contract has been breached, and Andy should recover his down payment.

Teeth Motors will reply that the delegation is presumptively valid under the U.C.C., and that since it hired all of Smiles's personnel, no substantial change has occurred: There is no reason to believe that Andy will not get the performance for which he contracted.

This case could be decided either way. Courts are more likely to uphold a delegation of duties by a corporation than by an individual, because corporations are not real persons to begin with. On the other hand, service is important to Andy and he may have legitimately had an interest in the expertise of the corporate management of Smiles. The new corporate management, being inexperienced, could change policies or personnel and thereby destroy the good service available to its customers. If Andy can convince the court that his concerns are substantial, his cancellation of the contract will be valid and he may recover his down payment.

Table of Citations

CITATIONS TO UNIFORM COMMERCIAL CODE

U.C.C. Section	Text Reference	U.C.C. Section	Text Reference	U.C.C. Section	Text Reference
1-102	§5	2-206(1)(b)	§§67, 71	2-308(a)	§145
1-102(3)	§13	2-206(2)	§74	2-308(b)	§145
1-103	§§5, 95	2-207	§§87, 88, 90, 111	2-308(c)	§398
1-106	§662	2-207(1)	§78	2-309	§86
1-201	§§5, 106	2-207(2)	§§35, 79, 85	2-309(1)	§146
1-201(10)	§279	2-207(2)(a)	§81	2-309(2)	§148
1-201(17)	§§48, 49	2-207(2)(b)	§83	2-309(3)	§149
1-201(19)	§§14, 32	2-207(2)(c)	§82	2-310	§452
1-201(23)	§557	2-207(3)	§§87, 89	2-310(a)	§§150, 151, 174
1-201(37)	§§744, 748	2-208(1)	§19	2-310(c)	§§153, 453
1-203	§§5, 13, 162, 234	2-208(2)	§20	2-310(d)	§§155, 156
1-204(3)	§425	2-208(3)	§20	2-311(1)	§§157, 159
1-205(1)	§18	2-209	§§162, 229	2-311(2)	§158
1-205(2)	§17	2-209(1)	§§161, 286	2-312	§§213, 214
1 205(4)	§20	2-209(2)	§164	2-312(1)(a)	§212
2-102	§56	2-209(3)	§163	2-312(1)(b)	§212
2-103(1)(b)	§§15, 32	2-209(4)	§165	2-312(2)	§§217, 218
2-103(1)(c)	§§152, 573	2-209(5)	§166	2-312(3)	§§215, 216
2-104(1)	§27	2-210(1)	§167	2-313	§226
2-105(1)	§§9, 37, 44	2-210(2)	§§168, 169	2-313(1)	§§221, 225
2-105(4)	§§50, 51	2-210(4)	§170	2-313(1)(a)	§219
2-105(6)	§447	2-210(5)	§170	2-313(2)	§§221, 223, 224
2-106(1)	§55	2-301	§§439, 451	2-314	§§33, 233, 257
2-106(4)	§§603, 604	2-302	§§21, 677, 681, 755	2-314(1)	§§234, 257, 262
2-107(1)	§42			2-314(2)(a)	§236
2-107(2)	§42	2-302(1)	§23	2-314(2)(b)	§237
2-201	§§34, 97, 103	2-302(2)	§24	2-314(2)(c)	§238
2-201(1)	§§100, 102	2-304(1)	§456	2-314(2)(d)	§239
2-201(2)	§109	2-304(2)	§§9, 457	2-314(2)(e)	§240
2-201(3)(a)	§119	2-305(1)	§124	2-314(2)(f)	§241
2-201(3)(b)	§120	2-305(1)(a)	§125	2-315	§§245, 256, 257
2-201(3)(c)	§§115, 116	2-305(1)(b)	§128	2-316	§§267, 268, 269, 275, 292
2-202	§§93, 268, 271	2-305(1)(c)	§129		
2-202(a)	§94	2-305(2)	§132	2-316(1)	§270
2-202(b)	§92	2-305(3)	§§133, 134	2-316(2)	§§275, 277, 284
2-204(1)	§57	2-306	§143	2-316(3)	§§275, 293
2-204(2)	§75	2-306(1)	§§137, 138, 140	2-316(3)(a)	§§288, 289
2-204(3)	§58	2-306(2)	§141	2-317	§§300, 302
2-205	§§60, 61, 62	2-307	§144	2-317(a)	§303
2-206(1)(a)	§64	2-308	§406	2-317(b)	§304

U.C.C. Section	Text Reference	U.C.C. Section	Text Reference	U.C.C. Section	Text Reference
2-317(c)	§305	2-503(5)(a)	§398	2-606(2)	§446
2-318	§§324, 325, 326	2-503(5)(b)	§§398, 400	2-607(1)	§448
2-319(1)	§382	2-504	§§422, 427	2-607(2)	§448
2-319(1)(a)	§383	2-504(a)	§377	2-607(3)(a)	§§330, 618
2-319(1)(b)	§385	2-504(b)	§379	2-607(5)(a)	§334
2-319(1)(c)	§384	2-504(c)	§378	2-608	§§449, 483
2-319(2)	§386	2-505	§740	2-608(2)	§489
2-319(4)	§389	2-505(1)	§395	2-609	§504
2-320(1)	§387	2-506(1)	§606	2-609(1)	§§502, 508
2-320(2)	§§387, 388	2-507(1)	§403	2-609(2)	§509
2-320(3)	§388	2-507(2)	§§171, 174, 553, 558	2-609(3)	§510
2-320(4)	§389			2-609(4)	§§507, 508
2-322(1)	§390	2-508(1)	§§424, 427	2-610(a)	§497
2-322(2)(a)	§390	2-508(2)	§426	2-610(b)	§498
2-322(2)(b)	§390	2-509	§535	2-610(c)	§499
2-324(a)	§§392, 393	2-509(1)(a)	§528	2-611(1)	§500
2-324(b)	§394	2-509(1)(b)	§529	2-611(2)	§501
2-325(2)	§463	2-509(2)(a)	§532	2-612	§§418, 427, 539
2-325(3)	§462	2-509(2)(b)	§534	2-612(1)	§418
2-326(1)(a)	§186	2-509(2)(c)	§533	2-612(2)	§419
2-326(1)(b)	§185	2-509(3)	§535	2-612(3)	§420
2-326(2)	§§199, 200	2-509(4)	§523	2-613(a)	§45
2-326(4)	§187	2-510(1)	§§471, 538	2-613(b)	§§46, 394
2-327(1)	§§196, 525	2-510(2)	§540	2-614(1)	§§422, 512
2-327(1)(b)	§§193, 194	2-510(3)	§541	2-614(2)	§464
2-327(1)(c)	§198	2-511(3)	§§177, 454	2-615	§§511, 520
2-327(2)	§524	2-512	§437	2-615(a)	§512
2-327(2)(a)	§188	2-512(1)(b)	§459	2-615(b)	§516
2-327(2)(b)	§§191, 192	2-512(2)	§438	2-615(c)	§517
2-328(2)	§§201, 203	2-513(1)	§§429, 430, 431, 432	2-616(1)(a)	§518
2-328(3)	§§206, 207			2-616(1)(b)	§518
2-328(4)	§§208, 209	2-513(2)	§433	2-616(2)	§519
2-401(1)	§359	2-513(3)(a)	§436	2-616(3)	§520
2-401(2)	§§364, 367	2-513(3)(b)	§435	2-702	§180
2-401(2)(a)	§369	2-513(4)	§431	2-702(1)	§§549, 550, 568, 607
2-401(2)(b)	§370	2-514	§401		
2-401(3)	§371	2-515	§§330, 622	2-702(2)	§§553, 555, 607
2-403(1)	§183	2-515(a)	§623	2-702(3)	§§562, 563, 564
2-403(1)(c)	§183	2-515(b)	§624	2-703	§632
2-403(2)	§§584, 730, 776	2-601	§§389, 416, 427, 465, 539	2-703(a)	§§549, 551
2-403(3)	§729			2-703(f)	§603
2-501	§360	2-601(c)	§446	2-704	§592
2-501(1)	§§372, 587	2-602(1)	§§442, 466	2-704(1)(a)	§588
2-501(1)(a)	§361	2-602(2)(a)	§473	2-704(1)(b)	§589
2-501(1)(b)	§362	2-602(2)(b)	§477	2-704(2)	§§499, 591, 592
2-501(2)	§§363, 374	2-602(2)(c)	§477	2-705	§583
2-502	§620	2-603(1)	§§478, 479, 480	2-705(1)	§§568, 569
2-503	§376	2-603(2)	§481	2-705(2)	§§573, 575
2-503(1)	§§380, 404	2-603(3)	§482	2-705(2)(b)	§574
2-503(1)(a)	§405	2-604	§§479, 482	2-705(2)(c)	§576
2-503(1)(b)	§428	2-605	§470	2-705(2)(d)	§577
2-503(3)	§380	2-606(1)(a)	§§193, 441	2-705(3)(a)	§578
2-503(4)(a)	§§411, 412	2-606(1)(b)	§§442, 443	2-705(3)(b)	§§580, 581
2-503(4)(b)	§413	2-606(1)(c)	§445	2-705(3)(c)	§582

U.C.C. Section	Text Reference	U.C.C. Section	Text Reference	U.C.C. Section	Text Reference
2-706	§§481, 601	2-723(2)	§§634, 635	5-106(a)	§462
2-706(1)	§§593, 630, 641 642	2-723(3)	§636	5-108	§461
		2-724	§633	5-108(a)	§§460, 463
2-706(2)	§§594, 596, 598	2-725	§§321, 323, 691	5-108(f)(1)	§459
2-706(3)	§595	2-725(1)	§690	5-109(b)	§459
2-706(4)(b)	§595	2-725(2)	§692	5-111	§463
2-706(4)(c)	§597	2A-103(1)(e)	§753	7-102(1)(d)	§709
2-706(4)(d)	§599	2A-103(1)(g)	§760	7-104	§707
2-706(5)	§600	2A-103(1)(h)	§742	7-104(1)(a)	§712
2-706(6)	§602	2A-103(1)(j)	§742	7-201	§726
2-707(1)	§607	2A-108	§755	7-202	§726
2-708(1)	§§631, 641, 642	2A-108(2)	§756	7-203	§726
2-708(2)	§§637, 640, 641	2A-108(4)	§757	7-204	§726
2-709	§769	2A-109(2)	§754	7-205	§726
2-709(1)(a)	§§626, 627	2A-201	§751	7-206	§726
2-709(1)(b)	§628	2A-209	§763	7-207	§726
2-709(2)	§628	2A-303	§§770, 772	7-208	§726
2-710	§641	2A-303(3)	§774	7-209	§726
2-711	§493	2A-303(4)	§773	7-210	§726
2-711(3)	§§481, 608, 610, 614	2A-303(5)(b)	§771	7-301	§738
		2A-304	§776	7-303	§582
2-712	§615	2A-305	§§775, 776	7-303(1)(b)	§709
2-712(1)	§§611, 613	2A-306	§779	7-403(1)	§728
2-712(2)	§§654, 663	2A-307	§§777, 780	7-403(3)	§§412, 711, 722, 728
2-712(3)	§616	2A-407	§764		
2-713(1)	§§655, 663	2A-407(1)	§764	7-404	§721
2-713(2)	§657	2A-503(3)	§758	7-501(1)	§714
2-714	§§450, 490	2A-508	§766	7-501(1)(2)(a)	§713
2-714(1)	§§336, 337	2A-509	§766	7-501(1)(2)(b)	§714
2-714(3)	§336	2A-510	§766	7-501(3)	§715
2-715	§§493, 615	2A-511	§766	7-501(4)	§734
2-715(1)	§§343, 662	2A-512	§766	7-502	§733
2-715(2)(a)	§§338, 659	2A-513	§766	7-502(2)	§585
2-715(2)(a)(b)	§329	2A-514	§766	7-503(1)	§727
2-715(2)(b)	§341	2A-515	§§764, 766	7-503(1)(a)	§728
2-716	§649	2A-516	§766	7-505	§719
2-716(1)	§648	2A-517	§766	7-506	§716
2-716(2)	§652	2A-518	§766	7-507	§§717, 718
2-716(3)	§§645, 646	2A-519	§766	7-508	§720
2-717	§§450, 617, 618, 619	2A-520	§766	9-203(1)(c)	§373
		2A-521	§766	9-301	§778
2-718(1)	§§673, 676	2A-522	§766	9-310	§779
2-718(2)(a)	§666	2A-523	§767	9-408	§749
2-718(2)(b)	§665	2A-524	§767		
2-718(3)	§§668, 669, 688	2A-525	§767		
2-719	§§296, 687	2A-525(3)	§767		
2-719(1)(a)	§680	2A-526	§767		
2-719(1)(b)	§§294, 684	2A-527	§§767, 768		
2-719(2)	§686	2A-528	§§767, 768		
2-719(3)	§§681, 758	2A-529	§§767, 769		
2-722(a)	§§545, 682, 683, 688	2A-530	§767		
		2A-531	§767		
2-722(b)	§547	2A-532	§767		
2-722(c)	§546	3-802(1)(a)	§178		

CITATIONS TO UNIFORM COMMERCIAL CODE—2003 REVISION

U.C.C. Section	Text Reference	U.C.C. Section	Text Reference	U.C.C. Section	Text Reference
1R-201(b)(20)	§14	2R-206(3)	§90	2R-705(1)	§571
1R-303(a)	§19	2R-207	§90	2R-710(2)	§643
1R-303(b)	§18	2R-313A	§231	2R-718(1)	§678
1R-303(c)	§17	2R-313B	§231	2R-718(2)	§667
1R-303(e)	§20	2R-316(2)	§285	2R-725(1)	§697
1R-303(f)	§20	2R-502(1)(a)	§62	2R-725(2)(c)	§698
1R-304	§13	2R-508(2)	§427	2R-725(2)(d)	§699
2R-103(1)(k)	§54	2R-608(4)(b)	§476	3R-310(a)	§178
2R-103(1)(n)	§698	2R-702(2)	§556		

Table of Cases

Index

Index

Subject	U.C.C. Section	Text Section
ACCOMMODATION		
See Shipment		
ACTION FOR PURCHASE PRICE		
See Seller's remedies		
ADDITIONAL TERMS		
See Acceptance of offer		
ADEQUATE ASSURANCE, DEMAND FOR		
See Assurance of performance, demand for		
ADMISSION OF ORAL AGREEMENT	2-201(3)(b)	§120
ANTICIPATORY REPUDIATION		
aggrieved party's rights upon	2-610	§§495-497
assurance of performance distinguished		§504
defined		§494
immediate right of action		§494
remedies	2-610(b), (c); 2-704(2)	§§498-499
retraction of	2-611(1), (2)	§§500-501
specially manufactured goods	2-610(c); 2-704(2)	§499
unconditional and unequivocal		§494
APPROVAL SALE		
See Sale terms		
ARTICLE 2, SCOPE OF		§§7-11
nonsale transactions	2-102	§56B
ARTICLE 2A		§56
See also Lease of goods		
"AS IS" DISCLAIMER	2-316(3)(a)	§§288-289
ASSIGNMENT OF RIGHTS	2-210(2), (4), (5)	§§168-170
ASSURANCE OF PERFORMANCE, DEMAND FOR		
after acceptance of goods or payment	2-609(3)	§510
anticipatory repudiation distinguished		§504
"customary in the trade"	2-609(2)	§509
duty to timely furnish	2-609(4)	§507
failure to supply—repudiation	2-609(4)	§508
grounds	2-609(1)	§§502-505
insolvency		§503
procedures	2-609(4)	§§506-508
right to demand	2-609(1)	§502
suspension of performance	2-609(4)	§508
written demand		§506
AUCTION SALE		
See also Sale terms		
bids as offers		§§202-203
forced sales	2-328(4)	§209
formation of contract	2-328(2)	§§201-203
seller's bid, effect of	2-328(4)	§§208-209
terms binding		§204
U.C.C. presumption	2-328(3)	§307
warranty of title	2-312(1)(a), (b)	§212
when title passes	2-328(2)	§§201-203
"with reserve"	2-328(3)	§§206-207

Subject	U.C.C. Section	Text Section
"without reserve"	2-328(3)	§206

B

BAILEE

acknowledges receipt of goods	2-705(2)(b)	§574
carrier distinguished		§575
risk of loss on bailed goods	2-509(2)	§§531-534
tender of bailed goods	2-403(3); 2-503(4)(a), (b)	§§411-413
wrongful procurement of bill of lading	2-403(2), (3); 7-403(1), (3); 7-503(1)(a)	§§728-731

BASIS OF THE BARGAIN
See also Warranty, seller's

	2-313(1)	§§225-226

BATTLE OF THE FORMS
See also Acceptance of offer

as counteroffer	2-207(1)	§§76-78
different terms	2-207(2); 2R-206(3); 2R-207	§§84-87, 90
explained		§76
international sales of goods (CISG)		§788
knock-out rule		§86
leases, inapplicable		§752
material alteration	2-207(2)(b)	§§83, 85
merchants—special rule	2-207(2)	§§80-83
exceptions	2-207(2)(a) - (c)	§§81-83
mirror image rule		§77
new terms, effect of	2-207(2)	§§79-83
performance, effect of	2-207(3); 2R-207	§§87-90
proviso clause	2-207(1)	§§78, 88
U.C.C. rule	2-207(1)	§78

BEARER BILL

definition	7-104(1)(a)	§712
negotiation of. *See also* Negotiable bill of lading	7-501(1), (2)(a)	§713

BILL OF LADING
See also Documents of title; Negotiable bill of lading

carrier's obligation	7-102(1)(d); 7-303(1)(b); 7-403(3); 7-404	§§708-709, 721-722
definition	1-201(b)	§702
drawn to seller or seller's order—divided interests	2-505	§§739-741
indorsement of	7-501; 7-506	§§715-716
negotiable. *See also* Negotiable bill of lading	7-104(1)(a); 7-403	§§703, 711-720
negotiation of. *See also* Negotiation	7-501(1), (2)(a), (b)	§§713-714
nonexistent goods	7-301	§§736-738
nonnegotiable. *See also* Nonnegotiable bill of lading	7-104	§§682-685
stoppage of delivery, effect on	2-705(3)(b), (c); 7-502(2)	§§582-585
"straight bill"	7-104	§§707-710
warranties on negotiation	7-507; 7-508	§§717-720

BONA FIDE PURCHASER

creditors not BFPs—stoppage in transit		§586
entrusted goods, purchase of	2-403; 7-503(1)(a)	§§728-731
from seller with voidable title	2-403(1)	§§183-184
of goods in transit	2-403(2); 7-502(2)	§§584-585
of negotiable bill	7-502	§§585, 728-735
precluding seller's right of stoppage in transit	2-403(2); 7-502(2)	§§584-585

BREACH OF CONTRACT

Subject	U.C.C. Section	Text Section
See also Anticipatory repudiation		
after acceptance of goods	2-607; 2-714	§§336-343
anticipatory. See Anticipatory repudiation		
damages. See Damages		
excuse. See also Excuse	2-615; 2-616(3)	§§511-520
installment contract	2-612	§§418-421
notice of excuse	2-615(c)	§517
notice to seller	2-607(3)(a); 2-608(2)	§§489, 618
remedies for. See Remedies		
risk of loss, effect on	2-510	§§537-542
shipping arrangements defective	2-504	§422
single delivery contract	2-601	§§416-417
upon repudiation. See also Anticipatory repudiation	2-610; 2-611(1), (2)	§§494-501
warranty. See Breach of warranty		

BREACH OF WARRANTY

Subject	U.C.C. Section	Text Section
contents of notice		§332
damages. See Damages		
filing of suit as notice		§333
no wrongful death action		§322
notice required	2-607(3)(a)	§§330-333
content		§332
filing suit as		§333
oral or written		§331
privity disfavored	2-318	§§311-328
tort liability		§§315-316
trend—strict liability in tort		§§317-323
proximate cause	2-715(2)(a), (b)	§329
reasonable time requirement	2-607(3)(a)	§330
remedies. See also Remedies		
after acceptance of goods		§§336-343
consequential damages	2-715(2)(a), (b)	§§338-342
"cover" limitation		§342
incidental damages	2-715(1)	§343
loss in value of goods	2-714(1)	§337
before acceptance of goods		§335
"vouching in," third party suits	2-607(5)(a)	§334

BUYER'S DUTIES

Subject	U.C.C. Section	Text Section
See also Shipping terms		
acceptance of goods. See also Acceptance of goods	2-301	§439
facilitating receipt of goods	2-503(1)(b)	§428
inspection of goods. See also Inspection, buyer's right to	2-513(1)	§429
notice of breach. See Notice		
payment for goods. See also Payment	2-301	§451
rejected goods. See Rejection of goods		

BUYER'S REMEDIES

Subject	U.C.C. Section	Text Section
accepted goods	2-714	§§336-343
consequential damages	2-715(2)	§§615, 657-661
conversion		§583
cover. See also Cover, buyer's right to	2-712	§§611-616, 661
damaged goods	2-613(b)	§§46-47
deduction of damages from price	2-717	§§617-619
incidental damages	2-715(1)	§662
nondelivery or repudiation, damages for	2-713	§§653-663

Subject	U.C.C. Section	Text Section
option to void sale	2-613(b)	§46
liquidated damages	2-718; 2R-718	§§670-678
recoupment. *See also* Recoupment	2-717	§§617-619
rejection. *See also* Rejection of goods	2-601	§§465-482
replevin	2-716(3)	§§644-646
resale	2-711(3)	§§608-610
restitution on buyer's default	2-718(2), (3)	§§664-669
revocation of acceptance. *See also* Revocation of acceptance	2-608	§§483-493
right to prepaid goods	2-502; 2R-502(1)(a)	§§620-621
security interest in rejected goods	2-711(3)	§608
seller's insolvency	2-502	§620
specific performance	2-716(1)	§§647-652
wrongful stoppage in transit		§§583, 708

BUYER'S WAIVER
See Waiver

C

C. & F.
See Shipping terms

CANCELLATION OF CONTRACT

definition and election of remedies	2-106(4)	§§603-604
seller's remedy of	2-703(f)	§603

CARRIER

as buyer's agent	2-705(2)(c)	§576
bailee distinguished		§575
duty under straight bill	7-102(1)(d); 7-303(1)(b)	§§707-709
duty upon transit stoppage	2-705(3)(b)	§§581-586
liability of. *See* Liability, carrier's		
negotiable bills, duties under	7-404	§§721-722
taking up the bill (cancellation)	7-404(3)	§722

CASH SALE

bad checks	2-507(2)	§§177-184
resale to BFP	2-403(1)	§§181-184
certified check as	3-310(a)	§178
defined	2-507(2)	§§171-173
presumption of	2-310(a)	§174
reclamation rights	2-507(2); 2-511(3)	§§177-180, 553
waiver of	2-702	§§175-180

CASUALTY TO GOODS
See Goods

CHECKS
See Payment

C.I.F.
See Shipping terms

C.O.D. PAYMENT	2-513(3)(a)	§436

COMMERCIAL IMPRACTICABILITY
See Excuse

COMMERCIAL UNIT

acceptance of	2-601(c); 2-606(2)	§§446-447

Subject	U.C.C. Section	Text Section
definition	2-105(6)	§447

COMMINGLED GOODS
See Fungible goods

CONDITIONAL

acceptance of goods	2-507(1)	§§171-403
acceptance of offer	2-207(1)	§78
delivery	2-507(1)	§171
payment	2-511(3)	§177

CONDUCT

as creation of warranty		§222
in acceptance of offer	2-206(1)(a); 2-207(3)	§§89, 440
in contract formation	2-204(1)	§57

CONFIRMATION

as acceptance of offer. *See also* Battle of the forms	2-207(1)	§§76, 109-113
defined		§111
effect of Statute of Frauds	2-201(2)	§109

CONFLICT OF WARRANTIES
See Warranty, seller's

CONFLICTING CLAIMS
See Delivery by carrier

CONSEQUENTIAL DAMAGES
See Damages

CONSIDERATION

for irrevocable offer	2-205	§§59-62
for modification	2-209(1) - (3)	§§161-164

CONSIGNEE

rights under nonnegotiable bill		§710

CONSIGNMENT SALE | | §705

CONSUMER GOODS

buyer's right to layaways	2-502; 2R-502(1)(a)	§§620-621
definition		§344
limitation of remedies involving	2-719(3)	§347
warranties *re. See* Consumer protection statutes		

CONSUMER PROTECTION STATUTES | 2A-108; 2A-109; 2A-503(3) | §§345-356
See also Federal Warranty Act

consumer goods		§344
consumer leases—U.C.C.	2A-108; 2A-109(2); 2A-503(3)	§§753-758
state statutes		§§355-356

CONTRACT

See also Acceptance of offer; Offer; Open terms

affecting right to inspect goods	2-513(3)(a), (b)	§§434-437
agreement required	2-204(1)	§57
assignment of rights	2-210(2), (4) - (5)	§§168-170
breach. *See* Breach of contract		
construction of	1-205(1) - (2); 2-208(1) - (3); 1R-303	§§16-20
definition	1-201(11)	§57
delegation of duties	2-210(1)	§167
formation, in general	2-204	§57
good faith obligation	1-203; 1R-304	§§13-15

Subject	U.C.C. Section	Text Section
installment. *See* Installment contract		
missing terms	2-205(1), (2); 2-208(1) - (3); 1R-303	§§16-20, 122-123, 160
modification	2-209	§§161-166
offers to. *See* Offer		
oral. *See also* Statute of Frauds	2-201	§§114-121
output contract	2-201; 2-306(1), (2)	§§103, 138-143
parol evidence. *See also* Parol Evidence	2-202	§§91-95
price. *See also* Open terms	2-305	§§124-135
requirements contract	2-201; 2-306(1), (2)	§§103, 137, 139-143
services and goods	2R-103(1)(k)	§§53-54
services, performance of		§52
statute of limitations	2-725(1), (2)	§§690-692
test for formation of	2-204(3)	§58
unconscionable. *See also* Unconscionable contract	2-302	§§21-25
voidable	2-302(1)	§23
waiver of. *See also* Waiver	2-209(4), (5)	§§165-166

COUNTEROFFERS
See Battle of the forms

COURSE OF DEALING
construction of contract	1-205(1)	§§16, 123, 160
definition	1-205(1); 1R-303(b)	§18

COURSE OF PERFORMANCE	2-208(1); 1R-303(a)	§§19, 123, 160

COVER, BUYER'S RIGHT TO
analogous to seller's resale remedy		§616
buyer's option		§656
damages pursuant to	2-712(2); 2-716(3)	§§645, 654-661
failure to, effect of	2-712(3)	§§614-615
in general	2-712(1)	§611
inability to	2-716(3)	§645
requirement for consequential damages		§661
substitute goods		§§611-612
time limitation	2-712(1)	§613

CREDIT SALE
definition		§172

CREDITOR
after-acquired goods	2-702(3)	§§564-565
fraud upon. *See* Fraud on creditors		
not a BFP		§586
sale on approval, rights upon	2-326(2)	§200
sale or return, rights upon	2-326(2)	§199
secured	2-702	§564

CUMULATION OF WARRANTIES
See Warranty, seller's

CURE
and buyer's failure to specify defect	2-605	§470
improper tender	2-508(1), (2); 2R-508(a)	§§423-427
notice of intent to	1-204(3)	§425
revocation of acceptance		§487

CUSTOM
See Course of dealing; Course of performance;
        Usage of trade

Subject	U.C.C. Section	Text Section
E		
"ENTRUSTING" GOODS	2-403(2), (3); 7-503(1)(a)	§§728-731
EVIDENCE		
parol. *See* Parol evidence		
preservation of	2-515	§§622-624
EXCLUSION		
of damages. *See also* Damages	2-719(1) - (3)	§§684-689
of warranties. *See* Warranty, seller's		
EXCUSE		
applied conservatively		§513
buyer fails to respond	2-616(2)	§519
buyer's alternatives	2-616(1), (2)	§518
commercial impracticability, doctrine of	2-615	§511
frustration of purpose	2-615	§511
grounds		§§513-515
higher costs		§515
impossibility of performance	2-615	§511
no waiver	2-616(3)	§520
notice of	2-615(c)	§517
partial performance possible	2-615(b)	§516
requirements	2-614(1); 2-615(a)	§512
strikes		§514
EXPENSES		
from resale, return, or storage of defective goods	2-603(2); 2-710; 2-711(3); 2-715(1)	§§481-482, 641, 662
of inspection	2-513(2); 2-715(1)	§433, 662
of return in "sale or return" contract	2-327(2)(b)	§192
overhead	2-708(2)	§640
saved, deduction of	2-706(1); 2-708(1); 2-712(2); 2-713(1)	§§642, 663
upon stoppage in transit	2-705(3)(b)	§580
EXPRESS WARRANTY		
See Warranty, seller's		
EX-SHIP		
See Shipping terms		
F		
FAIR DEALING	2-103(1)(b)	§§15, 32
F.A.S.		
See Shipping terms		
FEDERAL WARRANTY ACT		
attorney's fees		§354
FTC rules		§§345, 349
implied warranty disclaimers void		§348
in general		§345
scope of		§§350-353
standards		§§346-347
state legislation, standards for		§§355-356
"FIRM OFFER"	2-205	§§59-62

Subject	U.C.C. Section	Text Section
FITNESS WARRANTY		
See Warranty, seller's		
F.O.B.		
See Shipping terms		
FORMATION OF CONTRACT		
See Contract		
FRUSTRATION OF PURPOSE		
See Excuse		
FUNGIBLE GOODS		
buyer's interest in	2-105(4)	§51
definition	1-201(17)	§§48-49
equivalent goods	1-201(17)	§49
merchantibility of	2-314(2)(b)	§237
unidentified	2-105(4)	§50

G H

Subject	U.C.C. Section	Text Section
GOOD FAITH IN SALES CONTRACT		
cover	2-712(1)	§§611-612, 656
definition		
by merchant	2-103(1)(b); 1R-201(b)(20)	§§13-15, 31-35
by nonmerchant	1-201(19); 1R-201(b)(20)	§§13-14, 31-34
determining prices	2-305(2)	§132
in proper tender and cure	2R-508(2)	§427
modification of contract	1-203; 2-209	§162
obligation of, in general	1-203	§§13-15
output contract	2-306(1)	§§140-142
rejection and resale of goods	2-603(3)	§482
requirements contract	2-306(1)	§§140-142
resale	2-603(3); 2-604; 2-706(1), (5)	§§482, 593
specification of missing terms	2-311(1)	§159
warranty of, collecting bank's	7-508	§720
"GOOD FAITH PURCHASER FOR VALUE"	2-702(3)	§563
See also Bona fide purchaser; Third party		
GOODS		
acceptance of. *See* Acceptance of goods		
after-acquired	2-702(3)	§564
as means of payment	2-304(1)	§456
attached to realty	2-107	§§38-42
casualty to	2-613	§§45-47
conforming to description or sample	2-313(1)(b), (c)	§§220-222
consumer. *See* Consumer goods		
crops		§39
damaged	2-613(b)	§§46-47
definition	2-105(1)	§37
disputed condition of	2-515	§§622-624
fixtures	2-107(1), (2)	§42
fungible. *See* Fungible goods		
identification of. *See* Identification of goods		
identified	2-105(1)	§37
inspection, testing, and sampling	2-515	§623

Subject	U.C.C. Section	Text Section
insurable interest in	2-501; 2-509	§§372-374, 535-536
international sale of. *See* United Nations Convention on Contracts for International Sale of Goods ("CISG")		
lease of. *See* Lease of goods		
minerals		§40
nonconforming. *See* Nonconforming goods		
nonexistent or destroyed	2-613(a)	§45
price payable in	2-304(1)	§456
"receipt of" defined	2-103(1)(c)	§152
rejection of. *See* Rejection of goods		
security interest in	2-506(1); 2-701(1); 2-702(3)	§§606-607, 564-565
service contracts and		§§52-54
severed from realty	2-107	§§40-41
shipment of to form contract	2-206(1)(b)	§§65-67
sold, secured creditor's rights against	2-702	§§564-565
specially manufactured. *See also* Statute of Frauds	2-201(3)(a)	§§118-119
substitute	2-712(1)	§612
suit against third party for damage to	2-722	§§543-547
software sales	2R-103(1)(k)	§54
timber		§40
unborn young of animals	2-105(1)	§44

I J K

IDENTIFICATION OF GOODS

See also Passage of title

buyer's interest pursuant to	2-501(1); 2-722	§§545-547
buyer's repudiation after	2-501(3)	§§541-542
definition	2-501	§360
layaway goods	2-502	§620
method of	2-501(1)	§§361-362
passing title	2-401(1)	§357
requirement of	2-401(1); 2-501(1), (2)	§§359-363
resale after	2-706(2)	§598
seller's interest pursuant to	2-501(2); 2-722	§§363, 545-547
seller's repudiation after	2-502	§620
seller's right of upon buyer's breach	2-704(1)(a)	§§587-590
substitution after	2-501(2)	§363
unfinished goods	2-704(1)(b); 704(2)	§§589-591

IMPLIED WARRANTY

See Warranty, seller's

IMPOSSIBILITY OF PERFORMANCE

See Excuse

IMPROPER TENDER, CURE OF

See Cure

INCIDENTAL DAMAGES

See Damages

INCONSISTENT TERMS

See Acceptance of offer

INDORSEMENT OF NEGOTIABLE DOCUMENT

inadequate or missing	7-506	§716

Subject	U.C.C. Section	Text Section
liability upon	7-505	§§717-720
negotiation, upon	7-501(3)	§715
right to compel	7-506	§716
types of	7-501(3)	§715
warranties on	7-505; 7-507; 7-508	§§717-720

Subject	U.C.C. Section	Text Section
INFRINGEMENT, WARRANTY AGAINST	2-312(3)	§215

INNOCENT PURCHASER
See Bona fide purchaser

INSOLVENCY

buyer's after shipment	2-705(1)	§568
definition	1-201(23)	§557
rights of assurance pursuant to	2-609	§§502-505
seller's—reclamation	2-502	§620

INSPECTION, BUYER'S RIGHT TO

acceptance of goods after inspection	2-606(1)(a)	§441
after payment	2-512; 2-513(3)	§§434-438
before payment	2-513(1)	§429
C.O.D. contract	2-513(3)(a)	§436
disputed goods	2-515(a)	§623
effect upon warranty	2-316(3)(b)	§§290-291
expenses of	2-513(2)	§433
in general	2-513(1)	§429
loss of right	2-513(3)(a), (b)	§§434-438
place	2-513(4)	§431
right to test and sample	2-513(1)	§432
time of	2-513(1)	§430
under documentary sale	2-513(3)(b)	§435

INSTALLMENT CONTRACT

definition	2-612(1)	§418
performance of	2-612(2), (3)	§§418-420
right to reject	2-612(2)	§§419, 539
U.C.C. policy toward		§421

INSURABLE INTEREST
See Goods

INSURANCE

C.I.F. & C. & F.	2-320(1), (2)	§§387-388
risk of loss	2-501	§§372-374

INTERNATIONAL SALE OF GOODS
See United Nations Convention on Contracts for
International Sale of Goods

L

LEASE OF GOODS

consequential damages limited	2A-503(3)	§758
consumer protection	2A-103(1)(e); 2A-108; 2A-109;	
	2A-503(3)	§§753-758
attorney's fees	2A-108(4)	§757
consequential damages limited	2A-503(3)	§758
option to accelerate	2A-109(2)	§754
unconscionability	2A-108(2)	§§755-757

Subject	U.C.C. Section	Text Section
LOST BILL OF LADING		
See Bill of lading		
LOST PROFITS		
See Seller's remedies		
LOT		
delivery of	2-612(1)	§418
M		
MEASURE OF DAMAGES		
See also Damages		
buyer's		
buyer's option		§656
"contract-cover"	2-712(2)	§654
"contract-market"	2-713(1)	§§655-656
market price, proof of	2-723(2), (3); 2-724	§§633-636, 658
seller's		
"contract-market"	2-708(1)	§§631-632
"contract-resale"	2-706(1)	§630
"lost profits"	2-708(2)	§§637-640
seller's option	2-703	§632
MERCHANTABILITY, WARRANTY OF		
See Warranty, seller's		
MERCHANTS		
acceptance of offers. *See also* Battle of the forms	2-207(2)	§§35, 80-83
definition	2-104(1)	§§26-30
demand for assurances among	2-609(2)	§509
duty owed by. *See* Good faith in sales contract		
nonmerchants distinguished		§§30-35
oral contracts. *See also* Statute of Frauds	2-201; 2R-201(1)	§§34, 96-97, 114-121
request for specification of defects	2-605	§470
risk of loss	2-509(3)	§§535-536
warranty against infringement	2-312(3)	§§215-216
written confirmations by. *See also* Statute of Frauds	2-201(2)	§§109-113
MIRROR IMAGE RULE		
See Battle of the forms		
MISDESCRIPTION		
See Liability		
MODIFICATION		
attempt acts as waiver	2-209(4), (5)	§§165-166
of contract	2-209(1) - (3)	§§161-164
of warranty	2-209(1); 2-316(3)	§§286, 293
N		
NEGOTIABLE BILL OF LADING		
See also Bill of lading		
bearer bill	7-104(1)(a); 7-501(1), (2)(a)	§§712-713
carrier's duties	7-403(3); 7-404	§§721-722
definition	7-403(3)	§711
"due negotiation" defined	7-501(4)	§734
effect of	7-502	§§733, 735

Subject	U.C.C. Section	Text Section
failure to indorse	7-506	§716
goods entrusted to bailee	2-403(2), (3); 7-503(1)(a)	§§728-731
innocent purchaser of	7-502	§§732-735
negotiated without authority	7-502; 7-501(4)	§§732-735
nonexistent goods	7-301	§§736-738
order bill	7-104(1)(a); 7-501(1), (2)(b)	§§712, 714
possession equals ownership	7-403(3)	§§700, 711
rights of third parties		§§727-741
divided property interests	2-505	§§739-741
forged document	7-503(1)	§727
types of	7-104(1); 7-501(1), (2)(a), (b)	§§713-714

NEGOTIATION

Subject	U.C.C. Section	Text Section
definition	7-501(4)	§734
form of	7-501(1), (2)(a), (b)	§§713-714
indorsements	7-501(3)	§715
requirements of	7-501; 7-506	§§713-716
to innocent purchaser	7-502	§§732-735
warranties upon negotiation	7-505; 7-507; 7-508	§§717-720
wrongful	2-403(2), (3); 7-301; 7-502; 7-503(1)	§§727-738

NO ARRIVAL, NO SALE
See Sale terms

NONACCEPTANCE OF GOODS, DAMAGES FOR
See Damages

NONCONFORMING GOODS

Subject	U.C.C. Section	Text Section
effect upon risk of loss	2-510(1), (2)	§§538-541
inspection expenses, effect upon	2-513(2)	§433
installment contracts	2-612(2)	§§419, 539

NONNEGOTIABLE BILL OF LADING (STRAIGHT BILL)
See also Bill of lading

Subject	U.C.C. Section	Text Section
carrier's liability under	7-102(1)(d); 7-303(1)(b)	§§708-709
consignee's rights under		§710
definition	7-104	§707
effect		§§707-708

NONRECEIPT, CARRIER'S LIABILITY FOR
See Liability, carrier's

NONSALE TRANSACTIONS
	2-102	§§55-56

See also Lease of goods; Warranty, seller's

NOTICE

Subject	U.C.C. Section	Text Section
acceptance of goods	2-606(1)(a)	§§440-441
acceptance of offer	2-206(2)	§74
breach of contract	2-607(3)(a), (5)(a)	§§330-334
breach of international sales contract (CISG)		§790
breach of warranty	2-607(3)(a)	§§330-334
claiming excuse by failure of presupposed conditions	2-615(c)	§517
destination contract	2-503(1), (3)	§380
imperfect tender, cure of	1-204(3)	§425
market price	2-723(3)	§636
"Nachfrist" notice		§794
nonconforming goods	2-717	§618
"reasonable"	1-204(3)	§425

Subject	U.C.C. Section	Text Section
recoupment	2-717	§618
rejection of goods	2-602(1); 2-605	§§466-470
resale	706(4)(b)	§595
revocation of acceptance	2-608(2)	§490
shipment	2-504(c)	§378
stoppage in transit	2-705(3)(a)	§§578-579
termination of contract	2-309(3)	§149

O

OFFER

See Acceptance of offer; "Firm offer"

ON APPROVAL

See Sale terms

OPEN TERMS

assortment	2-311(1)	§157
construction of	2-2-5(1), (2); 2-208(1) - (3); 1R-303	§§16-20, 122-123, 160
credit	2-310(d)	§§154-156
delivery	2-307; 2-308(a), (b)	§§144-145
gap filling rules	2-205(1), (2); 2-208(1) - (3); 1R-303	§§16-20, 122-123, 160
one party to specify	2-311(1)	§159
payment arrangement	2-310(a), (c)	§§150-153
price		
agreements to agree	2-305(1)(b)	§§126-128
contract silent	2-305(1)(a)	§125
good faith price determination	2-305(2), (3)	§§131-133, 135
inoperative reference	2-305(1)(c)	§129
intent determinative	2-305(1)	§124
maximum-minimum price		§135
reasonableness	2-305(1)(a) - (c)	§§125, 128-129
reserved right to fix	2-305(2)	§§130-134
quantity	2-201(1)	§136
requirements and output contracts	2-306	§§137-143
shipping arrangements	2-311(2)	§158
time	2-309	§§146-149

ORAL CONTRACT

See Contract; Statute of Frauds

ORDER BILL

definition	7-104(1)(a)	§707
negotiation of	7-501(1), (2)(b)	§714
warranties	7-505; 7-507; 7-508	§§717-720

OUTPUT CONTRACT	2-306(1)	§§138-140

OVERSEAS SHIPMENT

See Shipping terms

P

PAROL EVIDENCE

common law		§§91, 95
disclaimer of express warranty		§§271-274
in general	2-202	§§91-95
sales contracts	2-202	§§92-95

Subject	U.C.C. Section	Text Section

R

REALTY

fixtures	2-107(1), (2)	§42
goods severed from	2-107	§§38-42
price payable in	2-304(2)	§457

RECEIPT OF GOODS

buyer's duty	2-503(1)(b)	§428

RECEIPT, WAREHOUSE

See Warehouse receipt

RECLAMATION OF GOODS

bad checks	2-507(2); 2-511(3)	§§177, 553, 558
bankruptcy, trustee not BFP		§566
bona fide purchasers, rights of	2-702(3)	§563
buyer's insolvency	2-702(2)	§§553-558
misrepresentation as to	2-702(2); 2R-702(2)	§§555-556
compared to buyer's right to capture	2-502	§620
exclusive remedy	2-702(3)	§562
failure to reclaim	2-702(2)	§§179-180
in general		§§552-553
procedure	2-702(2)	§§555-561
written demand		§559
secured creditors	2-702(2)	§§564-565
time limitation	2-702(2)	§§551, 553
transfer to bona fide purchaser	2-702(3)	§563

RECOUPMENT

deduction of damages by buyer	2-717	§617
notices	2-607(3)(a); 2-717	§618
"same contract" limitation	2-717	§619

REJECTION OF GOODS

buyer's duties upon		
expenses	2-603(2)	§481
no acts of ownership	2-602(2)(a)	§§445, 472-476
revision—reasonable use	2R-608(4)(b)	§476
perishables	2-603(1)	§480
resale	2-603; 2-604	§§478-482
return of goods	2-604	§479
storage of goods	2-602(2)(b), (c)	§477
buyer's right to	2-601	§§465-482
after acceptance of goods. *See also* Revocation of acceptance	2-607(1), (2); 2-608	§§448-449, 483
installment contracts	2-612(2)	§419
rightful rejection	2-601	§465
effect of on duty to pay	2-510(1)	§471
notice of	2-601	§§466-470
contents		§468
general rejection	2-602(1)	§469
reasonable time	2-602(1)	§§466-467
unreasonable time, effect of	2-602(1); 2-606(1)(b)	§§442-444
when specific defects required	2-605	§470
risk of loss pursuant to	2-510(1), (3)	§§465, 530-531, 533
surprise	2-508(2)	§426

Subject	U.C.C. Section	Text Section
wrongful	2-706(1)	§§465, 551, 593

REMEDIES

See also Breach of warranty; Buyer's remedies; Seller's remedies

Subject	U.C.C. Section	Text Section
accepted goods	2-714; 2-717	§§448-450
action for the price	2-709	§§625-629
anticipatory breach	2-610(b), (c); 2-704(2)	§§498-499
buyer's insolvency	2-702; 2R-702(2); 2-705(1)	§§550, 554-558, 568
cancellation of contract	2-703(f)	§§603-604
election of	2-702(3)	§562
exclusivity provision	2-719(1)(b)	§§684-685
limitation. *See also* Damages	2-718; 2-719	§§670-689
minimum adequate remedy requirement	2-719	§687
nonacceptance of goods	2-706(1); 2-708(1), (2); 2-710; 2R-710(2)	§§629-643
reclamation	2-507(2); 2-702(2); 2R-702(2)	§§552-566
recoupment	2-717	§§617-619
rejection	2-601	§§465-482
replevin	2-716(3)	§§644-646
resale	2-603; 2-706; 2-711(3)	§§475-482, 593-602, 608-610
restitution	2-718(2)(a)	§§664-669
revocation of acceptance	2-608	§§483-494
salvage	2-704	§592
security interest	2-505(1); 2-711(3); 2-716(3)	§§395, 608, 646
specific performance	2-716(1), (2)	§§647-652, 791
statute of limitations. *See* Statute of limitations		
third party, remedies of	2-506; 2-707; 2-722	§§543-547, 605-607

REPLEVIN

See Buyer's remedies

REPUDIATION

See also Seller's remedies

Subject	U.C.C. Section	Text Section
buyer's	2-706; 2-708; 2-710; 2R-710(2)	§§629-643
in general	2-610; 2-611	§§495-501

REQUIREMENT CONTRACT

Subject	U.C.C. Section	Text Section
	2-306(1)	§§137, 139-143

RESALE

Subject	U.C.C. Section	Text Section
buyer's right *re* rejected goods	2-603; 2-604; 2-711(3)	§§478-482
compared to buyer's remedy of cover		§616
effect on title to goods	2-706(5)	§§600-601
good faith	2-603(3); 2-604	
procedure	2-706(2) - (4)	§§594-599
public vs. private sale	2-706(2)	§594
seller's right		
damages upon	2-706(1)	§593
profit pursuant to	2-706(6)	§602
to purchase at sale	2-706(4)(d)	§599
unfinished goods	2-704(1)(b), (2)	§§587, 589-590

RESCISSION

See also Cancellation of contract; Revocation of acceptance

Subject	U.C.C. Section	Text Section
by acceptance of repudiation	2-611(1), (2)	§§500-501
by revocation of acceptance	2-608(1)	§488

Subject	U.C.C. Section	Text Section
by agreement	2-509(4)	§523
casualty	2-613	§§45-47
catch-all rule	2-509(3)	§§535-536
consignment		§395
destination contract	2-509(1)(b)	§§384, 529
effect upon right to sue third parties	2-722(b)	§§535-538
goods held by bailee	2-509(2)	§§531-534
"on approval" sale	2-327(1)	§§197, 525
"sale or return"	2-327(2)(b)	§§191, 524
shipment contract	2-509(1)(a)	§§383-384, 387-388
title immaterial		§521
upon buyer's breach	2-510(3)	§§541-542
upon seller's breach	2-510(1), (2)	§§538-540

S

	U.C.C. Section	Text Section
SALE, DEFINED AND DISTINGUISHED	2-106(1)	§55
SALE ON APPROVAL		
"approval"	2-606(1)(a)	§186
creditors' rights	2-326(2)	§200
definition	2-326(1)(a)	§186
expenses on seller	2-327(1)(c)	§198
merchant buyers	2-327(1)(c)	§198
no sale until approved		§195
risk of loss		§197
time of payment	2-327(1)	§196
trial use	2-327(1)(b)	§194
SALE OR RETURN		
creditors' rights	2-326(2)	§199
definition	2-326(1)(b)	§185
expenses on buyer	2-327(2)(b)	§192
risk of loss	2-327(2)(b)	§191
time for return	2-327(2)(a)	§§188-189
writing required	2-326(4)	§187
SALE TERMS		
See also Open terms; Shipping terms		
auction. *See also* Auction sale	2-328	§§201-209
cash sale. *See* Cash sale		
credit sale		§172
missing from contract. *See* Open terms		
"no arrival, no sale"	2-324	§§391-394
"on approval." *See also* Sale on approval	2-326(1)(a)	§187
"sale"	2-106(1)	§55
"sale or return." *See also* Sale or return	2-326(1)(b)	§185
to be specified in future	2-305(2); 2-311(1)	§§130-134; 159
SALVAGE		
of unfinished goods	2-704(2)	§§587, 592
SECURITY INTEREST		
after-acquired goods	2-203(1)(c)	§564
attachment to identified goods		§373
buyer's remedy	2-711(3)	§§482, 608

Subject	U.C.C. Section	Text Section
cure of improper. *See* Cure		
effect upon buyer's duty to pay	2-310(4); 2-507(1); 2-601	§§389, 403
methods of		
constructive		§410
manual	2-503(1); 7-403(3)	§§404-409
where goods held by bailee	2-503(4)	§§411-413
perfect tender rule	2-601	§§414-416
substantial performance exceptions	2-504; 2-612	§§417-422
risk of loss	2-509	§§521-534
seller's duty of, in general	2-503; 2-504	§§375-380, 402
substantial performance		
installment sales	2-612	§§418-421
shipping arrangements	2-504; 2-614(1)	§422
under documentary sale	2-503(4), (5); 2-504(c); 7-403(3)	§§379, 397-400, 412-413

THIRD PARTIES

Subject	U.C.C. Section	Text Section
beneficiary of express warranty	2R-313A, B	§§230-231
creditors, rights of after sale	2-326	§§199-200
document for nonexistent goods, rights under	7-301	§§736-738
financial interests in sale, remedies for	2-506(1)	§§605-606
liability for damaged goods	2-722	§§543-547
"person in position of seller"	2-707(1); 2-702(2)	§607
priority of bankruptcy trustee		§566
rights of vs. seller's reclamation	2-403(1); 2-702	§§181-184, 563-566
wrongfully issued bill of lading, rights under	2-403; 7-503(1)	§§727-731
wrongfully negotiated bill, rights under	7-502	§§732-735

THROUGH BILLS
See Bill of lading

TIME PROVISIONS

Subject	U.C.C. Section	Text Section
formation of contract	2-201(1)	§§101-102
lack of	2-309(1)	§146
open time for payment	2-310(a), (c)	§§151-153
payment	2-301	§451
rejection	2-602(1)	§§466-467
tender	2-503(1)(a)	§§405-409
to cure	2-508(1)	§424

TITLE
See also Bona fide purchaser; Passage of title; Unauthorized
                transfer; Warranty, seller's

Subject	U.C.C. Section	Text Section
purchaser of entrusted goods	2-403	§§728-731
rights on negotiation	7-403(3)	§711
voidable	2-403(1)	§183
warehouse receipt	7-201; 7-210	§§725-726
warranty of	2-312; 7-507	§§212, 717-720

TORT

Subject	U.C.C. Section	Text Section
liability		§§315-323
statute of limitations		§321

TRANSFER, UNAUTHORIZED
See Unauthorized transfer

U

UNAUTHORIZED TRANSFER

Subject	U.C.C. Section	Text Section
USAGE OF TRADE		
construction of contract	1-205(2)	§§16-17, 123, 160
definition	1-205(2); 1R-303(c)	§17
excluding implied warranties	2-316(3)	§293
title warranty and	2-312(2)	§217
V		
"VOUCHING IN"	2-607(5)(a)	§334
W X Y Z		
WAIVER		
as revision of contract	2-209(4), (5)	§§165-166
of express warranty	2-316(1)	§§267-274
of implied warranty	2-316(2), (3); 2R-316(2)	§§267, 275-294
of objections, buyer's	2-605	§470
of title warranty	2-312(2)	§218
WAREHOUSE RECEIPT		
See also Documents of title		
compared to bill of lading	7-201; 7-210	§726
definition		§723
purpose		§724
transfer of, effect		§725
WARRANTIES FOR LEASE OF GOODS	2A-209	§§762-763
WARRANTIES REGARDING DOCUMENTS OF TITLE		
collecting bank's	7-508	§720
upon negotiation	7-507; 7-508	§§717-720
WARRANTY, SELLER'S		
See also Consumer protection statutes; Federal Warranty Act; Privity		
breach of. *See* Breach of warranty		
construction of		§§299-305
cumulative and consistent	2-317	§300
express warranties, effect of	2-317(c)	§305
parties' intent	2-317(a) - (c)	§§302-305
samples	2-317(b)	§304
specifications	2-317(a)	§303
disclaimers		
by limitation of remedies	2-719(1)(b), (2)	§§294, 686-687
express warranties		
narrow construction	2-316	§§268-269
parol evidence permissible		§§271-274
fraud		§273
lack of agreement		§273
unconscionability		§272
unreasonableness of	2-316(1)	§270
implied		
"as is" language	2-316(3)(a)	§§288-289
buyer's examination of goods		§§290-292
custom or usage		§293
specific conspicuous language	2-316(2)	§§276-286
consumers—revision	2R-316(2)	§285

NOTES

NOTES

NOTES

NOTES